# "WHAT CAN THE MATTER BE?"

# Tavistock Clinic Series
Margot Waddell (Series Editor)
Published by Karnac Books

Other titles in the Tavistock Clinic Series

Acquainted with the Night: Psychoanalysis and the Poetic Imagination, *edited by Hamish Canham & Carole Satyamurti*
Assessment in Child Psychotherapy, *edited by Margaret Rustin & Emanuela Quagliata*
Borderline Welfare: Feeling and Fear of Feeling in Modern Welfare, *by Andrew Cooper & Julian Lousada*
Creating New Families: Therapeutic Approaches to Fostering, Adoption, and Kinship Care, *edited by Jenny Kenrick, Caroline Lindsey, & Lorraine Tollemache*
Facing It Out: Clinical Perspectives on Adolescent Disturbance, *edited by Robin Anderson & Anna Dartington*
Inside Lives: Psychoanalysis and the Growth of the Personality, *by Margot Waddell*
Internal Landscapes and Foreign Bodies: Eating Disorders and Other Pathologies, *by Gianna Williams*
Looking into Later Life: A Psychoanalytic Approach to Depression and Dementia in Old Age, *edited by Rachael Davenhill*
Mirror to Nature: Drama, Psychoanalysis, and Society, *by Margaret Rustin & Michael Rustin*
Multiple Voices: Narrative in Systemic Family Psychotherapy, *edited by Renos K. Papadopoulos & John Byng-Hall*
Oedipus and the Couple, *edited by Francis Grier*
Organization in the Mind: Psychoanalysis, Group Relations, and Organizational Consultancy, *by David Armstrong, edited by Robert French*
Psychoanalysis and Culture: A Kleinian Perspective, *edited by David Bell*
Psychotic States in Children, *edited by Margaret Rustin, Maria Rhode, Alex Dubinsky, & Hélène Dubinsky*
Reason and Passion: A Celebration of the Work of Hanna Segal, *edited by David Bell*
Reflecting on Reality: Psychotherapists at Work in Primary Care, *edited by John Launer, Sue Blake, & Dilys Daws*
Sent Before My Time: A Child Psychotherapist's View of Life on a Neonatal Intensive Care Unit, *by Margaret Cohen*
Surviving Space: Papers on Infant Observation, *edited by Andrew Briggs*
The Anorexic Mind, *by Marilyn Lawrence*
The Learning Relationship: Psychoanalytic Thinking in Education, *edited by Biddy Youell*
The Many Faces of Asperger's Syndrome, *edited by Maria Rhode & Trudy Klauber*
Therapeutic Care for Refugees: No Place Like Home, *edited by Renos K. Papadopoulos*
Understanding Trauma: A Psychoanalytic Approach, *edited by Caroline Garland*
Unexpected Gains: Psychotherapy with People with Learning Disabilities, *edited by David Simpson & Lynda Miller*
Working Below the Surface: The Emotional Life of Contemporary Organizations, *edited by Clare Huffington, David Armstrong, William Halton, Linda Hoyle, & Jane Pooley*

Orders
Tel: +44 (0)20 7431 1075; Fax: +44 (0)20 7435 9076
Email: shop@karnacbooks.com
www.karnacbooks.com

# "WHAT CAN THE MATTER BE?"

Therapeutic Interventions
with Parents, Infants, and Young Children

THE WORK OF
THE TAVISTOCK CLINIC UNDER FIVES SERVICE

Edited by
*Louise Emanuel & Elizabeth Bradley*

Foreword by
*Margaret Rustin*

KARNAC

First published in 2008 by
Karnac Books
118 Finchley Road
London NW3 5HT

Copyright © 2008 by Louise Emanuel & Elizabeth Bradley

The rights of the editors and contributors to be identified as the authors of this work have been asserted in accordance with §§ 77 and 78 of the Copyright Design and Patents Act 1988.

All rights reserved. No part of this publication may be reproduced, stored in a retrieval system, or transmitted, in any form or by any means, electronic, mechanical, photocopying, recording, or otherwise, without the prior written permission of the publisher.

**British Library Cataloguing in Publication Data**

A C.I.P. for this book is available from the British Library

ISBN: 978–1–85575–340–2

Edited, designed, and produced by Communication Crafts

Printed in Great Britain

www.karnacbooks.com

# *CONTENTS*

| | |
|---|---|
| SERIES EDITOR'S PREFACE | ix |
| ABOUT THE EDITORS AND CONTRIBUTORS | xi |
| ACKNOWLEDGEMENTS | xv |
| FOREWORD | |
| *Margaret Rustin* | xvii |
| PREFACE | xxi |

**Introduction**     1

## I
### THEORY AND PRACTICE

**Early developments**     11

1    Brief work with parents of infants
       *Isca Wittenberg*     15

| | | |
|---|---|---|
| **2** | The relation of infant observation to clinical practice in an under-fives counselling service<br>*Lisa Miller* | 38 |
| **3** | Infant–parent psychotherapy: Selma Fraiberg's contribution to understanding the past in the present<br>*Juliet Hopkins* | 54 |

**Later developments** 67

| | | |
|---|---|---|
| **4** | The process of change in under-fives work<br>*Paul Barrows* | 69 |
| **5** | A slow unfolding—at double speed: therapeutic interventions with parents and their young children<br>*Louise Emanuel* | 81 |
| **6** | A sinking heart: whose problem is it? Under-fives work in the surgery of a general practitioner<br>*Beverley Tydeman & Janine Sternberg* | 99 |

## II
### COMMON THEMES IN WORK WITH UNDER FIVES

**Challenging and disruptive behaviour** 117

| | | |
|---|---|---|
| **7** | Anger between children and parents: how can we help?<br>*Lisa Miller* | 121 |
| **8** | Disruptive and distressed toddlers: the impact of undetected maternal depression on infants and young children<br>*Louise Emanuel* | 136 |
| **9** | Where the wild things are: tantrums and behaviour problems in two under-fives boys<br>*Cathy Urwin* | 151 |

## The parent couple and oedipal issues — 167

**10** Locating the ghost in the nursery: the importance of the parental couple
*Paul Barrows* — 171

**11** Father "there and not there": the concept of a "united couple" in families with unstable partnerships
*Louise Emanuel* — 187

**12** Oedipal issues in under-fives families: creating a space for thinking
*Michi Gurion* — 200

## Separation and loss; weaning and growth — 211

**13** Spanning presence and absence: separation anxiety in the early years
*Meira Likierman* — 215

**14** Sleeping and feeding problems: attunement and daring to be different
*Dilys Daws* — 237

**15** Holding the balance: life and death in the early years
*Elizabeth Bradley* — 254

GLOSSARY — 269
REFERENCES — 273
INDEX — 283

# SERIES EDITOR'S PREFACE

*Margot Waddell*

Since it was founded in 1920, the Tavistock Clinic has developed a wide range of developmental approaches to mental health which have been strongly influenced by the ideas of psychoanalysis. It has also adopted systemic family therapy as a theoretical model and a clinical approach to family problems. The Clinic is now the largest training institution in Britain for mental health, providing postgraduate and qualifying courses in social work, psychology, psychiatry, and child, adolescent, and adult psychotherapy, as well as in nursing and primary care. It trains about 1,700 students each year in over 60 courses.

The Clinic's philosophy aims at promoting therapeutic methods in mental health. Its work is based on the clinical expertise that is also the basis of its consultancy and research activities. The aim of this Series is to make available to the reading public the clinical, theoretical, and research work that is most influential at the Tavistock Clinic. The Series sets out new approaches in the understanding and treatment of psychological disturbance in children, adolescents, and adults, both as individual and in families.

*What Can the Matter Be?* has been gestating through several generations of Tavistock child and adolescent psychotherapists for about thirty years. This final text constitutes a comprehensive compendium of what might be described as the Clinic's "Under Fives Model", both in theory and in practice.

A central and invaluable emphasis is on the inestimable therapeutic significance, for later individual, parental, and family development, of early intervention on a time-limited basis.

The respective clinical chapters speak, each in their distinctive and vivid voices, to a range of problematic experiences that will resonate with parents and professionals alike. One way or another, they address the kinds of factors that foster an infant and young child's development and those that impede, or even arrest it. The theoretical chapters draw on an extensive literature on, for example, the legacy of past, unresolved familial difficulties; on current unstable parental partnerships; on oedipal issues; and on the nature of change itself.

The appropriateness of the title will be evident to any reader, for it encompasses the pain of parental incomprehension in the face of the troubling or challenging behaviour so typical of many infants and toddlers, while also casting illumination on the possible dynamic sources of it. The problems are not so much that "Johnny's so long at the fair", but the equivalently worrying and inexplicable ones of sleeplessness, tantrums, eating difficulties, and separation anxieties and of what could possibly explain them. In the course of the book, the hapless, helpless question of the original rhyme—"Oh dear, what can the matter be?" stirred, as it is, by fears of betrayal, abandonment, or being dropped or passed over—finds a range of compelling and accessible suggestions of what may lie behind them. The book also offers ways of thinking that help to discriminate between those situations in which change can be effected over a relatively short period of time and those where further intervention is indicated.

This volume is both scholarly and humane and a tremendously important addition to the world of infant mental health.

## ABOUT THE EDITORS AND CONTRIBUTORS

PAUL BARROWS is a Consultant Child Psychotherapist working in Bristol. He was until recently Chair of the Association for Infant Mental Health (UK), Editor of the Newsletter of the World Association for Infant Mental Health, and Editor of the *Journal of Child Psychotherapy*. He is Organizing Tutor of the MA in Infant Mental Health offered in Bristol in collaboration with the Tavistock Clinic, London.

ELIZABETH BRADLEY is a Consultant Child Psychiatrist at the Tavistock Clinic, where she has been a leading member of the Infant Mental Health Workshop for over twenty years. She is a psychoanalyst with a special interest in applying psychoanalytic ideas to the understanding and treatment of parents and families; in particular, unconscious aspects of parenting and emotional life in pregnancy and motherhood.

DILYS DAWS is Honorary Consultant Child Psychotherapist at the Tavistock Clinic, and Visiting Child Psychotherapist at the Baby Clinic of the James Wigg Practice, Kentish Town. She was the Founding Chair of, and is now Advisor to, the Association for Infant Mental Health. Publications include *Through the Night: Helping Parents and Sleepless Infants* (reprinted 1993).

LOUISE EMANUEL is a Consultant Child Psychotherapist working in the Child and Family Department of the Tavistock Clinic. She is Chair of the Under Fives Service and Co-Convenor of its training forum, the Infant Mental Health Workshop. She has a special interest in work with under fives, "looked-after" children, and children with disabilities. She also undertakes organizational consultancy. She lectures on training programmes in the UK, Europe, Israel, and South Africa. She has written a book, *Understanding Your Three Year Old* (2005), as part of the Tavistock Clinic's Understanding Your Baby series.

MICHI GURION is a Consultant Child Psychotherapist at Enfield Child and Mental Health Service, where she works with adolescents at risk and also coordinates a service for looked-after children. She has a special interest in work with under fives and their families and teaches infant observation at the Tavistock Clinic.

JULIET HOPKINS is an Honorary Consultant Child Psychotherapist at the Tavistock Clinic and a psychotherapist in private practice. She has specialized in working with children under the age of 5 years and their families and has a special interest in infancy and attachment. She has published widely in this field.

MEIRA LIKIERMAN is a Consultant Child Psychotherapist at the Tavistock Clinic and a staff member of the Child Psychotherapy training. She has worked with children under the age of 5 years and their families for twenty-five years and also has a private practice with adult patients. She lectures on psychotherapy training programmes and university courses in the UK, the US, and Europe. She has published numerous clinical and theoretical papers in professional journals and has spoken in conferences worldwide. Her book, *Melanie Klein: Her Work in Context*, was published in 2001.

LISA MILLER is a Consultant Child Psychotherapist who ran the Under Fives Service at the Tavistock Clinic for many years and chaired the Infant Mental Health Workshop, which underpins it. She is now semi-retired but continues to supervise, teach, and lecture at the Tavistock and the UK and in a range of countries abroad. She is Editor of the *International Journal of Infant Observation*.

JANINE STERNBERG is a Consultant Child Psychotherapist at the Portman Clinic, Tavistock and Portman NHS Trust, having worked for many years at the Tavistock Mulberry Bush Day Unit, a small unit for children with complex difficulties. She is also an adult psychotherapist. She has a long standing interest in under-fives work and worked for some years in a GP surgery. She has written a book, *Infant Observation at the Heart of Training* (2005). She was until recently Editor of the *Journal of Child Psychotherapy* and is now Editorial Coordinator for the *British Journal of Psychotherapy*.

BEVERLEY TYDEMAN is a Consultant Child Psychotherapist working at the Marlborough Family Service. She has an interest in infant mental health and for many years worked in GP surgeries alongside health visitors and GPs, offering consultation to families with young children. She also teaches at the Tavistock Clinic, where she is the Organizing Tutor of a course in Therapeutic Communication with Children. She is interested in contributing to the development of child mental health skills for a variety of front-line workers in the community, including nursery staff, special needs workers, and mentors in schools, as well as social workers and family support workers.

CATHY URWIN is a psychotherapist with children and adults working in the NHS and in private practice. She holds the post of Consultant Child Psychotherapist and Research Fellow at the Tavistock Centre, having previously worked for a number of years in East London. She has a background in teaching and research in developmental psychology and is especially interested in working with infants and under fives and children with communication difficulties and in the impact of trauma and deprivation on parenting

ISCA WITTENBERG was a Consultant Child Psychotherapist at the Tavistock Clinic and still holds an honorary post there. She continues to teach at the Tavistock and in countries all over the world. She has a special interest in infant–parent interaction, as well as in brief work with clients of all ages at points of crisis. She has published two books: *Psychoanalytic Insight and Relationships* (1970) and *The Emotional Experience of Learning and Teaching* (1983), as well as many other publications.

## ACKNOWLEDGEMENTS

We would like to acknowledge the hard work and support of:

Sophie Boswell
Janice Cormie
Dawn De Freitas
Margot Waddell
Margaret Rustin
Karnac Books

And all those who contributed chapters to the book.

# FOREWORD

*Margaret Rustin*

This is a long-awaited and highly readable collection of contributions by some of the best-known clinicians in the field of work with under fives and their families and networks. The stories told in the course of quite brief interventions are skilfully woven together from conversations with parents and the many communications, verbal and nonverbal, made by their children. The consulting-room setting allows much to be perceived: within a set time-frame, the essence of the current impasse in the parent–child relationship emerges with often startling clarity. The conjunction of the parental narrative, the child's behaviour and play, and the use that can be made of the opportunity to talk in depth with someone outside the family enables a great deal to happen.

Observation of the intricacies of family relationships as revealed in the room, and hypotheses about the inner worlds of both children and parents, tumble over themselves as one turns the pages. It is not hard to see why the opportunity to provide brief early interventions is very attractive to clinicians who combine interest and knowledge of babies' development and parental anxieties with a commitment to a health-promoting use of NHS resources (which is not as widespread as one would like) and the vital place in community mental health of support for parents of babies and young children.

The Under Fives Service at the Tavistock Clinic was born when two thoughts came together in my mind in the late 1970s. We had noticed that it was not easy to find ways to encourage families and community-based early-years professionals to refer to our child and family mental health clinic, despite the fact that we had unusually rich resources within our multidisciplinary teams to tackle early difficulties and that we could provide longer-term specialist treatment, including child psychotherapy, when this was indicated. Our belief in the efficacy of early intervention suggested the importance of shifting this reluctance to refer, which was often based on the belief that children would be "pathologized" (i.e. seen only as people with problems rather than in the round) and that most early childhood symptoms disappear with time. Clinical experience indicated, by contrast, that some early difficulties persist and indeed worsen when neglected. More recent empirical research has very much confirmed this clinical impression.

This issue of under-referral of the under fives could perhaps be tackled, I thought, if we could provide a fast-track response to the worries of the parents of young children which would be somewhat outside ordinary referral systems and offer something quickly enough to match the high level of anxieties engendered in the parents of babies and young children when things go wrong.

What has grown from the initial pilot project has gone far beyond the original conception. A great many families are helped by a brief intervention at a crisis moment, which can relieve anxiety and unblock developmental potential in children and parents and open up that relationship. More serious problems are also sometimes in evidence, when more substantial longer-term input will be needed and can be set in train before things get too stuck. Professionals from a range of disciplines have responded with great enthusiasm to this model of an under-fives service, and interesting variants of it have been established elsewhere in Britain and in many other countries. It has been one of the strands in the recent enormous growth of interest in infant mental health and parent/infant psychotherapy.

The widening scope of professional—and, indeed, of social and political—concern about supporting young families means that the ideas explored in this book enter a lively field of debate. Evidence from practice and evidence from research both point strongly in the direction of the benefits of early intervention. The contributions in this book range from closely observed clinical case studies with much eloquent and compelling detail, to broader engagements with the question of focus in parent/infant work, the nature of change achieved in brief work, and potential service developments. The increasing numbers of "early-years" professionals are a group with whom child and adolescent mental health practitioners need to engage as fully as possible. This book is a splendid text to set out for a wide audience some of the work of an imaginative and experienced group of clinicians. The stories of the families and the intensity of parent–child relationships in the early years stay powerfully in the mind and will no doubt resonate for many. It is a pleasure to see in print a record of some of the work done over thirty years and to envisage further developments to come.

## *PREFACE*

The Under Fives Service, together with its corresponding seminar, the Infant Mental Health Workshop, has been running as a clinical specialist service within the Child and Family Department at the Tavistock Clinic for over twenty years. It originated from a growing interest in infant and young child observation and its clinical application to psychoanalytic work with families with babies and children under the age of 5 years . This book is an attempt to describe the development of the model of clinical work by clinicians within the service and by practitioners who have adapted the model elsewhere. It is a compilation of papers that have been written over the years for publication in professional journals or as conference lectures by past and present members of the Service.

The range of clinical material, ideas about technique, duration, and frequency of interventions, and theoretical understanding is rich and vast. This diversity is also reflected in the differences in styles of writing, the authors varying in their ways of discussing theoretical and clinical approaches to the work. The unifying factor—the setting and underlying conceptual framework of the model—is outlined in the Introduction. The chapters in Part 1, "Theory and Practice", elaborate on the development of the model with clinical illustrations. Part 2 focuses on the many common themes that emerge in work with under fives: understanding challenging and disruptive behaviour; work with parents; and coping with separation, weaning, and loss.

Child psychotherapist Martha Harris was a great proponent of infant observation as an important training skill for psychoanalytically trained child psychotherapists. She saw the value of applying these skills to work with under fives and began offering what she termed "therapeutic consultations" to families with babies or young children (Harris, 1966). The Under Fives Service and multidisciplinary workshop was set up for interested colleagues, and over the years a model of brief psychoanalytically informed interventions for under fives was created; this was adapted by practitioners seeking to develop their own under fives services worldwide and was written about extensively in the *Journal of Child Psychotherapy* and other publications. The child psychotherapists who have contributed to this book were all trained at the Tavistock Clinic and, like consultant psychiatrist and psychoanalyst Elizabeth Bradley, work in the tradition of the British object relations school of psychoanalysis. They also apply a variety of useful theoretical concepts that supplement their theoretical framework.

Some aspects of this work have changed over the years as a host of outside influences and pressures have come to bear on the service. The service has always offered consultations to staff working in nurseries or day care centres and has provided clinical input in community settings. Some of the most well-known papers, such as Dilys Daws's (1985) "Standing Next to the Weighing Scales", arose from work in a local baby clinic, and Juliet Hopkins's paper (1988) "Facilitating the Development of Intimacy between Nurses and Infants in Day Nurseries", from work in a local nursery. Recent changes in the National Health Service (NHS) have increased the emphasis on clinical input within community-based settings, so that families can be seen in general practitioner surgeries or community centres, and clinicians may work jointly with other health professionals in these settings.

The Government initiative Sure Start was set up to ensure that families of all social strata have access to children's services, and this has had a strong influence on ways of delivering services. As part of the local Sure Start programme, the Tavistock Clinic Under Fives Service, together with other health and voluntary sector agencies, formed the "Emotional Support Service", providing psychological help to families with young children in the community.

There has been a recent increase in research in infant and child development, and advances in neuroscience research; together, these are increasingly informing the thinking about parent–infant interventions. The writings of Cramer (1995), Palacio-Espasa (2004), Lieberman (2004), Thomson-Salo et al. (1999), and others offer a range of approaches to this work. This book is intended to describe the particular approach to clinical work with under fives that has been developed at the Tavistock Clinic. It is aimed at early years professionals and clinicians working with this age group who have an interest in enhancing their understanding of young children's emotional and behavioural difficulties. It elaborates on many of the ideas that have been clearly described for interested parents in the Tavistock Clinic's *Understanding Your Baby Series* (the relevant volumes in the series are listed at the end of the Reference section).

The Service often sees families where domestic violence, trauma, and abuse underlie the children's difficulties. Several of the chapters allude to a background of violence in the home or, at the least, severe marital discord. Parent/couple work is a central focus of the Under Fives Service, and there has been an increasing demand for interventions with families where parents are separating or undergoing a divorce. The interface between parent and couple work is a matter for delicate clinical negotiation, and this is a developing area of expertise in the team. Work with single parents to help them to internalize both paternal and maternal functions in their parenting, is highlighted in the section "The Parent Couple and Oedipal Issues".

The substantial input of the Specialist Perinatal part of the Under Fives Service for families whose babies have been born prematurely, are ill, have disabilities, or have died is referred to in Elizabeth Bradley's chapter, "Holding the Balance". We have attempted to reflect the broad range of work undertaken by the Service with ethnic-minority groups, refugees, and asylum seekers: reference is made to the impact of displacement from their country of origin experienced by immigrants (Juliet Hopkins) and the additional cultural dimension inherent in many of these families regarding sleep, feeding, and maintaining discipline in the family (Beverley Tydeman & Janine Sternberg).

Readers may note that the gender balance of clinical cases described is biased towards boys. In general more boys are referred to the service than are girls, as to all child and adolescent mental health services (CAMHS), which may account for this difference.[1] Many theoretical and clinical issues explored in this book relate to children of both genders and gender is not likely to be the main factor determining a particular mode of intervention. We know from clinical experience that girls often internalize their conflicts, whereas boys tend to externalize their distress and are more likely to be referred for behaviour difficulties.

For the purposes of this book, the terms "infancy" and "infant mental health" refer to the 0- to 5-year age range unless specifically stated. It will become clear that within this age range, different types of intervention will be required for babies under 18 months, for toddlers, and for children rising 5 years making the transition to school. "Intensive" individual child psychotherapy implies three or more treatment sessions per week. Definitions of psychoanalytic theory and terminology are to be found in the Glossary, elaborated on in the introductory section, and often explained in the chapters themselves. We have sought to avoid unnecessary technical terms and jargon. In this way we hope to make the detailed stories of the clinicians' encounters with families, and their efforts to offer a theoretical framework for thinking about their experiences, what Rustin (1998) describes as "theory in action", as accessible and meaningful as possible.

## Note

1. For this reason as well as for grammatical simplicity, in general discussions children are referred to with masculine pronouns and therapists with feminine pronouns.

# "WHAT CAN THE MATTER BE?"

# Introduction

*The Under Fives Service*

The Under Fives Service was set up in recognition of the importance of prompt early intervention for families with babies and small children. The multidisciplinary team consists of a consultant child psychiatrist, child psychotherapists, family therapists, child psychologists, and a couple therapist. It offers quick-response psychoanalytically based interventions to families, carries no waiting list, and offers up to five sessions of focused work, which can be extended as required. The underlying approach requires the clinician to maintain a thoughtful and observant attentiveness when seeing families, without a set structure for interventions. This framework, combined with a flexibility of approach, may allow for a range of decisions to be made about frequency, duration, and the appropriate type of intervention, based on clinical judgement. This may also include some form of practical advice.

In addition to work undertaken in the clinic, the Under Fives team offers a service to families who are more difficult to reach, seeing them in outreach community settings. Group work and parenting skills courses are also offered both within the Clinic and in the community. A specialist perinatal project, focusing on pregnancy and the early weeks, offers support to families who have had fertility problems, miscarriage, premature babies, or a bereavement. Consultation to staff of nurseries and other day-care provision for infants and pre-school-age children is also offered as part of the service, including telephone consultations. There is also involvement in consultation on policy issues—for example, what contributes good nursery care arrangements, and the separation of mothers from their babies in the prison population.

Referrals fall into three categories: babies under 18 months, toddlers, and children from the age of 3 to 5 years. Common problems in the first year are feeding, weaning, and sleeping difficulties, excessive crying, and "failure to thrive". Later on separation anxiety, hyperactivity, aggressive behaviour, and temper tantrums are more common. Phobias and nightmares, sibling rivalry, as well as concerns about developmental delay or obsessional behaviours are common referrals. Psychosomatic symptoms—such as eczema, asthma, incontinence, and encopresis—lead to referral once medical investigations have ruled out physical problems. In the main the underlying issues tend to point to difficulties within the parent/infant/ child relationship and within the parent/couple relationship. Sometimes separation difficulties or problems around attachment and bonding lie at the heart of the problem, both for parents and for child. In many cases, the parents bring to the parenting situation their own experience as a child and may repeat a cycle of neglect or abuse with their own children.

The brief five-session structure often brings into focus the key issues within a family. For example, in cases of babies with eating difficulties, the sense of urgency transmitted to the therapist may lead her to address the pressure placed on everyone by the five-session model. The need to "get something into" the parents quickly and resolve the situation may, paradoxically, contrast with their often limited capacity to "take in" a lot of what is offered. This may reflect their baby's eating patterns—a very little at a time—and may indicate the need for longer-term work.

In many less urgent situations, the request for instant solutions and strategies is a constant one. Helping parents to recognize that we are not averse to giving advice but resist substituting thoughtfulness with action—we need to get to know and understand how the family functions first—is an important aspect of the work.

Some families may use the service for repeated brief consultations at points of difficulty, often at a new developmental milestone, relating to weaning, separation, and loss. This form of "serial" consultation (Stern, 1995) can be a valid way of using the service, although a question might remain about whether some underlying difficulty is being missed and brought back time and again for further work.

Audit and evaluation exercises over the years have indicated positive outcomes for the five-session model. However, the service has expanded to include longer-term work, reflecting the increasing complexity and greater levels of disturbance of referred cases, requiring multi-agency liaison. There are occasions when an initial piece of brief work may bring about change but may also function as an assessment for long-term work for one or more members of the family, including individual, group, or parent/couple work. It is often hard to ascertain from the initial referral the level of severity of the problem and the nature of the intervention that may be required.

## Theoretical framework

The psychodynamic framework presupposes an awareness (for which we are indebted to Freud, Klein, and many others) of the power of unconscious processes, and the way in which they can be expressed through nonverbal and verbal communications in the consulting room. Such awareness involves an understanding of, for example, the concepts of unconscious phantasy, splitting and projection, projective identification, and transference and countertransference phenomena (see the Glossary). Also at the heart of the framework is the application of observational skills to clinical work with families with young children (Miller, 1992; Miller, Rustin, Rustin, & Shuttleworth, 1989; Reid, 1997; Sternberg, 2005; Waddell, 2006; see also all issues of the *International Journal of Infant Observation and Its Applications*). An understanding of attachment theory, child development, and neurosciences research offers multiple perspectives to the work, and ideas stemming from systemic family therapy may also contribute to clinical practice with under fives.

Of central importance is Bion's concept of container/contained (1962a, 1962b) and his notion of "maternal reverie". He recognized that the baby's psyche is not developed enough to contain powerful feelings of any kind. Using the digestive system as a metaphor for the processing of emotion, Bion described how the infant requires an attentive carer, who is able to "take in" and think about his unbearable feelings of distress without becoming overwhelmed by anxiety. When the carer has made sense of the infant's communications in her own mind, she is then able to respond appropriately to the infant and tend to his needs. This process of "containment" is achieved when the parent is able, in a state of "reverie", to attend closely to the infant and to "digest" what the baby has put into her—the contained.

Gradually, the infant learns, through repeated experience of a thoughtful parent, how to make sense of his own experiences, to think for himself. This shift—from evacuation of overwhelming sensory data to a capacity to investigate his own feelings—is vital for a baby's emotional and cognitive development. It is the beginning of his development of "symbol formation"—the ability to internalize a picture of helpful parents to whom he can turn in his mind in times of distress.

Excessively long periods of inattention or inconsistent unpredictable responses by the main caregiver may result in the infant unconsciously developing defensive forms of behaviour as a means of coping with this lack of containment. He may find ways of "holding himself together" through excessive muscular development, sensory stimulation, or kinetic activity, creating his own "second-skin containment" (Bick, 1968). By turning away from the carer and becoming prematurely self-sufficient, he may develop a version of Winnicott's "false self" (1960). In attachment theory terms (Ainsworth, Blehar, Waters, & Wall, 1978), the child would manifest insecure or disorganized attachment patterns, which can often be observed in the clinical setting. At times, despite adequate attentiveness and attempts to contain the infant, his overwhelming states may be too much for the carer to process. This mismatch in the early parent–infant relationship may, therefore, be linked not only to the quality of parental care, but also to the infant's temperament and responsiveness to the caregiver.

Much of the understanding of young children's behaviour and communications, as well as that of their parents, is based on a recognition that these unconscious infantile defence mechanisms may be resorted to at times of stress or anxiety throughout their development. Symptoms such as sleep problems, tantrums, crying, biting, or hair pulling may originate in very early experiences in infancy, relating to the lack of an adequate container for the infant's internal and external experiences that might become intensely persecutory.

The experience of a reliable adult thinking about a child's feelings, struggling to make sense of and to understand them as a meaningful communication, enables him to gradually take into himself or internalize a model of thoughtfulness, attention, and curiosity. This, in turn, can help the child to be able to "say" what he is feeling and experiencing, as well as to play out "symbolically" his anxieties and preoccupations and can facilitate his emotional, cognitive, and social development.

When a young child projects his emotional states into his parents or carers, they may become filled up with the child's feelings, making it difficult for them to think clearly. By "giving" his carers an experience of his emotional discomfort at first hand, via the mechanism of "projective identification", a child conveys his states of mind nonverbally to those who are most likely to be receptive to his communications. The carer will hopefully identify with the child's emotional predicament and, reflecting on it, understand the nature of his experience. Thus, the mechanism of projective identification can be used as a means of communicating emotional experience in a nonverbal yet powerful way. A clinician may make use of these unconscious projections (via the mechanism of projective identification) to consider their impact on her own emotional state, a helpful gauge of her clients' state of mind.

Just as we recognize the "infant" in the child, we can notice the "child" in the adult, observing infantile feelings of rivalry, exclusion, envy, and anxiety relating to "not knowing" or feeling "small". This is especially pertinent as parents often feel a failure by coming to the clinic in the first place, and they may be confirmed in this by their own parents' views. The transgenerational transmission of failures in emotional containment may lead parents themselves to develop infantile defences, passing on these methods of coping to the child. Young children are at risk of becoming the "receptacles" (Williams, 1997) of their parents' unprocessed projections. This can lead to disruptive behaviour as they attempt to discharge this burden through whatever means available to them. The tension between acknowledging infantile states of mind in parents whilst simultaneously supporting their capacity to function as adults is a recognizable feature of the work.

In addition to a psychodynamic framework, an awareness of neurosciences research can be of particular importance when working with children traumatized in infancy who are hyper-reactive and are prone to apparently unprovoked outbursts of aggression. An understanding of the autonomic conditioned fear response (Emanuel, 2004) offers us a framework for thinking about the bodily processes involved in infants' responses to trauma, a heightened awareness of the body as the "theatre" for the emotions (Damasio, 1999). The trauma of chronic abuse and violence resulting in hyper-vigilance and an overactive bodily response to fear, triggered in the brain, can be recognized in the consulting room, and an explanation involving this understanding can offer relief to parents or carers who may be bewildered by their young child's behaviour. This research confirms the importance of emotional containment for the infant's social and cognitive development.

*Intervention process*

Access and acceptability have always been important features of the service. The aim remains to respond to referrals quickly, often by telephone, to arrange a mutually convenient appointment. Meetings are arranged on a regular basis, initially weekly or fortnightly, but the frequency may vary after the initial meetings, with longer intervals if this is felt to be the best option. In brief work the structure and the setting are important and need to provide a safe environment for both the therapist and the family.

In approaching the session the therapist has in mind the theoretical framework, a receptivity to observing all details of the way the family present themselves, and an awareness of the emotional impact of the family on her. The attitude is one of openness to exploration of all communications from parents, infants, and child, until a "selected fact" (Bion, 1962b) and focus for the work emerges. The therapist will attempt to make contact with the infant or child, observing his play and attempting to understand the meaning of his communications, while also engaging the parent. The way in which young children dramatically enact their predicament and that of the family through their play, their drawing, and their interactions with family members contributes to the "speed and spectacular nature of the therapeutic effect" (Watillon, 1993) in this work and enables a "slow unfolding" of the material within a brief time frame (see chapter 5). This is likely to include a gradual exploration of the parental background and its implications for the family. Detailed discussion about the daily routine of the family (Daws, 1989) can offer a valuable "port of entry" to understanding the nature of the difficulties and their impact on the family.

Although the therapist may be acutely aware of transference manifestations in the room, she is sparing in addressing this, unless drawing attention to it is likely to facilitate the development of a therapeutic alliance with the parents. A flexibility of approach, taking into account the unique needs of each family referred, seems to be important. This is possible when the therapist has an internal theoretical framework on which to draw, enabling her to provide a containing structure to the interventions.

Nearly all of the work of the Under Fives Service is done in the presence of one or both parents or carers, together with the child, and, on occasions, the parents on their own. Often the focus is on helping the parents to gain the insight and strength to function together as a benign parental couple, despite sometimes conscious or unconscious attempts by the child to split the couple. In other cases, work may centre on helping a single parent understand her child's need for her to exercise both paternal and maternal functions: to maintain in her mind, and to cultivate in the child's mind, the notion of a well-functioning parental couple. The role of the father and an ability to keep him in mind, whether absent or available to attend the clinic, is increasingly seen as essential to the therapeutic process (Barrows, 1999b; Emanuel, 2002b; Von Klitzing, Simoni, & Burgin, 1999).

Clinicians often offer a model of family work alternating with separate parent meetings. The latter enable parents to consider parenting/couple issues separately with the therapist, in parallel with family meetings in which they can observe, together with the therapist, how young children's play and behaviour communicate their emotional preoccupations and often those of the family.

Therapists may work on their own or with a co-worker, depending on the nature of the referral. Co-workers ensure that there is a built-in opportunity to discuss the impact of the family's projections on the therapists and how they are perceived in the transference. There may be requests to join other professionals in the network when there are concerns about parenting capacity, with a view to assessing whether an intervention from the Under Fives Service could help support parental functioning. Health visitors, who offer an invaluable service to parents with young children, make use of our services for referral and consultation purposes and, if practical, may accompany referred families to a first meeting.

Families who only want advice and instruction are unlikely to benefit from the service, which does require some interest in thinking about or exploration around the problem rather than a direct problem-solving approach. Medication is rarely prescribed for children and only very occasionally considered to be helpful for a parent, and this would then be discussed with the parent and the GP.

Finding explanations for children's difficulties in early life is a challenge. Growing up involves developmental steps that can seem insurmountable at the time and may require careful understanding and help from the wider family or professionals. In the first years of life these steps come in rapid succession. Trying to work out "What the matter can be" is a joint project that the family and clinicians undertake together to come to a shared understanding of the underlying problem. There will always be further developmental tasks ahead, but each one accomplished gives more confidence and hope for the future.

# PART I

# THEORY AND PRACTICE

# Early developments

This section contains versions of three previously published papers written respectively by Isca Wittenberg, Lisa Miller, and Juliet Hopkins, who participated in the establishment and growth of the Under Fives Service and corresponding workshop. These chapters give a historical perspective on the developing influences and underlying theoretical framework informing the authors' work with under fives, touching on major themes running through this book. They are "classic" in the sense that the authors illustrate clearly the underlying psychoanalytic framework gained through their training as child psychotherapists, while adapting this to the requirements of mainly brief interventions with parents and families.

The debt to Melanie Klein and her description of an infant's primitive states of persecutory anxiety and "terror of annihilation", later described by Bion as "nameless dread", is evident in the way in which the authors capture the essence of a baby's early experience, his states of persecutory anxiety and moments of fragmentation. The concepts of "containment" (Bion, 1962b), "holding" (Winnicott, 1963), and "second-skin containment" (Bick, 1968) underpin the clinical work. The capacity to reflect, to think rather than to act, to maintain an attentive presence in the face of overwhelming projections, is central to this work.

These early chapters focus on the younger end of the "under-fives spectrum", with Isca Wittenberg describing work with parents of young babies, and Lisa Miller and Juliet Hopkins including clinical examples of babies and toddlers Perhaps this is not a coincidence, as so much of what follows in later sections and work with "rising fives" is rooted in early parent–infant interactions. Some themes when working with parents of young children seem to be universal, and many of us will have had an experience, as Isca Wittenberg puts it, of a mother exclaiming incredulously: "Do you really think that babies think?"! Differences in technique and emphasis in the work depending on the age of the child—infant, toddler, or "rising 5"—are explored in the latter half of the book.

Isca Wittenberg elaborates her technique of working psychoanalytically with parents of babies, within a brief time frame. Her suggestion that "we can best help the baby by the help we offer to the infantile aspects of mother and father" is convincingly supported by the case examples, although she also cautions against transference interpretations that only take account of infantile aspects of the parents at the expense of their adult capacities.

Wittenberg describes work with parents whose baby's crying was proving to be too much for them. The power of the intervention seemed to lie in her capacity to interpret for the parents and to help them to empathize with what their baby might be feeling, as well as to acknowledge their own ambivalent feelings towards this baby and the impact he was having on their life and relationship. Fraiberg sums up this dynamic: "The primary focus of the work was on understanding the parents' negative transference to their baby, rather than on understanding their transference to the therapist" (quoted by Hopkins, in chapter 3).

With this example Wittenberg introduces a recurring theme in the book, that of the baby or young child who is perceived as a "monster" by his parents, in their belief that he is intent on wrecking their lives. This perception can begin *in utero* and may be linked to the parents' phantasies about their own and their baby's destructiveness. The transgenerational transmission of phantasies of "monster-like" babies and parents elaborated by Wittenberg occurs frequently in clinical material—one wonders whether the "ghost" in the nursery is more specifically, a phantom "monster"!

Isca Wittenberg and Lisa Miller both highlight the importance of infant and young child observation as a core training tool for clinicians undertaking psychoanalytic work with parents and infants. The experience of finding a role within a family where one is observing, of exercising "restraint" (Miller, chapter 2) by resisting intervention and advice giving, and of becoming aware of our own prejudices, judgemental attitudes, and identifications is invaluable training for clinical work.

Lisa Miller describes the two main factors influencing her work with under fives as the "formative experience" of undertaking an infant observation and her ongoing work with parents of children being seen by colleagues for individual child psychotherapy. This is evidenced in her clinical examples, which illustrate Miller's attentive observation of parent and baby and her ability to tolerate unbearable feelings of distress and depression while continuing to think about the family's predicament. Her observing eye, which enables parents themselves to begin noticing their babies' needs, provides the "holding"(Winnicott) and "containment" (Bion) that Juliet Hopkins describes in some detail in her chapter (chapter 3). By "receiving the broadcast" of both the parent(s) and the baby's primitive anxieties, Miller announces herself as "emotionally available", perhaps one of the most important aspects of this sort of work.

This chapter also touches on the delicate balance of working with the "needy child in the parent" as well as "entering into a conversation with the adult in the parent". Awareness of transference phenomena with parents of referred children is essential, even if not directly commented upon. "We only have a limited mandate to work in the transference", yet to "disregard [it] is dangerous; the work may be wrecked on a sea of unconscious responses unless we have an idea of what is going on in the infantile transference and can find a way to address it". Miller's caution about interpreting transference phenomena is echoed by Wittenberg who interprets only when it seems essential, "unless they present an obstacle to the work".

Finally, in her chapter Juliet Hopkins gives an interesting perspective on Fraiberg's work with parents and infants in her groundbreaking book *Clinical Studies in Infant Mental Health*, using case examples to convey how Fraiberg and Winnicott and later Bion offered her a framework for thinking when she began working with mother–infant couples and young families. Her case examples include situations we find increasingly common in our service, where the loss of the "mother country" experienced by immigrant and refugee families reinforces earlier losses in the parents' lives. Hopkins illustrates how, by working in the here-and-now of the session, she enables a mother to make an emotional link between her present difficulties and her childhood experiences, resulting in immediate improvements in the mother–infant relationship.

The worry about the risk of harm or violence, intimidation, and abuse being enacted towards a baby or of self-harm by a parent is present in each of these three chapters. The dilemma about whether, when, and how to involve social services or emergency medical services is an ever-present concern with parents of babies, when situations can become volatile so quickly. All three authors describe having to contain their anxiety about the level of risk posed to babies and to parents themselves, and at what point to intervene, but in these cases the situation was "held" by the therapeutic work. Wittenberg quotes the mother in her final case illustration saying: "I don't know what would have happened if I had not had this opportunity to come and talk to you. . . . I feel I might have hurt the baby . . . or committed suicide."

One of the common themes that emerges in all three chapters is the extraordinary speed of change and "cure", which, in some cases, occurs within two or three sessions. The question of how to give a "succinct description" of this clinical work and the factors that may have contributed to such rapid change without it sounding "magical" is raised by Juliet Hopkins and implicitly by all three authors. Paul Barrows also refers (in chapter 4) to this problem of gaining credibility for what sound like "miracle cures" obtained by very brief interventions.

This important issue is one that the authors attempt to address by giving detailed descriptions not only of clinical material illustrating their technique in the consulting room, but of their thought processes before, during, and after sessions, revealing their internal struggles to "eschew irritable reaching after fact and reason". Maintaining a state of "negative capability"—a concept of Keats's, elaborated by Bion (1977)—involves the therapist's ability to tolerate the uncertainty of "not knowing" or fully understanding a situation and allowing her "free-floating attention" to receive the full emotional impact of a family's projections. The therapist considers her countertransference experience and her observations of conscious and unconscious processes in her attempt to arrive at an understanding of the "selected fact" that has been communicated in a session. As Lisa Miller has said, every encounter is an encounter with the unknown and to be able to understand it properly we need to come to it without having made up our minds in advance, ready to experience what the encounter has to offer.

CHAPTER 1

# Brief work with parents of infants

*Isca Wittenberg*

My interest in brief work began when I was asked to spend a day a week at Sussex University Student Health Service as a Student Counsellor. Having so little time available and wanting to see as many students as possible, I offered a three-session consultation to each of the young people referred to me by the doctors. It proved a wonderful learning opportunity.

I was impressed by how clearly a core problem emerged not only from what the client said, but also from his or her behaviour during the interview and how the very difficulty that had brought about the present impasse sometimes became enacted. This enabled me to observe, feel, think about, and comment on what was happening between us in the here-and-now and how this might be a way of communicating what was also going wrong in other relationships.

The interviews were mainly unstructured, but I felt free to ask questions if some statement needed clarifying. Also, unless such information emerged spontaneously, I would usually within the first session enquire about the client's family and what had prompted him or her to seek help at this particular time. I would be quite active in commenting on the feelings in the room and what seemed to be expected of me. On the basis of this, I might begin tentatively to formulate something about the nature of the underlying problem and how it might relate to present and past experiences. A great deal of work went on in my mind between the first and second session, especially an examination of the feelings and thoughts that had been aroused in me or appeared to have been lodged in me. These gave a clue as to the nature of the emotions and anxieties that were intolerable for the client to bear and hence had been projected into me. I encouraged the student to do some homework, too—namely, to think about our conversation and bring to the next session any further thoughts that had come into his or her mind in connection with it. The second (middle) session was the one where earlier hypotheses as to the nature of the anxieties and difficulties and their possible origin could be tested and new understanding take place. In the final session, I learnt how such understanding had been used and I summarized what we together had discovered. We would explore what the ending of our contact meant to the client and whether more help might be needed and desired, or not.

When, some time later, the Adolescent Department of the Tavistock Clinic set up a Young People's Counselling Service (which offers up to four sessions), I used a very similar model and was able to tell my colleagues about the method I had found useful in doing brief work—namely, a particular way of using the transference and countertransference to highlight a problem and promoting the client's adult capacity for thinking about feelings rather than gathering the infantile self into the relationship with me. An offer of a few sessions is particularly useful in working with adolescents and young people because many of them are afraid of dependency involved in long-term treatment. Few will be able to commit themselves to the latter unless, through an initial brief encounter with it, they have a taste of what analytic understanding is about. In some cases a crisis or block in development may be alleviated by the insight gained within the four sessions.

I do not wish to overrate the benefits that derive from brief work. It is not a panacea or quick fix that can replace long-term analytic work. However, my previous experiences of brief work have convinced me that at critical points of transition in a person's life, such as having a baby or facing the problems of retirement, disability, bereavement, death, even a few interviews can be extremely useful. The new situation often produces an inner turbulence and may drive the individual urgently to address previously undigested anxieties. To be able to talk about their worries and fears, to be listened to by someone who can bear to stay with psychic pain and help them to think about their feelings in depth, may give clients some understanding of the nature of their problem. In some cases this may lead to a realization that more ongoing help is required, but often the insight gained and the experience of being understood is enough to enable clients to manage their lives more constructively and to undo a block in their development. Brief work is most likely to be of benefit where the person coming for help is not generally disturbed but is stuck with a particular problem, especially if it is one that has come to the fore recently due to some inner or outer change.

## *The value of early intervention with parents and their infants*

Having a baby is a most disturbing as well as a very exciting event. New parents in particular are undergoing major life changes. Up to this moment they have been a twosome, but now they need to make space for a third person. This new entrant into the couple's life radically alters the nature of their relationship, requiring them not only to care for each other as partners, but to be jointly responsible for the baby they have created. A mother is likely to harbour some fears about the kind of baby inside her, of what it might do to her body, as well as worrying whether she can provide a good-enough environment for its growth. In the last few months, the burden of carrying the baby, anxieties about the birth, and the responsibilities facing her may weigh heavily. After the baby is born, the wonder and joy at having produced a live baby have to be matched with the realities of the ongoing strain of looking after a physically and emotionally demanding little one. Not only is the actual work of taking care of a vulnerable young infant physically taxing, but the baby's communication of his/her terrors of helplessness, of falling apart, of struggling to survive will put to the test the parents' capacities to be in touch with, tolerate, and attend to such extreme primitive anxieties with sympathetic understanding. In each partner the nature of their relationships to their own father and mother and siblings as well as their infantile anxieties will be evoked. What they have internalized on the basis of their own experience of having been babies, children, and in their parents' care will deeply affect the way they perceive the new baby, how they interpret the baby's behaviour, and the way they deal with it.

While the mother is likely to be the main caretaker, the father, too, is called upon to take on a new role, helping with the care of the baby and supporting his wife with his understanding, thus parenting the mother. He will have to cope both with the jealousy that may be evoked by the closeness of the nursing couple and with envy of the mother's ability to feed the baby from her breasts. All these upheavals, external and internal, while likely to cause distress, may also lead to a spurt of emotional growth and deep satisfaction for one or both parents. If the burden becomes too great, however, and the anxieties aroused too unbearable, temporary or even more long-term breakdown may ensue. Alternatively, past unhelpful defensive patterns of dealing with feared emotions may become re-enforced, to the detriment of the parent–child relationship.

When the Child and Family Department of the Tavistock Clinic set up an Under Fives Service offering up to five sessions to parents of children under the age of 5 years, I was keen to participate, hoping particularly to see parents of infants. Psychoanalysis as well as research in developmental psychology has shown that the foundations of mental-emotional health are laid in infancy. To offer understanding to parents burdened or unable to manage the disturbing feelings aroused by their young baby seems to be, therefore, of quite particular importance, a piece of preventative mental health work of the first order. Because of the intimate, interactive relationship between parent and baby, any upset in one is easily communicated to the other and can quickly develop into a vicious cycle of mounting distress. I hoped that an early, brief intervention (up to five sessions were offered), might alleviate an escalation of difficulties or resolve a crisis that had arisen. To witness relief, greater tolerance of the difficulties involved in being a parent, and the ascendancy of love towards the baby arising out of greater insight is a wondrous, humbling, and gratifying experience for any therapist. I have often asked myself how the little I have done could have brought about such a change. Part of the answer, I believe, lies in the fact that looking after an infant reawakens very primitive, overwhelming anxieties, and hence there is a great urgency to seek and make use of understanding. The concern for the baby and the wish to be good-enough parents further promotes working at the difficulties.

### *The importance of infant observation as a training tool for clinicians working with parents and infants*

The study of infants, which includes detailed observation of babies within their own families for a period of some two years, has made us aware of the intricate interplay between the mental states of infant, mother, and father. One learns at first hand about the most primitive anxieties and the defences against them, observes how adjustments and maladjustments come about, and watches character in the making. The responsiveness of mothers and fathers to the baby's needs and anxieties plays a vital role in laying the foundation for the children's emotional growth, the structuring of their personalities, and the specific vulnerabilities that they may be subject to throughout life. But the baby's endowment also plays an important part. Moreover, a lovingly responsive baby may help to pull the mother out of a depressed state, while a "difficult-to-satisfy" infant may undermine a mother's confidence in her ability to care for her baby and may precipitate a vicious cycle of persecutory behaviour between them. Infant observation also helps one to study one's own feeling responses to the triad of baby, mother, and father. We need to become aware of the strength and nature of the emotions evoked in us in order to empathize with parents and infants and not to allow prejudices and judgemental attitudes to interfere in our professional work. The following are likely to be some of the chief hazards:

1. Over-identification with the baby. There is a tendency to identify with the infantile wish never to be frustrated, to have a perfect mother. This attitude tends to show itself in being impatient when the new mother is at first clumsy in her feeding or keeps the baby waiting for a feed, expecting her to provide instant relief, be constantly available, infinitely patient, never tired, never having needs of her own. There is an assumption that all distress in the baby is due to inadequate mothering and could therefore be avoided.

2. Jealousy of the baby is often less obvious but probably always present to some degree. We all harbour an infantile wish to be nursed, fed, carried about, and given exclusive love and attention, and we may therefore feel jealous of the baby, noticing only the satisfactions rather than the distresses that are part and parcel of being an infant. Sometimes this leads to the view that the baby is being indulged too much—for instance, that the mother feeds him too long, or should not let him go to sleep at the breast.

3. Competitiveness with the mother has its roots in childhood rivalry with our own mothers and the wish to have babies of our own. It shows itself in a judgemental attitude towards the way the mother and father handle the infant and in unfounded doubts about the parents' capacity to be good caretakers. We tend too readily to be

critical and need to be aware of an inclination to step in and rescue the baby (which is only seldom necessary). We may feel inclined to give advice rather than being supportive and understanding of the difficulties of parenting a baby twenty-four hours a day.

It is essential to be aware of such tendencies in ourselves when we engage in counselling parents. There are a number of ways of setting about this task. My own approach is based on insights gained from psychoanalytic work. I attempt to get in touch with and understand the parents' feelings, their unconscious phantasies, and the nature of the anxieties that interfere with their ability to care for the baby in the way that their more adult selves would wish to do. The work is intense and emotionally demanding. It requires of the client availability and awareness of feelings in depth and the capacity to reflect upon them anew. The therapist needs the experience of ongoing psychoanalytic work in order to be able to discern quickly the nature of the underlying anxiety and to have the conviction that it is helpful to name it and face it openly with the client. Sometimes we may have to weigh up whether the baby is in any physical danger, but usually it is the emotional development that is at stake. I am convinced that we can best help the baby by the help we offer to the infantile aspects of mother and father, thus setting a model for them of being interested in thinking about and containing infantile feelings.

The following examples will illustrate some of the stresses experienced by parents and the way I found of working with them. I find it useful to allow up to 1¼ hours for the first meeting in order for a relationship to the therapist to develop and the main problem and its history to emerge.

### *The Monster Baby*

I was asked to see Mr and Mrs B urgently. The mother had phoned the secretary of the Counselling Service, saying that she was absolutely desperate and must talk to someone this very day because the baby's crying drove her mad. As she was speaking, the secretary could hear the baby screaming in the background. She told me: "It was such a terrible sound, it went right through me." The impact of this communication was to make me feel that something absolutely dreadful was happening and that I was going to be confronted by such a disturbed mother–baby relationship, perhaps involving violence, that it might necessitate hospitalization. I agreed to see the family that evening.

When I met Mr and Mrs B, I felt at once reassured. I found them to be a charming young couple who behaved lovingly towards each other and towards their 8-week-old baby boy, who remained asleep throughout the interview. Mrs B sat on the couch, holding the wrapped infant close to her body, while father took the chair next to mine. Mother told me that she feeds the baby frequently and plays with him afterwards, but within minutes of being put down he starts screaming and she cannot get on with anything else. Having agreed that this was difficult to bear, I asked the parents to tell me about the history of this baby. Both parents reported that there had been difficulties from the start. Mrs B had been very sick for much of the pregnancy. Then, in the last few weeks before confinement, the doctors became worried about the baby not gaining weight. Mother was eventually hospitalized, and when there were signs of foetal distress, two weeks before the baby was due, a Caesarean operation was decided upon. The baby was lying in a transverse position and had the cord around his neck. The mother was told that he was very thin because her placenta had not given him adequate nourishment. The father added: "He looked emaciated, like a concentration-camp baby—just skin and bones." They were advised that he needed to be given a lot of milk, so the mother fed him at frequent intervals. Her nipples became sore, and she became progressively more exhausted. She wondered whether he was getting enough at the breast, so she had weaned him the week before and bottle-fed him, yet he still continued to scream whenever she put him down. She mentioned that when she is not alone in the house the baby cries less, and when her mother puts him in his cot and rocks him for a while he settles and sleeps longer.

Mrs B added: "I haven't time for all that; I've got to get on with my work. I'll soon have to get back to my job, my maternity leave will be up then, and they will not give me more time off or let me work part-time. I don't want to neglect the baby and leave him all day, but my career is important to me." I said she seemed to feel that he never gave her any peace and would continue like this, and she would never be able to return to her career. Perhaps this made her want to get away from him and start work now. Her worry about the future might also have made her more tense and impatient with the baby. She asked in surprise: "Can my nervousness and my wish to get away from him really affect him? Do babies pick up such feelings?" She then spoke of feeling ashamed if he screams while they are out: "All the other mothers know what to do with their babies and how to satisfy them." Mrs B had dissolved into tears by now, crying pitifully; Mr B had moved over to his wife, was comforting her, and had taken the baby from her. I commented that the baby made her feel a failure. Father said: "I feel the baby is trying to tell us something. We are trying to be good parents, but what is the baby feeling?" Mother added: "Does he feel we are monsters? He seems so violent when he closes his little fists and beats my breasts. Can babies be violent?" I said she had no doubt that he was very angry with her sometimes, but she felt that it was worse than that; that perhaps he was accusing her of having been a mother who had starved him when he was inside her and that he had now come to avenge himself for that.

Mother continued to cry but became very thoughtful. Towards the end of the interview, the parents asked for advice about how they should handle the baby. I said I was sure they would find their own way of comforting him, and I reminded them that they had told me that he sleeps better when mother feels supported by father's presence and also when he is rocked after being put down by Granny. This led to Mr and Mrs B speaking about their parents. They both came from broken homes. In fact, this couple had put off marrying and starting a family because they felt that having children had led to discord and the marriage break-up in their childhoods. We parted after having fixed a meeting for the following week, but I indicated that they could get in touch with me earlier if they felt this to be necessary.

As I came away from the meeting, I reflected on the fact that they had not been able to learn from the way Mrs B's mother handled the baby. Did that suggest a lack of recognition of Granny's mothering capacity, a feeling of superiority on their part in terms of their intellectual and very impressive professional achievements? Was the baby felt to be an intruder who would destroy their careers and their marital relationship? Had the pregnancy, the birth, and the baby's appearance been so terrifying that they felt guilty and utterly persecuted, convinced that either they or the baby were monsters? I suddenly realized that I was having a corresponding experience of seeing either the parents or the baby in extreme terms. Having expected to meet a hostile mother, I felt very positive towards the couple during and after the interview and sorry that their parenthood had got off to such a difficult start. Instead, I was left with a very eerie feeling about the baby. I pictured an extremely angry, unforgiving baby, the kind of child that not only shakes the parents' confidence in being able to produce a good baby but gives them such hell that they regret they ever gave birth to it. Was this baby, in fact, such a sort of monster? This phantasy perturbed me at times throughout the week, and so I approached the second interview with much trepidation.

When I collected them from the waiting room, the couple looked more relaxed. The baby was crying but in not too distressed a way, and he quietened as soon as mother fed him. I noticed that he was scratching the bottle at first but then held onto it firmly. The parents were smiling as they told me that the situation had changed "out of all recognition. It is a complete success story." Mother said she had at first felt drained after the interview last week, but it was marvellous what had happened since. She reported that she was spending longer in putting him down and was rocking him for a while. He often slept for three hours at a time. He still awoke sometimes after a few minutes, but if she held him for a little while he would fall asleep again. She had stopped worrying about work. She said that she used to want him to fit into her schedule so that she could get on with her typing, but actually now that he was sleeping more she was able to get more work done. He was even sleeping for seven hours at night, and so she felt more rested. Father got him a little rocking chair made out of canvas, and the baby was enjoying sitting in it. Mother could put her foot on it and rock him while she continued working. "And when he smiles at me, I feel so rewarded." Father said that the baby followed him with his eyes. We talked about how they and the baby managed to keep in touch with each other in these various ways. "But," father added, "he doesn't always want to look at you. For instance, when he has been lying on his bed on his own and I come into the room, he sometimes seems deliberately to look away." A moment later, he added: "It occurs to me now, as I am telling you, that perhaps the baby is cross that we left him on his own." I said: "That may well be so—isn't it interesting to think about what baby's behaviour might mean?"

Mother burst out: "Do you really think that babies think?" She had read that it was all a matter of physical stimuli. I reminded her that she and her husband had wondered last week what the baby was trying to tell them with his crying. Perhaps, when she expected a terrifying message to come from him, it was preferable to consider him as incapable of thought. She said that he still cried piercingly when the bottle didn't come at once. He seemed to know when she put the muslin on him that food was on the way; he would look around, but it did not seem to come fast enough. She then began to reflect that when she had breastfed him, the milk had been there right away. "It's different with the bottle—perhaps he wonders whether the food will ever come." She looked astonished at her discovery. Perhaps thoughts about his experience *in utero* crossed her mind, as it did mine. She said she knew now how to handle him and went into some detail about how she fed him, held him for some time in the position he liked best, played with him afterwards on the bed, gently put him down and rocked him. "It's all so much better," she exclaimed. She said she wanted to see how things developed with the baby before deciding what to do about her work. She wondered whether she could not, after all, persuade her colleagues to accept her back on a part-time basis. She told me that she used to be very ambitious, a "high-flyer", but added: "It's not so important any more since I find more pleasure in the baby." Father said: "It's really wonderful what has happened since last week, we are so grateful." I asked: "What do you think did happen?" Mrs B replied: "When we came I thought that either I had done something terrible to the baby, he had such a dreadful time inside me. At other times I thought that there was something very wrong and disturbed about him, something really nasty and dangerous. I thought that if he is so violent now, how would he be when he is five, ten, and fifteen!" I said that they had been afraid that he would never get better, afraid that they had produced a cruel, monstrous child, full of destructiveness.

They then told me that for years they had not really wanted to have a child, they were so happy together, so fulfilled in their work and marriage. They then realized that time was getting on and that, if they were to have children at all, they could not postpone it much longer. However, it came as a shock that Mrs B fell pregnant at once. She was just about to get promotion in her job. Mrs B said: "I suppose we were selfish, we had such a good life, just the two of us, we wondered whether the baby would put an end to all that. We wanted him to fit into our lives and not to take over. Instead, he did take over and was controlling us. I was both angry and frightened, and it all got into a vicious circle. I feel we are on a much better footing now. I feel easier, he feels happier, and I feel so happy that I can make him happy". She thought for a moment before adding: "We have been seeing much more of my parents. I have come to appreciate my mother more, we are closer now, able to share the love and worry about the baby." Both Mr and Mrs B again expressed their gratitude and said they would write to let me know how they were managing. They sent a letter two months later, which stated that the baby was happy and contented and so were they—mother was working part-time. They again expressed their appreciation of the work we had done together.

I was very touched in the second interview to witness how the parents were beginning to observe and think about the baby's behaviour and emotional experience. Why, I asked myself, had these intelligent parents not been able to do this before? What had enabled them to do so now? It seemed that, on the one hand, a division had been established in their minds between adulthood and work, which were highly regarded, and, on the other hand, babies, which were looked down upon. I may have represented for them a maternal or grand-maternal figure who was a professional woman and also had the capacity to feel for and think about infants. This may have enabled them to bring their adult, thinking capacity to be used also in the service of parenting.

Discussion

While this may be part of the picture, I believe that we have to look in greater depth at the change that took place in this couple. What is so striking about this case is the way the parents' feelings about themselves and the baby were transmitted to me in such a powerful way that I was taken over by them—first, the feeling that they were monsters, and then that their baby was a monster. Yet the interesting fact is that this did not happen in the parents' presence or in the presence of the baby. I had these thoughts about the couple before I met Mr and Mrs B, and I was obsessed with thoughts of a destructive baby before I had seen him awake. I kept on wondering about this phenomenon. It did not fit in with what we so often describe as countertransference: our emotive response to what a patient projects into us in the consulting room, in the alive encounter in the here-and-now. It made me aware of the need to extend the concept of countertransference to include what we feel is lodged in us before and after a session. With hindsight I feel it was a twofold fear of their and their baby's destructiveness which invaded me in such a powerful way before and after the first session. I think the dread of a "monster" child had its roots in the parents' unconscious fantasy of having been responsible for the break-up of both their parents' marriages after they had had children and led to the fear of having a child who, in turn, would destroy their life together. To what extent such anxiety affected the pregnancy one can only speculate, but I am certain that the newborn looking like a "concentration-camp baby" aroused the frightening fantasy in the parents of being "monsters" themselves who had inflicted such harm on the baby.

In turn, the actual behaviour of the baby, his demanding a great deal of feeding and holding and his "eerie" cry, was not felt by them to be arising due to his neediness (linked to the inadequate nourishment *in utero*), but led to the belief that he was a tyrant who wanted to punish them and control their lives forever.

So a vicious circle of persecutory anxiety was set up between baby and parents, each interaction seeming to confirm the idea that they were monsters. I believe that the parents' phantasies were so powerful that they interfered with their capacity to see, observe, and think about the reality of their baby and themselves. What I think I was able to do was to alleviate the phantasy of being, or having, a monster by pointing at the interconnectedness of the baby's persecutory anxiety, anger, and demanding-ness and their fears, guilt, and consequent feelings of persecution. The parents were able to experience me as someone who appreciated their wish to be good parents, someone who empathized with the burden of caring for a young infant and was able to tolerate and try to understand their angry and despairing feelings. This alleviated their worst anxieties and created a space to see themselves and their child in a more realistic light rather than distorted by their phantasies. Instead of being caught up in a vicious circle of persecutory phantasies and anxieties, they were able to study the baby's behaviour, think about him with understanding, and thus to parent him in a way that engendered mutual satisfaction. A safer, happier basis was thus laid for his and their development.

## Unresolved mourning and its effect on the baby

The family doctor wrote as follows: "I would be grateful if you would send this family an appointment. Lisa and John, both in their early twenties, have been together for some years now. Their little boy, Robbie, died earlier this year aged 17 months, after a long illness involving many months of in-patient treatment. Lisa was heavily pregnant at the time, and Zena was born six weeks after Robert's death. Initially they seemed to be coping well with both the grief and the arrival of the new baby, but it has become apparent that the stress has become enormous and neither of them is coping. John has become rather destructive, which made Lisa leave home. She is angry with him and with the hospital. I am worried about them and how their bad feelings might affect the new baby, who is 7 months old now."

I saw the couple within a few days; they were half an hour late. Father had a round soft baby face. He was blonde; she was dark. He wore two earrings in his left ear and looked depressed. She was pretty, with dark rings under her eyes and an angry, withdrawn expression.

They sat down on opposite sides of the room. I said that I had heard from their doctor that there had been difficulties in their relationship since their older child's death. They both said emphatically that it had nothing to do with Robbie's death, they had often quarrelled before, but they then added that recently they seemed to argue about every silly little thing. I commented that they seemed troubled by this, and I thought the fact that they had come together indicated that they were both interested in doing something about their relationship. I wondered, though, why they had arrived late. I learnt that they had had a disagreement on the way to the clinic. Lisa was angry that John had gone across to the other side of the road; she had understood this to mean that he didn't want to come. John said firmly that there was never any question of his not wanting to come.

I said that perhaps this incident showed how easily they misunderstood each other at present and that it also indicated Lisa's doubts about John. John said he got violent sometimes and hit her. Asked what made him feel violent; he replied that Lisa didn't listen to him or want to understand him. Lisa said: "But when I ask you what the matter is, you just sit there and don't answer." I said they were telling me that the communication between them had broken down and each of them felt hurt and rejected by the other. Lisa said John had been wonderful with Robbie. When I wondered whether Robbie had been a bond between them which was now broken, Lisa quickly denied this, saying she had left John once when she was six months pregnant, but they always got together again because when they were close it was wonderful. Now, however, it was worse than ever before. I could sense a great deal of anger in the room and therefore ventured that perhaps they were angry with each other because they had not been able to keep Robbie alive.

From this point onwards, Robbie was at the centre of our conversation. John said he was very angry with the hospital; it was unbelievable how many mistakes had been made. Robbie was a wonderful child, he was so proud of him. Zena was nice, Lisa said, but "ordinary—Robbie had been special". Would I like to see photographs? she asked. Lisa produced a photograph of Robbie, showing a charming blonde, blue-eyed fellow crawling in his cot, smiling and animated. Zena was dark-haired, a fat, rather solid and solemn-looking baby. I commented on Robbie's friendly smile, and John said that was how he was all the time, in spite of all he had had to go through. He was so intelligent too. John became very animated as he spoke about Robbie, whereas Lisa showed little emotion. I spoke about John's pride in his son and then asked about the illness. They said he had seemed fine when he was born, but just when they were due to leave the hospital, the doctor had told them that Robbie had been diagnosed with aplastic anaemia and would need blood transfusions every six weeks. He was fine for the first six months, then not so well but recovered again, and in his second year began to have periods of illness. But much of the time they had thought he'd be okay. When he was 15 months old, a specialist told them that they had to be prepared for the likelihood that he had no more than two to four months to live. He was put on chemotherapy, and John said he had to keep a careful watch because the nurses often made mistakes. When I asked whether he was blaming the hospital for Robbie's death, John replied, "I can't help wondering. They moved Robbie to another room, then he just went downhill and after six days he gave up." I asked whether they also felt disappointed and angry with Robbie for giving up the struggle when they were trying everything to keep him alive. John agreed, saying, "Why, when he had fought so hard, did he have to give up just then?" I said they must have felt very helpless and as if someone must be to blame for the death.

They both said it was unfair what had happened to them. I said that perhaps their anger and blaming had got into their relationship. Lisa then said that at first they had been inseparable—they had met a lot of couples at the hospital who left their partners because of the illness of their child but "we were regarded as the ideal couple". The doctor had been worried that Lisa would reject the new baby and told John to look after her, but in fact it was John who wasn't interested in Zena, while Lisa had taken to her. "If it had been a boy," John said, "it would have been quite impossible." I said that perhaps it felt disloyal to his son to like the new baby. Turning to Lisa, I said that she seemed to find some comfort in having a healthy baby that she could help to grow, while John seemed to feel that he had lost both a son who was like him and also the closeness to her, and thus felt left out and angry. I asked about his work. He had lost his job on a building site, and then he hadn't bothered because of Robbie's illness. He would like to get back to work; it had given him satisfaction in the past, but it wasn't easy to get employment. I said the absence of work must add to his feeling helpless and doubtful about being wanted, useful, and productive. It did seem important to feel that he had a contribution to make to the family. I said I hoped they would find time to talk to each other as they had done today, and we agreed to meet again two weeks later, after Christmas.

At the second interview I hardly recognized Lisa; she looked so much better, with red cheeks and pretty make-up. John also looked less depressed. They told me that they had had a very good Christmas. John said he had felt so much lighter when he had walked out of my room than when he had come in last time; he felt a heavy burden had been taken off them. Things between him and Lisa had been so stuck, but ever since then they had gone on talking to each other. When he felt hurt or angry, he told Lisa what it was about. Lisa agreed that the relationship was great now. John had been very caring, but she was still not sure of him. She said he seemed to need to be reassured about being loved, even when she thinks that things are going well between them. She said she was rude to him sometimes and called him stupid, but she didn't really mean it. He said that at times he felt he could not get through to Lisa, though this was less so now. I remarked on his vulnerability to feeling unwanted and unloved, and I remembered that they had told me that Lisa gets help from her mother but that John was not close to his family. It emerged that his father had died when John was a child, and that he finds he cannot communicate with his mother. I commented that it seemed he had quite a history of not feeling listened to, and that this might make him especially sensitive in relation to Lisa's availability. Lisa said: "He wants me to be his Mum much of the time, but I have got the baby to look after." I said that this might leave John feeling rather excluded, especially after the loss of Robbie. John said: "I feel such a failure with no work—and not able to save Robbie." I said that all that made him especially need and want Lisa's approval—and at that, Lisa looked across to him warmly, as if this was a really new insight for her. John brightened up. He said they had done a lot of things together recently. They had been decorating their flat. He had gone to two building sites this week to offer himself for work. I said these were very important ways of proving to himself that he had something good to contribute. Lisa had had the advantage of being reassured by her ability to feed the baby, while he had not had as much opportunity to prove to himself that he could be creative.

They then talked about Zena, and John told me that he was enjoying her more although Robbie was always part of their conversation. He now shared some of looking after Zena, whereas before he had spent almost all day watching television while Lisa was busy with the baby, and so they had hardly communicated. I said it seemed as if they now felt that not everything had come to an end with Robbie's death, that they could invest in the new baby while keeping Robbie alive in their minds. Lisa said she could express her feelings to John more now because she was less frightened of him. There had been no hitting recently. John said he did not let himself get into such a state; he realized it was better to talk rather than to act on one's feelings. Lisa said he used to drink too much and then be violent. I asked when the drinking problem had started, and John thought it was about two years ago. I said it sounded as if that was the time they began to worry about Robbie's illness, and that television, like drink, might be a way of escaping from worry and sorrows. John said that he had gone drinking because it made him feel more alive, and I added that it was to counteract the dead feelings and depression. Having talked about these matters, they again stressed how greatly things had changed and that they really felt very close and good together. I said they seemed to have done a great deal of thinking and working things out together, and I wondered whether they wanted to carry on by themselves rather than continue to meet with me. They agreed that this is what they would like to do. I said that I hoped they would contact me if their relationship deteriorated or if they wanted to talk further with me. They both firmly shook my hand, and John gave me a big wink and smile as they went out.

It seemed to me that having a new baby had helped Lisa to invest in life again after her son's death but that, in order to cope, she was projecting her feelings of anger and sorrow into her husband. The more the father carried the anger, guilt, and depression, the more Lisa rejected him. The more she rejected him, the more John felt excluded by the closeness of mother and baby, and, in turn, he got angry to the point of violence. I was impressed by John's capacity for insight. I think that our work enabled them to verbalize their anger and depression and to come together to repair both the house and their relationship. Having faced their mourning, I hoped that the new baby could receive love in her own right, rather than being loaded with disappointment and depression and being perceived as only a second-class, "ordinary" person.

*Post-natal depression*

When Mrs D rang the Counselling Service saying that she wished to consult someone about difficulties over her baby's birth, our sensitive secretary gained the impression that she was severely depressed and therefore arranged for her to come to see me a few days later.

First interview

A pleasant looking woman, Mrs D immediately delved into the terrifying birth experience with Debbie. She cried throughout the interview, drying her tears with the many tissues she had brought with her. She had not expected the birth to be difficult. Contractions had been normal, but then the baby became "stuck". Neither the epidural nor the anaesthetic worked, and she was in severe pain. Eventually the baby was extracted by suction, and "it all felt like being tortured". When I commented that it sounded a very frightening experience, she nodded agreement. She had talked with many friends, who had passed it off as "just a difficult birth", not understanding how dreadful it had been. She lost a great deal of blood, was severely bruised, and required extensive stitching. The following morning she was asked to get up but fainted on the way to the bathroom. Everyone had told her that she was brave and strong, yet "I was in the most terrible pain and feeling dreadful." I said she must have been very shocked and have thought that nobody understood how awful she felt. Perhaps she might be afraid that I, too, would simply be reassuring instead of appreciating what a frightening experience she had had and that she was still feeling dreadful. I added that it sounded as if she had thought that she was dying. Mrs D began crying more copiously now, saying that she still suffered from the consequences of the birth. The episiotomy had left her not only very sore but so damaged internally that she had had to undergo a laser operation recently. She had not been able to have intercourse because it was too painful. She and her husband were close, and she had missed the sexual relationship. She said that it was all so dreadful; they had not in any way had a normal life since Debbie's birth. I commented that Debbie's arrival seemed to have disrupted everything.

Mrs D said her husband and his family, with whom they were staying, adored the baby and could not understand why she found Debbie so difficult. She herself could hardly bear to be with her. She found the baby demanding and could not stand her crying. I said she might feel that it was she, mother, that needed looking after. She agreed, saying that for weeks and months she thought, "There is this bundle that I am supposed to nurse, feed, and clean up, and I feel I cannot. I just want to turn away and do nothing." I said it seemed that she could not provide for the baby when she felt her own needs, especially her emotional needs, were not attended to. I also wondered how angry she might be with the baby whose birth had caused her so much pain and disrupted her relationship with her husband. She replied, "I know it is irrational, but I blame the baby for all this and I don't trust myself to be alone with her." I said it sounded as if she were afraid she might hurt the baby. Mrs D cried for some minutes. She said sometimes she felt that she could not go on any more, but until now nobody had understood how she felt. Everyone had been trying to be nice, telling her how well she was doing, but that had not helped. Her husband was kind, and he was wonderful with the baby. She was glad to be out of the home much of the day and liked her work in an accountancy firm. Debbie was looked after by a minder who was good with her and had only one other child to attend to. I said she seemed to feel that this was safer for the baby and herself. Mrs D said that every time she looked at the baby she went over and over the birth experience in her mind. She added that it was good to be able to talk to me. She reiterated that she did not feel that anyone had listened to her before like this and understood how dreadful it had all been and how awful she still felt.

She asked whether she could come again soon, and we fixed another appointment four days after the initial one. I ended by saying that I thought it might be helpful to try to find times when she and the baby were more at peace, so that they could meet on some basis of pleasure, instead of distress, which was such a reminder of what agony had been involved in her birth.

Second interview

Mrs D looked a little brighter and said she was relieved to be able to come. There was one thing in particular that I had said that had been important to her. Every time she thought about the birth, she now remembered that I had said that she had thought that she would die. This summed up just how she had felt, and it was a comfort that somebody had recognized this. She had been able to look at the baby more and feel less angry, although the thoughts about the birth still went on and on in her mind. She then told me how resentful she had been last Christmas, when nearly all the presents she received had been for the baby. I said that even before the baby was born she had been afraid that the baby was robbing her of what had been hers. I asked about her family and learnt that she had a sister who was married and had two children. I wondered whether Debbie was felt to be more like a sister than a baby of her own—a rival baby who had robbed her of her mother's attention. I also referred to the fact that it was going to be Christmas now and perhaps she felt that I was giving presents and attention to a child of my own rather than more of my time to her. She replied that she thought this Christmas might be a bit better than the last. I suggested that maybe when her needs and her painful experiences were given attention here, she was able to give more of herself to the baby. She told me that they were planning to buy a house of their own and hoped to move the following month.

Third interview

Mrs D reported that, although she was still crying when she came to see me, she was doing so much less at home. What emerged in this session was primarily that Mrs D had been very efficient and successful in her work and had thought of herself as a "superwoman". It became clear that the birth had disrupted this notion of herself as so capable and in control. I said that the delivery had thrown her back into a state of feeling helplessly dependent on others, like a small child. She seemed also to feel that these others had inflicted the pain and suffering on her on purpose, like torturers.

Fourth interview

Mrs D reported that she felt much better. They had moved, and she felt very pleased to be in her own home rather than staying with her in-laws. She now had more space and freedom. Debbie was crawling up and down the corridor. I commented that there seemed to be a feeling of more space for both of them, that she and the baby could be near, yet not too close to each other. Mrs D talked of her love of gardening and hoped that Debbie might enjoy sharing this activity with her. She sounded altogether more hopeful. I agreed to Mrs D's wish that the fifth and last interview should take place after Debbie's birthday, a day she was dreading.

Fifth interview

Mrs D immediately started crying but said she had not done so for some time. It was good to have a home of their own, the sexual relationship with her husband had returned to normal, and she was enjoying Debbie. She mentioned that the baby was becoming very independent, was developing well, and had begun to sleep through the night. Mrs D looked proud as she told me that everyone finds her delightful. The baby-minder had commented that Debbie seemed so much better these days. She was no longer restless and fretful. Mrs D thought this might relate to her feeling less upset and more at ease with the baby. I said the move and the birthday were quite a big event, marking the fact that they had all survived this very difficult first year. She seemed to have begun to enjoy her family. She said her husband had been thinking about another addition to the family, but she was in no hurry to have another baby. It was nice, though, to see Debbie settling down to toys, and she liked playing with her. I asked about the birthday, and Mrs D said it had all gone very well, and a good time had been had by everyone. They had invited friends, and Mrs D had made a big birthday cake.

Then she started to cry as she told me that she had been terribly upset by a dream she had had the night after Debbie's birthday. In the dream, *she had seen the baby sitting inside the gas oven they had recently acquired. The baby was trapped and screaming, but she had just stood by looking on and did nothing.* Mrs D cried heartrendingly, saying she was still terribly upset about the dream, it was so awful. I said what felt awful was that the dream showed her murderous feelings towards the baby, allowing it to be tortured. I thought the birthday had once more aroused her anger at the terrible birth experience. I reminded her that at one point we had talked about Debbie feeling more like a baby sister/younger sibling to her than her baby. Perhaps the birthday had brought up in Mrs D early childhood feelings about her own mother's baby who was to stew in mother's stomach, to have no life, so that it should not rob Mrs D of her mother's attention. Maybe she felt that such hidden early feelings were the reason for her having such a punishing labour when she had thought that the baby might kill her. I recognized that she was feeling dreadful and very miserable about such murderous phantasies. I thought that alongside such thoughts she also felt very sorry for the baby, who was trapped inside and whom she had not been able to help to get out. This too must have made her feel helpless at the time of baby's birth. I thought that she was able to deal better with her feelings during the daytime and that these thoughts had now become contained within a dream.

Perhaps, as this was our last meeting, she might also feel angry with me, as if I were a mother who now replaced her with the next baby. Mrs D gathered herself together and told me the interviews had been extremely important to her. "I don't know what would have happened if I had not had this opportunity come and talk to you," she said; "I feel I might have hurt the baby," and after a pause she added, "or committed suicide." We talked about whether it was appropriate for this to be the last time we met. Having given it some thought, Mrs D said she felt it was. We agreed that if she continued to be worried, she would contact me. I also suggested that when she became pregnant again, this might well be a time when she would wish to have further help. Mrs D asked me to write to her new doctor. She wanted me to explain about the birth and about her depression. She wished the doctor to know that she had been to the Counselling Service and that if she got depressed again this was the kind of help she wanted, rather than to be sent off to a psychiatric hospital or treated with antidepressant drugs.

Comment

We see that Mrs D's experience of giving birth to a baby not only was felt as an attack on her body, but shattered the omnipotent image she had of herself as a "superwoman". This resulted in a life-and-death struggle between the strict internal voice, which demanded that she be perfect, and the rage with her child who had forced her to confront her vulnerability and her negative feelings about mother's babies. It was hard for me to decide during the course of the fifth interview whether it was safe for this to be our last meeting. But I trusted Mrs D neither to act on her feelings not to push them out of her mind, but to seek further help if necessary. I think it is important to remember that uncertainty about what has been achieved and worry about the future are always present and are integral elements of the burden of anxiety carried in brief counselling work. It is essential that enough trust has developed during the course of the intervention for the client to feel that one is truly interested and concerned and therefore available to be contacted again when needed.

## *Conclusion*

I hope that the examples presented here in a brief form convey something of the variety of problems parents brought and the kind of interaction that took place between us. The comments show some of my reflections at the time of seeing the parents as well as subsequently.

I have found working with parents of infants to be deeply moving and rewarding. One becomes aware of how prone parents are to feeling inadequate, helpless, persecuted, enraged, depressed, and guilty. When there is no one to unburden themselves to, these emotions escalate, and anxiety quickly becomes overwhelming. It seems, therefore, important to provide a readily available counselling service, where parents can talk over their difficulties without being given reassurance, offered facile solutions, or infantilized by an expert. I think the clients I saw experienced me as someone genuinely interested in helping them to understand themselves as well as their babies, someone who respected their adult strivings to be good parents while helping them to examine the more infantile and destructive feelings that interfered with their task.

I set out with no rigid technique in mind and found myself working a little differently with every case. My experience of infant observation and psychoanalytic work helped me to be able to listen, to encourage the exploration of the roots of the current anxiety, to stay with psychic pain, and to believe in the emotional strength derived from facing the truth. It always seemed to me that I was doing very little, and I was astounded at the dramatic improvement that often resulted. Of course, many questions remain unanswered, and the degree of long-term benefit the client derived is uncertain. Yet I have no doubt that in many instances a dynamic shift did in fact occur. In speculating about the reason for this, I would suggest that the clients were locked into an unhelpful pattern of relating, feeling persecuted and being persecuting. Conversations with me opened up a new channel of communication between destructive and loving aspects of themselves, between their infant and adult selves, and this led to a better understanding between husband and wife, between parent and baby. As a result, hope was restored, and a benign circle of interaction emerged, which produced satisfaction and in turn increased the parents' confidence in their capacity to look after their babies and help them develop.

It seems to me appropriate to work briefly with parents so as not to encourage dependency and to avoid the danger of disturbing the new intimate relationship developing between parents and their offspring. On the other hand, it may be important to offer ongoing help where the parent has little internal containment or external support. Long-term help is likely to be essential where destructive feelings towards the infant dominate, and this may be the case if the parent has had a deprived childhood or been abused. There is another group of parents who, while they may be helped in their relationship with their baby, may indicate their need for therapy for a wider range of problems and can be encouraged to refer themselves to the appropriate agency.

The parents I have worked with on a brief basis, although they experienced anger and at times hatred towards each other or their babies, showed great concern and were primarily worried lest their negative feelings would take over. While it may be wise to be cautious about what may be expected from a few interviews, I suspect there are many parents who could use such an opportunity to develop their own resources to understand themselves in their struggle to find a better relationship with their babies and thus lay a sounder basis for their emotional growth.

Because they are in the midst of an enormous change in their lives, feelings are stirred up in the depth, alive to be worked with and seeking to be understood. It is always a surprise to me how even a little help given at this early stage can go a long way, and that this can prevent problems getting established and becoming a serious interference in the relationship between the couple and their baby. The countertransference is bound to be strong, as our own baby-feelings, as well as those associated with us being mothers or fathers, are stirred up by this work. Hopefully, we can develop an attitude of being able to listen and trying to understand the emotions and fantasies about the parents themselves and their baby as they are presented to us. Our client may fear that we will be like the interfering and criticizing parental figures in their external or internal world; alternatively, they may turn to us in the hope that we have some magical solutions to offer. While I am aware of such transference phenomena, I tend not to interpret them when dealing with parents of infants unless they present an obstacle to the work, because it seems to me unhelpful to encourage infantile dependency at a point in a couple's lives when they are being called upon to be at their most adult. It is essential, however, that we do not fit in with the parents' fantasy of being all-knowing, nor that should we only consider the baby. It is our task to encourage the adult part of the parents to look themselves at the primitive anxieties that have been stirred up by having a baby, so that they can test them against the reality and thus enable their worst fears to be modulated. It is a privilege to be allowed to play a small part in such a process, one that fills those of us who work in this field with a deep sense of joy.

## Note

This chapter is a modified version of two earlier publications: I. Wittenberg, "Brief Work with Parents of Infants", in: R. Szur (Ed.), *Extending Horizons* (London: Karnac, 1991), pp. 80–107; and I. Wittenberg, "Brief Therapeutic Work with Parents of Infants", in: F. Grier (Ed.), *Brief Encounters with Couples* (London: Karnac, 2001), pp. 69–85.

CHAPTER 2

# The relation of infant observation to clinical practice in an under-fives counselling service

*Lisa Miller*

This chapter gives an account of a method of working and a service developed in the Child and Family Department of the Tavistock Clinic. It presents some thoughts on the use of observation in psychoanalytically orientated work.

I need to describe the services offered in the Child and Family Department under the title "The Under Fives Service". We offer brief help—up to five sessions only, which may be variously spaced out over a number of weeks—to families whose concern is focused on anxiety about their baby or small child. For example, we have mothers and fathers with babies who will not sleep, who will not eat, who cry incessantly; we have couples where the mother is depressed; we have parents anxious about the effects of bereavement or divorce; we have babies who refuse to be weaned, toddlers who suffer tantrums and jealousies; and of course we have those who come with nameless and inexplicable anxieties. This service differs from the rest of the provision made in the department in so far as here we do not regard ourselves as having a referred patient. We have parents coming for counselling; they come to think with an experienced outsider about the problems they perceive in their child or their children. The worker comes from a multidisciplinary workshop where psychiatrists, social workers, psychologists, and child psychotherapists meet regularly to discuss some of these cases and other aspects of work with very small children.

Flexibility, promptness, and informality characterize the service. We see family members in various groupings; we like to see both parents, but we are quite willing to take what comes. We pride ourselves on being able to give an appointment quickly—sometimes very quickly—believing that in a case where anxiety involves a baby or small child, help is needed now and can be used at once. The relative informality of the service means that self-referrals predominate. A mere telephone call secures a session. Certainly the parents need to have decided that they have a problem, and it requires some courage to pick up the telephone and to come. But beyond that we try to put as few obstacles as possible in people's paths.

In the main, the very appearance of a family at the Clinic means that the parents are aware that something is going wrong with their capacity to be a mother or a father in these circumstances to this child. Our job is, through observation at all levels, to promote states of mind conducive to thinking. Indeed, we are fostering the parents' capacity to observe themselves and their own children. The work relies upon the knowledge that a good deal of change can be brought about in a family where the children are still very small. It is a time of naturally high-speed growth and development. It is a time when much emotional heat is generated in the family, and the potential for development in parents exists in relation to the potential for development in the baby. Interventions can be highly effective in the intimacy of the nursery.

I have already implied that one of the sources of inspiration for setting up this service lies in the tradition of infant observation as part of the child psychotherapy and other trainings. As is widely known, for the student who visits a baby once a week in the baby's own family setting for the first two years of life, the aim of the exercise is twofold. First, the student gains highly privileged and detailed access to the processes whereby a child grows up emotionally, socially, and intellectually within a family. Second, the student is enabled to develop the capacity to observe, and to observe in a rich and total sense. Watching and listening, developing an eye and an ear for detail and the power subsequently to record it, must be allied to the highest possible degree of emotional receptivity. The observer has to allow him/herself to stay in touch with primitive infantile emotion and anxiety. Our method of observation, of course, puts emotionality at the centre of the picture. Conventionally in the past, the observer has tried to be an impartial recorder, putting aside feeling and involvement lest these interfere with some process of noting objective truth. But here the truths that interest us are emotional truths. The observer cannot register or record them without being stirred.

There is clearly a link between this sort of observation and the concepts of transference and countertransference. As always, we owe a debt to Freud, who at first regarded all the complex and passionate feelings for the analyst that arise in the patient as something of a nuisance. But soon he seized and embraced the fact, seeing that transference and countertransference can be used in a central way to investigate what was happening in his patient's mind. Here, too, we as observers are investigating mental activity and mental states. We are asking ourselves not only to observe what appears to be happening, but also to observe the effect that it is having upon them. Correctly grasped, the emotional factor is an indispensable tool to be used in the service of understanding. Students observing an infant can become sensitive to infant modes of communication; they need to think about body language and about nonverbal or preverbal experiences and how to describe them. It is easy to see how useful all these capacities will be to someone who is attempting therapeutic work with a baby in the room.

Naturally, infant observation involves much note being taken of the baby's family. In the sort of brief work I am about to describe, the attitude towards the family as a whole, which is fostered during an observation, is also helpful and relevant. The observer gradually has to find her way to an attitude that is receptive, attentive, and nonjudgmental. In infant observation, she finds herself as a newcomer in a family; she has to establish a position for herself that is interested, friendly, but at the same time neither intrusive nor intimate. It seems to me that this is also a good position to adopt when starting to observe a family, which one hopes to help in any therapeutic way. Two things come together in the under-fives work: first, the formative experience of doing and, in my case, teaching infant observation; and second, the long-standing experience we have of working with the parents of children who are referred for psychotherapy. By this I do not mean under-fives cases; I am referring to the range of children who are sufficiently damaged or disturbed to be referred as therapy patients. We offer ongoing work to the parents of these children. I think we have learnt that to do this we need a particularly delicate response. With parents of referred children, unconscious anxieties and impulses including the whole range of transference phenomena may be called out in all their strength. Yet we only have a limited mandate to work in the transference. Parents are here on their child's ticket, and we must bear in mind the child in treatment, whose needs may sometimes be experienced as competing with the needy child in the parent. To disregard the transference is dangerous; the work may be wrecked on a sea of unconscious responses unless we have an idea of what is going on in the infantile transference and can find a way to address it.

We must also enter into conversation with the adult in the parent. This involves distinguishing between the part of the parent which is an adult and that which is a child or a baby and catering for both parts, and to see and work with the family as a whole.

## *Ella*

I should like now to describe a case that I saw under the aegis of the Under Fives Service. Our secretary took a call that she judged to be urgent. A young woman had rung the Service in tears, saying that her baby girl, born six weeks before, had cried incessantly all her life. I saw the mother and baby next day.

Afterwards, I thought that even the circumstances of our first meeting fitted in with some of the underlying themes that emerged in our first session. I often find that the way the family gets itself to my room demonstrates something important about themselves and their expectations, so it is useful if observational skills can be sharpened and employed from the first moment of contact. Ms B and her little girl were late. They were so late that I thought they would not come, and I decided to run briefly down to fetch something from my car. As luck would have it, I bumped into Ms B and the baby as they came in through the main doors. Thus, although I recognized her as probably my patient, she had no means of recognizing me, and I had a sense of misfit.

As we went upstairs, I had a chance to observe Ms B and Ella. Ms B looked beautifully turned out. She was carrying Ella, who was, surprisingly enough, asleep. Ella was lying not in but on her mother's arms, spreadeagled on a folded shawl of immaculate and dazzling whiteness. Ella, who looked a fine big baby and not at all sickly or thin, was dressed in a way that caught my attention. Instead of wearing the sort of clothes you expect a tiny baby to wear, she was wearing a miniature dress of red tartan—a small version of what you expect an older child to wear.

So even before we reached my room, I had some observational data, and some questions were forming in my mind. Why, for example, was

Ella asleep if she was said to be so sleepless? Could it be that already a process had been started by her mother's decision to come for help and the hope of receiving that help? I did not know. Why was mother so exquisitely dressed? And why was Ella disguised as a 4-year-old? There was an incongruity here. Most women who have had a baby six weeks ago do not look elegant, even when they are full of happiness. The impact of raw infantile emotion upon the skinless availability of the new mother means that she is in the full experience of what D. W. Winnicott (1963) calls "primary maternal preoccupation". This preoccupation is more often with insides rather than outsides: she is thinking about what is going on inside the baby, what is going into the baby, what is coming out of the baby. Yet there seemed a complete denial of all this, despite the alarming telephone story.

I settled down to listen. Ms B began to talk, quite quietly, rather hesitantly, but without real pauses. Ella lay loosely across her lap, still asleep but unsupported. Ms B told me that Ella was so restless and cried so much that everyone around her had become panic-stricken. She especially screamed at night. She could neither sleep not let anyone else sleep. The screaming had such an unnerving quality that the whole household became infected with anxiety. Ms B said that she was a nurse herself. Her mother was also a nurse. She and Ella were living in the same house as her mother, aunt, and two cousins, and none of them had heard anything like it before. They had called the doctor out more than once in the middle of the night. Ms B had taken Ella back to the hospital where she was born, and she was a constant attendee at the local baby clinic. Although all the medical people consulted had united at first in saying that there was nothing physically wrong with Ella, it sounded as though they were beginning to waver and to wonder what medical investigations they could consider. Ms B said that her mother thought that there must be something seriously wrong with this child. All this was relayed in an alarmingly flat, depressed monotone. Ms B sounded hopeless. She said she was getting very little sleep and felt she couldn't cope much longer.

I will confess to feeling curious about what Ella's amazing cry could sound like. But I had no chance to hear it, because the moment that Ella stirred Ms B looked anxious and frantically began preparing to breastfeed her. It was as though I could not be expected to put up with any noise at all. At this point Ms B launched into an account of her current situation. I was soon feeling that there was every reason for Ms B to be feeling agitated, angry, unsupported, and grief-stricken, and I was not at all surprised that she was finding it hard to care for

Ella. Ms B came from abroad but had been living here for some years. This was her predicament: she had been engaged to be married to Ella's father, a professional man from her own country who had more recently arrived in England. Wedding plans were in the air for June, the actual month of Ella's birth as it turned out. House buying was on the horizon. Then the couple went on holiday together, and on holiday Ms B became pregnant. Her fiancé wanted her to have an abortion but she demurred. He seemed to agree, but from then on his ardour waned and his interest cooled. As her pregnancy proceeded, he saw her less and less. He stopped discussing marriage. All this seems to have happened without any real acknowledgement or discussion of the way in which things had changed. The pair drifted further and further apart. Since the baby was born, the father had shown some interest. He had paid for baby clothes and equipment. But this was, of course, nothing like the degree of interest Ms B wanted. She felt betrayed, but proud and angry; she did not wish to beg for anything. Her own mother, the baby's grandmother, was beside herself with fury. She was bursting to get at Ella's father to force him to shoulder his responsibilities. To complicate matters, Ms B did not get on with her mother, from whom she had been separated for six years between the ages of 7 and 13. They had had an uneasy relationship ever since being reunited. Now they were forced by circumstances to live together, disagreeing in many ways over the baby and at absolute loggerheads over the baby's father.

This story was told in a low-key, disjointed, and elliptical way. Sometimes one will hear an observer say that an observation was difficult to remember and record, and it will be clear that some sort of unconscious forces were at work interfering with the continuity of the memory. Similarly, I found it hard work to join up and to make sense of Ms B's story, which I have written in a processed form. I also had to work to infuse it with some emotionality, because it was so flat. All I could do was to comment very simply on how angry, depressed, and above all preoccupied Ms B might feel. I mostly felt helpless and overwhelmed. What could I possibly do? I could hardly make sense of the story, let alone make comments that satisfied me.

As the talk progressed I took the opportunity to observe Ella. As her mother told her tale disjointedly, so Ella fed disjointedly. She never sucked continuously for any length of time. It looked as though she was unlikely to be experiencing a feed that had a beginning, a middle, and an end—the sort of experience that has shape and form and can acquire depth and meaning. Ms B did not hold Ella firmly and collect her arms and legs together. Poor Ella, achieving a noteworthy degree of muscular coordination, had to hang on to the nipple for dear life. She was too young to hold on to anything with her hands and arms, and she could not get a purchase on anything to push at with her feet. All her energy went into holding herself together by her mouth. She continued to lie unsupported across her mother's knee. Occasionally Ms B seemed to do the reverse of what I felt Ella needed. Instead of gathering the baby up, she shifted her legs or her body underneath Ella, or gave her little prods. Ella would give little shakes and flutters of miserable insecurity. She would slide off the nipple and make efforts to regain it. These efforts were only sometimes helped by her mother.

Our conversation changed course. We spoke now not only of all the distressing circumstances of their lives, and also of how full Ms B must be of preoccupations that stopped her from concentrating on Ella. We talked about Ella's crying and how it might mean that Ella was frightened and upset; we discussed the fact that it was worst at night when, I suggested, Ms B herself might feel more lonely and bereft. Ms B gradually warmed to the topic of Ella's panic. It seemed to make some sense to her to think about a new baby's bewilderment and fear when confronted with inexplicable experiences. Ms B's mood remained depressed, but she became rather more involved; she smiled and cried and agreed, while still leaving me dubious about how much she was absorbing of what we said. She seemed to have some sense of relief when I said Ella might be frightened rather than ill, emotionally rather than physically distressed.

Towards the end of the interview, Ms B was talking about how intolerant Ella was of being put down. I must admit that only when writing about it did I think that Ms B was also talking about a part of herself, which did not want to let go and leave the room now that she had established a conversation. However, even if it had come into my conscious mind, I probably would not have said it. What I did was to draw upon my unspoken observation of how unheld and unfocused Ella looked, and to say that people sometimes find that tiny babies like to be held firmly while they are fed and that it may give them a feeling of being able to hold on to something reassuring when they are put down if they are wrapped in a blanket. This sounds as if I am not only addressing Ms B as a parent, but also giving her advice. In fact, we avoid giving advice in a prescriptive sense; unless an idea springs organically from the conversation and is in tune with the unconscious preoccupations of the moment, it will be rejected now or later as useless. Here, Ms B gave no particular sign of taking it in, and soon afterwards time was up.

Ms B gathered Ella up. She handled her as if she were an older baby, I thought, not like a vulnerable child of 6 weeks. She rose to go, accepted an appointment for the next week, and left me alone with my thoughts.

I felt depressed. I felt at this point that I had seen a mother and baby failing to meet. I felt that I had also failed to meet a need; I felt that there was something fundamentally lacking and that the whole mess was too great for me to sort any of it out. It seemed ridiculous to try to do so within the limited confines of brief counselling. Both I and the setting were inadequate. I feared I was left with discomfort and dissatisfaction. Ms B had been hard to contact, hard to get a grip on, and I thought it was likely she had not felt understood. I had a sensation of having had to grapple with something passive, like a large smooth object on which one cannot find a handhold. I reflected on how the whole history was full of faulty connections. Ms B and her fiancé had been unable to engage: nobody in Ms B's household or among the professionals she consulted had been able to get to grips with the problem. You will notice—as I did not fully while I was experiencing it—how I identified with both the mother and baby. I left my room and went out into the corridor where I met a colleague. I said something about having just seen such a difficult depressing case, and my colleague said something about the force of projections in these cases. Once more, we can look to infant observation for some practice in absorbing the sheer strength of the infantile projection of anxiety and the difficulty in containing it, which seems to require in marked fashion the presence of a third person to help: in my case, my colleague; in the case of a student observer, the seminar where the material is presented; and in the case of Ms B—nobody.

Ms B returned a week later. Despite my apprehensions, she seemed to have made some real use of our first session. Ella, I observed at once, was not lying on a shawl in the precarious way I saw previously. She was firmly encased in a neatly fitting baby sling. Her mother took her out, made a sort of little bed on the couch, put Ella down to sleep properly, and then turned her attention to me. Before she had even spoken I could see a change. Boundaries had been re-established. Ms B was behaving like a mother to Ella rather than like a helpless girl. Ms B began to talk in a more animated way. She said that things had improved a lot. Ella was sleeping better. She did not scream at night any more, and she was feeding very well. I began to see that Ms B had gone away and thought about what we said. She told me that she had had an idea herself which, she felt, was the key to the whole improvement. She had been turning over in her mind things she remembered from our talk. I did not particularly recall this remark, but I had apparently spoken about a baby's need for attention. She had realized that while she fed Ella, she was not looking at her. From this moment on she made a deliberate attempt to focus her gaze on the baby while Ella was at the breast. Ella clearly felt better as a result. The nipple alone is not sufficient to focus a baby's emotional state; it must be supported by the seeing eye. One might conjecture that Ella no longer felt alone with her experiences. She felt accompanied by a thinking mind, and things began to make more sense to her. You will see, of course, that all this can be connected up to the idea of observation. Even in an ordinary infant observation, where we have no therapeutic intention at all, the mother frequently feels that her own interest in the baby is matched by that of the observer. In some families, we see that interest in the baby seems to develop and become stronger and richer as the observation proceeds. We must be careful about attributing this to the presence of an observer, but perhaps we can cautiously say that a good observer, by his or her very presence, can underline and support the seeing eye in the parents. I observed Ella, and so did Ms B.

I want to concentrate upon this first session for the purpose of this chapter, but I shall rapidly summarize the outcome of this piece of brief work. In all I saw Ms B five times with her baby, and the third and fifth interviews included Ella's father. Many cultural, social, and psychological difficulties were glimpsed as these two people tried to find resources to make sense of their predicament. But from the point of view of describing this sort of work, I wish to emphasize that although Ms B was left with serious, widespread, even intractable-looking problems to face in straightening out her life, these problems came to be seen as separate from Ella. For the time being, Ella enjoyed the necessary protected status of the infant. She grew into a strong, cheerful baby who ate a great deal and slept soundly. Her mother's problems would be bound to impinge upon her life soon. Indeed, at the time I last saw them Ms B's return to work was imminent; it was forced upon her out of financial necessity and certainly would make a great difference to Ella's life. However, that first connection between mother and baby had been formed. At our last meeting Ms B thanked me warmly. She said emphatically that she felt I had understood her, and she told me, "When I first came here to the Clinic I thought I was going mad."

I should like to consider this benign connection that has been potentiated between Ella and Miss B in terms of the containment of infantile emotion. To begin with, we have a graphic picture of how Ella's original distress entered into so many adults (including doctors and nurses) without being checked, held, and understood. People were starting to wonder if she had an undiagnosed life-threatening condition. It seems to me that Ella was indeed terrified out of her life. She was projecting primitive panic; but it was a psychic, not physical, state. With an infant, the two are very close and frequently undifferentiated by the baby. The point is that they need to be differentiated. Ella needed someone to realize that her distress was primarily mental. The basic conditions for containing infantile anxiety were not being met. Containment, as I see it, has two aspects; these are holding and focusing. The structure of the mother's arms and body around the baby provides shape, framework, and support, and her attentive gaze attributes potential meaning to the child's experience. Poets have called the eyes the gateway to the mind. This expresses a truth from the baby's point of view: through the mother's look the baby makes connection with her mental state and her thinking mind. The baby learns about mental contact.

Ella's undifferentiated primitive emotion was being broadcast out, but no receiving station was on the air. You could say that perhaps the essence of the message at length received by her mother was, "Look at me!" Certainly behind this lay some fear, again long preverbal, of non-existence, of death. It is no accident that so many infant observations disclose mother's fear that their babies may be dying. For example, the stable mother of a healthy new baby, the fourth in a family, confided to an observer that although all was going well, she had had a dream *where she saw her little boy surrounded by white lilies* and feared he might die. Phantasies like this seem fuelled and accentuated by projections from the infants themselves. We can easily conjecture in the circumstances that Ms B was entertaining death-wishes towards Ella, who symbolized so much that was unwelcome in her life, but we can also think that Ella was projecting fears of death.

Why could no one tolerate Ella's projections? It seems that when a small baby's projections are not received by its mother or primary caregiver, it can be hard for others to perceive what is happening. Understanding cannot be achieved without a degree of identification with the baby. We all have a tendency to protect ourselves from feeling infantile pain. Direct contact with strong infantile emotions tends to awaken similar feelings in those who make the contact. This can happen even at a distance. I gave a lecture on the emotional development of babies, which prompted a woman in the audience to ask questions. These questions were based on something that during the lecture had begun to worry her. She suddenly remembered how often she had heard a baby crying in the flats where she lived. Was the baby neglected and suffering? Once she had been put in touch with the notion of infantile pain, and to be somewhat aware of the importance of infantile experiences, this woman became quite severely anxious. The critical nature of adult responsibility became plain to her. We can see how the discipline of infant observation can help us to consider ways in which adults can learn to bear to be sensitive to infantile anxiety and pain. It was in some sense too painful for the adults around Ella to feel the anxiety of a baby who was out of touch with her primary object and suffering a degree of anxiety so primitive that it amounted to the psychotic.

Her mother's identification with Ella was not lacking. Paradoxically, it was so strong that she was bowled over by it. Ms B could not receive projections of distress, absorb them, consider them, and maintain some adult perspective. At one point Ms B told me she had been a screaming baby in the early weeks herself. I could conjecture that, because she felt so utterly unsupported, so let down from all sides, her adult self was felt to be disintegrating. She dressed carefully, she made her face up beautifully, but the grown-up woman in her could not be maintained. It fragmented and dissolved and ran away like quicksilver. Ms B found her own infantile self—similar to Ella's and drawn into identification with the baby—reawakened with alarming intensity. She was in the grip of violent infantile emotions herself at a level just below the conscious. Her state of mind was so inadequate and so inappropriate to what she herself thought of as the state of mind necessary to being a capable mother that she felt crazy.

At this point Ms B was in no condition to look into the problem, to investigate it, and to sort out the mess Ella felt she was in. It is interesting to note that after I saw Ms B, I was full of anxiety. Specifically, I felt hopeless about my capacity to make sense of the problem and despairing about the possibility of doing anything to ameliorate it. Depression engulfed me. I felt inadequate and alone with the case. I believe that the service I performed was to identify with the anxious infant in Ms B, to receive her broadcast, and yet, despite the difficulty, to do my best to puzzle away and to keep thinking. By implication I announced myself as emotionally available. This is probably the single most important facet of this sort of work, and again infant observation provides training in emotional availability. Once Ms B felt that the communication had been received, she was enabled to receive Ella's communication in its turn. Having been thought about, she could think. Having experienced my eyes as having been on her in a comprehending rather than a persecuting way, she could look at Ella. The adult in Ms B was recovering its ordinary capacity to think as the infantile aspect had some attention, and simultaneously Ella, the real baby, began to feel properly looked after.

The question is one of locating and addressing the unconscious infantile anxiety before adult thought processes can be freed and development can proceed.

## Henry and Margaret

I should like now to proceed to another case, again one in the emotional heat of the nursery, and again one where what we learn from infant observation is directly relevant. Once more it is a case where the first interview did much to contain anxiety and to release some thinking capacity. Mrs H rang the Counselling Service in a state of agitation. She told the secretary that she had felt quite unable to manage her son Henry, aged 2¾, since the birth of his sister, Margaret, a month ago. She felt he was getting monstrously jealous and demanding. She feared her control would snap and that she might do him some harm.

I rang back as soon as I could, to find that Mrs H was out. Her husband was there, and he brightly greeted me by my first name as though I were an old friend, although he did not know me and had only barely grasped the fact that his wife had requested an appointment. I could not help thinking that communication between them was at present rather poor. Their moods were so different, and one did not seem to know what the other was thinking or doing.

Next day they all came. Mr and Mrs H were a good-looking young couple, but tired, harassed, and not very well. They stumbled through the corridors. It seemed a long way to my room, and they were carrying large numbers of burdens—a pushchair, a baby seat, bags. When they got to my room, it struck me as being oddly full. This was partly because they grouped themselves towards one end, placing Margaret in her reclining chair on my office desk and distributing parcels all about. Mrs H had had Margaret and Mr H had followed with Henry who looked a sturdy, attractive, but gloomy toddler. Mrs H put Margaret down and, before her husband could do anything with Henry, began to pour out a half tearful story about Henry. Henry wouldn't do anything he was told. He was obstinate and contrary. He kept trying to attack Margaret. He wanted Mrs H's attention all the time, and even at playschool the teachers had started to say that Henry kept getting into fights—into stubborn, insoluble wrangles. Mr H, by contrast, was patient and kindly with Henry and settled him with toys and crayons at my small low table. This did not really seem to make Mrs H feel any better. Indeed, I thought I observed her shooting irritable glances at him and wondered whether she saw Mr H as helpful or competitive.

They both joined to describe life in a tiny, too-full flat. There weren't enough rooms, they chorused. Neither parent could agree on who was to do which jobs. Mrs H felt desperately unsupported. She said she was bearing the brunt of the new situation since Margaret's birth; she fed the baby, woke at night, struggled with Henry, cooked the food— but then we heard Mr H, who felt that his wife didn't appreciate how hard he was trying; not only did he look after Henry, rock Margaret, do the shopping, tidy up, but he was also the breadwinner and trying to have time and space for his own work. I felt I was hearing a familiar story, where the internal situation overrode external reality. Practical problems could not be tackled because of the unconscious meaning attached to them. I also began to wonder whose anxiety belonged to whom: again there was something familiar about this family where turbulence had been stirred up by the advent of a new baby, and where the anxiety produced by this was being handed about, passed on from one person to another.

Next, both Mr and Mrs H described how they had not wanted Mrs H's mother to come to look after things as she had done at the time when Henry was born. They wanted to manage without her; on the last occasions Mrs H had got on beautifully with her mother to her face, but was left with irritation and rancour, which she felt unable to direct at her mother and vented on her husband. They both agreed they did not want her to come again. But they were both nervous about having hurt her feelings and had recently written her a letter explaining their decision; they were rather dreading the reply. This mother was divorced when Mrs H was 10 years old, and all her children had assumed a protective role.

Anyway, they told me, things were so different with Margaret. With Henry, they had just felt he fitted in with the pair of them. They could go to a party and put him to sleep on a bed; they could travel the world with him on their backs (and had done so). What was going to happen to them all now? Mr and Mrs H conveyed graphically to me that they felt that an enormous responsibility had suddenly been thrust upon them. From being a carefree young couple, rather Bohemian, they were behaving as though they had been catapulted into a world of harsh reality and harder work for which they were totally unprepared.

I thought that, with two children, they felt themselves required to be "real" parents for the first time. At this point we can observe what is happening in the room. Henry is playing concentratedly and quietly with toy animals. Margaret is lying sleepily in her chair. Neither child is exhibiting any demanding behaviour, but Mr and Mr H are together seizing my attention and filling my ears. On the one hand, they both seem hopeful and needy, if rather desperate, cooperating in describing their problems. On the other hand, this alternates with rather competitive rivalrous behaviour as they vie for my attention and each describes the other one as lacking in some necessary quality.

We started to discuss the particular significance of the birth of a second child. At the back of my mind was a picture of this young couple who with their first baby had not quite emerged from projective identification with their internal parents—or, to put it another way, had been prepared to be looked after by Mrs H's mother and not to feel fully adult. Like two adolescents with a magic baby, they indulged their wish to wander the world. I never found out, I may add, how exactly this was financed. However, with the second pregnancy both seem to have felt a thrust forward; they settled, Mr H started to work seriously, and they turned down the idea of Mrs H's mother. But once Margaret was born, they found themselves facing sibling rivalry for the first time. Not only did they have to manage it in Henry, but they found it re-evoked in both of them. Each parent was identified with Henry, and a rivalry broke out between the parents as though they were brother and sister competing for part of a rather limited good object. There was not, it seemed, enough of anything to go round—not enough time, space, money, energy, affection, or sleep, and only just about enough of me.

That there was enough of me during this part of the session was entirely due to the fact that Henry and Margaret were so well behaved. Where were these two demanding infants? I believe that Henry in particular was gaining very marked relief from the feeling that his parents were being looked after, and, of course, he was freed from their projections—we were to see how they tended to invest him with aspects of their infantile selves.

Henry began to move around and to show expressively how dangerous he felt himself to be. He seized Margaret's hand and leg, waking her, making her cry, and drawing forth a feeble, impotent response from his parents. His mother seemed about to cry. His father begged him not to do it. Neither parent briskly stopped him. Henry had an eye on me, as though he was demonstrating what was wrong. I started to speak about how worried Henry must be feeling, looking at him but talking to his parents and hoping to address them all. Henry started to draw a self-portrait: "Henry," he said, showing me a picture of an enormously round fat face to which he added a colossal greedy mouth. I was able to continue, saying that Henry must feel scared if he thought he was so big. Would his parents remember that he was still small? Would there be any parents around to be the big ones? Could anyone get them out of this pickle, or were they just four children in it together? All four of them, even Margaret, were listening avidly.

I had been thinking that their small flat had become one big nursery. Mr and Mrs H had temporarily lost adult status. Henry was receiving the projections I spoke of a minute ago—projections of infantile greed and violence. He had taken on the significance of a huge baby who could never be satisfied, whose appetite increased as he fed, whose destructiveness could never be appeased. I spoke about how hard it was to feel like parents in the circumstances. Henry said he wanted to go to the lavatory. Mr H jumped up in a nice, fatherly way and took him. Mrs H burst into tears and said how much she loved Henry but that she was afraid she would hit him and hurt him. She was clearly temporarily reduced to the state of a big sister left in charge of a baby who was too much for her. The necessary agent for reviving her adult self—her adult relationship with her husband—was for the time being in abeyance.

I shall not pursue this case further here. During the time we met, both aspects of the maternal transference to me emerged—the helpful mother and the highly irritating one who had to be placated. Indeed, they failed to turn up for their last appointment—partly, I think, because they really felt better, but partly because they were avoiding me and the negative transference. But work had been done: Henry was better, Mr and Mrs H were working together as mother and father, and they were going to move house. The case, like the former one, illustrates what can be achieved in certain cases involving small children:

when the infantile anxiety can be located, contained, and transformed, then adult thinking can start. And the adult needs cannot be truly met unless infantile needs are also satisfied. The adult in us cannot function properly if it is being interfered with by the obtrusive unsatisfied demands of a baby in need of attention.

This chapter is based on a paper originally given in 1992 at a conference in Turin entitled "With a Reference to W. F. Bion. To Observe to Understand and to Share, without Memory or Desire." What relevance does the paper have to the title? I hope the first part explains itself. I have tried to demonstrate two examples of some work where observation leads to understanding and where, once the understanding has coalesced in the worker's mind, some decisions can be made about how to share this understanding with the families. The act of sharing the understanding makes demands upon one's judgement because, as in all work with an interpretative basis, one has to gauge how best to frame the communication—what can be put into words, what sort of words to choose, what is better left understood but unsaid. And what about that rather mysterious phrase "without memory or desire"? I am sure that we can interpret this at many levels. To me, in this kind of work, it means much as it means when we are thinking about the best frame of mind to approach infant observation: we need open minds, free on each new occasion from hampering preconceptions, able to see what is there even if it disquietingly fails to fit in with what we expect. We must not be too eager to see our wishes fulfilled, whether these wishes are to have our theories corroborated or to see the family we observe or treat turn out to be the kind of family that would give us pleasure. We have to try to see things as they are.

## Note

This chapter is a modified version of an earlier publication: L. Miller, "The Relation of Infant Observation to Clinical Practice in an Under Fives Counselling Service", *Journal of Child Psychotherapy*, Vol. 18, No. 1 (1992): 19–32 [Special Issue: Work with children under five].

CHAPTER 3

# Infant–parent psychotherapy: Selma Fraiberg's contribution to understanding the past in the present

*Juliet Hopkins*

Infant–parent psychotherapy was first named and developed by an American child psychoanalyst, Selma Fraiberg. She described the work in a ground-breaking book, *Clinical Studies in Infant Mental Health*, published in 1980. Since then many significant clinical and theoretical contributions (e.g. Stern, 1995; Lieberman & Zeanah, 1999; Barrows, 2003; Baradon et al., 2005) have been made to this field. The subject has expanded to include a wealth of complexities of interpretation and technique, but the value of Fraiberg's original psychoanalytic insight remains unchallenged.

Fraiberg relied on the assumption that there is no such thing as individual psychopathology in infancy. This does not mean that babies do not contribute difficulties from their side of the relationship. It does mean that symptoms in the infant can best be treated by treating the infant–parent relationship, rather than by treating either infant or parent separately. Like all short-term therapies, infant–parent psychotherapy is focused, and the focus is on the development of the infant, who is always present in the sessions. The infant's presence ensures that parental feelings towards him are readily available in the here-and-now for exploration and interpretation. Interpretation, as practised by Selma Fraiberg, utilized a combination of "object relations" and "attachment theory" to understand the ways in which the parental past interfered with relating to the baby in the present. The symptomatic infant was found to be the victim of negative transference, haunted by "ghosts in the nursery" (Fraiberg, Adelson, & Shapiro, 1975, p. 165). Infant–parent psychotherapy was the treatment of choice whenever the baby had come to represent an aspect of the parental self which was repudiated or negated, or when the baby had become the representation of figures from the past. The primary focus of the work was on understanding the parents' negative transference to their baby, rather than on understanding their transference to the therapist.

However, interpretative work was only part of Selma Fraiberg's therapeutic approach. She combined it with what she termed "developmental guidance", a rather misleading name, since it very rarely involved giving advice. Developmental guidance comprised a multiplicity of interventions aimed to support the parents emotionally, to demonstrate their own unique importance to their child, and to help them observe and think about the reasons for their child's behaviour. The infant's presence allowed the therapist to witness the infant's own contribution to the problems, to appraise his development, and to share his achievements with his parents. "We move back and forth, between present and past, parent and baby, but we always return to the baby" (Fraiberg, Adelson, & Shapiro, 1975, p. 61).

The clarity with which Fraiberg formulated the essentials of infant–parent psychotherapy offered me security when I made my first tentative move from working exclusively with individual children and parents to working with mother–infant couples and young families. In addition to Fraiberg's ideas, I brought from my British psychoanalytic tradition the benefits of working with the therapist's countertransference, a development within psychoanalysis which Fraiberg did not explicitly recognize. In the clinical examples that follow I shall supplement my illustration of Fraiberg's method with reflection on the clinical significance of my countertransference experience as evoked in sessions.

## Case illustration 1

Kiran K, aged 24 months, was referred by a paediatrician who had been seeing her regularly as an outpatient for the past six months. She had gained no weight for this period and was persistently unhappy, crying and whining all day, and unable to sleep at night unless her mother shared her bed.

The family were Kenyan Asians who had come to London when Kiran was 8 months old. There was an older sister, Sandip, aged 4 years, who was said to be no trouble at all. I invited the whole family, but Mr K did not come because he felt unable to leave his shop. When I collected Mrs K and the two little girls from the waiting room, Mrs K insisted that Kiran should walk unaided down the long corridor in spite of her repeated pleas to be carried. In my room Kiran plaintively demanded her mother's lap, but Mrs K put her briskly on the floor, demanding that she be a "good girl". Mrs K's first communication to me was a placating expression of gratitude for the move to live in England, "your lovely country". I aimed to reassure her that criticism was also acceptable by pointing to the pouring rain and saying that I knew some things, like the weather, were better in Kenya. Sandip at once settled silently to draw, while Kiran made constant overtures to her mother, which were all rejected. Mrs K was eager to talk, but from time to time I turned from her to the children to bring them into our conversation and to encourage their play. Mrs K told me of her anxieties about Kiran's failure to thrive, her insatiable demands, and her persistent misery. As a baby, Kiran had mainly been cared for by an ayah, until the move to London when she was 8 months old. Then Kiran had begun to cry, whine, and to refuse food, problems which steadily grew worse. Mrs K had left behind many loved relatives in Kenya and a luxurious life with servants. She was now largely alone, performing the servants' duties herself and seeing little of her husband, who worked long hours. She sounded gleeful when she said that Kiran doesn't even allow her to sleep with her husband any more. It was a painful interview in which I found Mrs K's rejection of Kiran hard to bear, while the extent of her depression and of her antagonism towards her husband made me feel despondent. I ended by saying that this was a problem that would take some time to solve and that we would need to include her husband in our next meeting.

Three weeks later, Mrs K returned with her daughters, explaining that her husband had not come because there was no need. She herself had only come to thank me and to ask what I had done. Kiran had been happy by day, was eating heartily, and was sleeping alone in her bedroom at night. I said I was as amazed as she was. In fact, I had noticed from the moment I met them that this time Mrs K had felt differently about Kiran, for she had swept her into her arms, carried her down the corridor, and sat down with her cradled in her lap. Kiran had then felt sufficiently secure to slither down to explore the toys with concentration. Mrs K explained that everything had changed because she had learned from me how to play with her children. She had never played with them before because in Kenya this was a job for servants, but now she knew how to do it and it had made them all happy. This surprised me further, since I had scarcely played with her children at all.

What had enabled this mother to change her attitude towards her own role and towards her children so dramatically? I do not know, but I think that in the course of talking with me she had discovered something new about herself: the extent of her grief about the loss of Kenya and her resentment towards her husband for bringing her here, depriving her of her extended family, and turning her into a servant. When she had told me about the move, I had given her permission to feel grief by commenting sympathetically upon what anyone would feel under the circumstances. After she was in touch with her loss, I suggested that Kiran might also have missed Kenya and her ayah, and since then had been complaining and grieving for both of them. A further significant moment occurred when I had drawn Mrs K's attention to Kiran's repeated approaches to her and had said that they were not only tiresome demands for attention, but also signs of Kiran's affection for her mother and of her wish to be close to her. Finally, there had been an opportunity to focus on Sandip by talking about her picture of nice and nasty spiders in terms of the way these two little girls had divided the nice and nasty roles between them, instead of each being able to be both nice and nasty.

The speed of Kiran's transformation in so many areas of development remains unique in my experience. Happily, it has made for a conveniently concise, if very atypical, account of brief work with infants. However, dramatic symptomatic changes do occur in this work although they certainly cannot be relied upon and some families need long-term intervention. What can seem surprising is that significant changes in behaviour can occur without the parent's or the child's behaviour ever having been a focus of attention. As Daniel Stern (1995) has said, infant–parent psychotherapy is not a behaviour-orientated therapy, but a representation-oriented one. In this case, Mrs K's self-representation as good and grateful was attributed to Sandip, while Kiran represented her own resentment and misery. As long as Mrs K needed to repudiate and negate these feelings in herself, she projected them onto Kiran who enacted them for her. Probably Kiran's initial distress about the move from Kenya, when she was 8 months old, had made her a natural target for her mother's projection. When my intervention had helped Mrs K to accept her resentment and to mourn her loss, she became able to empathize with Kiran, to comfort her, and to reciprocate her affection. As Selma Fraiberg has described, when someone hears a mother's own cries she becomes able to comfort her baby. In retrospect, I realized that Mrs K had left me feeling so despondent after our first meeting because she had been able to communicate her cries at an emotional level. I have learned that parents who can communicate their distress at this level are more likely to benefit from the therapeutic encounter with me.

These changes were made in the context of a positive relationship to me, which led Mrs K to identify with me as someone other than a servant who could enjoy playing with children, thus giving her permission to enjoy this activity as a mother and not a servant to her children. This could be called a transference cure. Such transference cures are not to be dismissed. They can prove more lasting in infant–parent psychotherapy than they might in individual work. Once the vicious cycle of the child enacting the parent's projections has been broken, the child is freed to develop other strategies and may not collaborate with a pathological enactment if called upon to do so again. In Kiran's case the referring paediatrician found that there had been no recurrence of her problems six months later.

*Case illustration 2*

My second case illustration is one in which the baby had become the representation of figures from the parental past as well as negative aspects of the parental self.

Sukie S, aged 24 months, and her single mother, Ms S, were referred by their health visitor. Ms S was worried that her little daughter was "a monster" and "exceptionally clinging". The health visitor was more concerned about Ms S's parenting. I learned that when Sukie was 9 months old, Ms S had entirely destroyed her own flat, in order, she said, not to destroy Sukie, and to get help with the care of her daughter. Since then Sukie had been on the "at-risk" register and had received daily foster care, while Ms S had had weekly support from a social worker. Ms S still found Sukie's company very hard to bear and particularly disliked being touched by her.

When Ms S and Sukie came to see me, I encountered a stout Irish woman and a small freckled child in a buggy. Upon entering my room, Ms S left Sukie in the buggy against the door and chose to sit as far away from her as possible. She at once embarked upon a tirade of hatred against her daughter and her extended family, as well as against social services and other authorities. She was furious that "they" hadn't let her have an abortion, that "they" hadn't allowed her to give Sukie up for adoption, and that no one had helped her with Sukie's care. Sukie seemed entirely unperturbed by this diatribe. She sat silently in her buggy, looking with great interest at the attractive toys that I had set out in the centre of the room. She made no flicker of protest. Mrs S's irate monologue continued. I found myself unable to listen. It required all my resolution simply to sit still and not to rescue Sukie from her mother's hatred and to free her to play with the appealing toys. I felt frightened of Ms S, battered by her onslaught, furious with her social worker (who clearly should have arranged for Sukie's adoption), and helpless to work with such a hopeless case. Minutes went by. I longed for rescue. I even found myself thinking how hard the countertransference is to bear in infant–parent psychotherapy in contrast to individual work. If only I had seen this mother on her own, I would have been able to listen to every word she had said.

I mention my feelings for two reasons. One is that in thinking about training for this work, the capacity to contain emotional distress while listening and without taking sides is something that has to be attended to and developed. I shall return to this issue later. The other reason is that these feelings, the countertransference, are valuable as a source of insight. We can use our countertransference to understand and to interpret the patient's transference, as proved to be necessary to gain Ms S's cooperation. And we can use it to help select the focus for short-term therapy. Stern (1995) has described how the baby's behaviour provides valuable cues to relevant themes on which to focus the therapy. So does the countertransference. In this case these two sources of information reinforced each other. Sukie's inability to protest at her confinement suggested themes of intimidation and abuse that were echoed by my feelings. In addition, my urge to enact the role of rescuer suggested a further and more hopeful theme.

While struggling with my own emotions, I looked at Sukie, who had started to rock gently back and forth. I thought at first that she was doing this for comfort, but then I realized that she was now gently inching her buggy towards the toys. Sukie's determination gave me courage to interrupt Ms S and to begin to work.

I began by acknowledging Ms S's anger and her disappointment that having a baby had proved such a terrible burden and that she had had no satisfactory help with it. I said I thought her anger about coming to see me was to do with her fear that yet another authority would fail to help; she might be afraid that I would only criticize her and make things worse, when she really needed rescuing. Ms S calmed down enough to begin to describe her exasperation with Sukie. "She follows me everywhere at home. She wants to suffocate me. She terrorizes people. She messes up the flat. She wrecks everything." It was hard to reconcile this picture with the inhibited child who had now moved her buggy to the table and was tentatively touching the tea set. Ms S went on to express her fear that she would flatten Sukie. She said that she had days of terrible depression when she could not get up for fear that she would batter her. She would lie in bed preoccupied with whether to give up Sukie for adoption or not. Sukie had learned to stay in her room when Ms S was "in a mood". She was always put to bed very early and had never called her mother in the night. Ms S said she had come to see me to make me tell social services that Sukie should spend an extended period in residential care to enable Ms S to finally decide whether she wanted her adopted or not.

Ms S was surprised to be asked about her own childhood. She described it with calm detachment as though it had happened to someone else. Her father had been extremely violent and had selected her from among her siblings to be the particular victim of his hatred. She had been hospitalized three times on account of the injuries that he had given her. He was a tyrant and a wrecker. Her mother had never protected her and had lied about the cause of her injuries to protect Ms S's father from the police. Her home was like a prison, and she ran away as soon as she was 16.

I asked if Ms S had ever wondered whether her present difficulties were related to her childhood experiences. She was astonished. I pointed out the similarities in what she had said about Sukie and about her father. At the moment when I mentioned the way she had felt imprisoned in turn by each of them, Ms S got up and unharnessed Sukie so that she was freed at last to play. At that point Ms S appeared to feel able to empathize with Sukie and did not have to force her to continue her own experience of imprisonment. This was a beautiful illustration of Selma Fraiberg's finding that remembering saves one from blind repetition because it enables identification with the injured child (Fraiberg, Adelson, & Shapiro, 1975, p. 197). It gave me hope for change and enabled me to suggest that we should have a few more meetings in order to explore the problems that lay behind Ms S's preoccupation with thoughts of giving her unbearable daughter away.

When Ms S and Sukie returned for their next appointment, Ms S told me that it had been "a mind-blowing experience" to think that her problems were related to her past. She had contacted her three siblings, and together they had shared memories of their childhood which they had never mentioned before. Ms S felt immense relief that her version of abuse was confirmed. She said she had stopped blaming herself for everything and no longer feared she might be mad.

Ms S was not willing to commit herself and Sukie to regular appointments. I saw them for eight appointments spread over ten months before Ms S dropped out of treatment without explanation or goodbye. In each of our meetings Ms S had recalled appalling events from her childhood with an increasing amount of feeling, and in each meeting she had shown an increasing capacity to relate positively to Sukie. In our fifth meeting she said she had realized that Sukie wasn't really a little monster, she had simply imagined her so. She recounted how for the first time she had done something other than routine care for Sukie's sake—she had taken her to the park. She also related, with embarrassment about being "so soft", that she now took Sukie on her lap when they watched TV together. Her own mother had never cuddled her. She said she had suffered no more depression, and for the first time she made no mention of adoption.

In what proved to be our last meeting, Ms S spoke warmly of feeling at last that she and Sukie belong together. She had lost the impulse to flatten her and had amazed herself by starting to play with her. These changes were achieved after Ms S visited her father in Ireland and confronted him with his violence towards her in childhood. Instead of denying it, as he had always done before, he acknowledged it and begged forgiveness. No doubt this moving encounter was responsible for another change that I saw that day. When Sukie fell and hurt herself, Ms S acknowledged that it hurt and comforted her with a cuddle. In previous sessions she had responded to all Sukie's bumps with laughter and remarks like, "She's faking tears" and "She's so clumsy she brings it on herself." It seemed that she could respond to Sukie's hurt now that her father had responded to hers.

As Ms S changed, so did Sukie. She became self-assertive and talkative. She listened increasingly to our adult talk and was pleased to be included. Ms S was surprised to realize how much Sukie understood, and she followed my lead by talking to her more. Sukie lost the compulsive compliance that was manifest in our first meetings and started to defy her mother. She also started to attack me when I ended the sessions, but she never risked trying to hurt her mother. Her sleep became disturbed by nightmares of monsters, and she took refuge in her mother's bed. It seemed that Ms S was beginning to become a secure base for Sukie, but a really secure attachment remained a distant prospect. Their relationship was still full of conflict, rebuff, teasing, threats, and slaps.

There is always the drawback, when trying to write a coherent account of therapy, that all sense of the anxiety and confusion that accompanies the work is lost. I should emphasize that I found this work stressful. I worried at first that I had made a bad situation worse by reducing the likelihood of adoption. I worried when I decided not to report an incident of battering. I worried when appointments were missed and I did not know if Ms S and Sukie would return. I worried when they drifted prematurely out of therapy and missed further opportunities for progress. Fortunately I have colleagues to turn to, since opportunities for discussion are essential in supporting this work.

## Understanding the past in the present

When trying to understand the many baffling problems that arise in infant–parent relationships, I have found it helpful to work with Benedek's hypothesis (1959) that the experience of becoming a parent evokes representations of the parent's own early infant–parent relationship. These representations, which may have lain dormant for years, become available for re-experiencing, for projection and enactment. They involve both sides of the parent's own early relationships. This means that the new baby may be experienced either as a representation of the parent's own childhood parent or of the parent's own childhood self, or both. This can be, and often is, an enriching experience. However, when the early representations are negative, their projection can lead to difficulties. Ms S provides a tragic example of a mother who appears to have experienced her daughter both as her father (tyrannical, imprisoning) and as her childhood self (hated, rejected). She also experienced herself both as her violent father and as her desperate childhood self, longing for rescue. The role of her uncaring mother who had failed to protect her seems to have been mainly attributed to the social services. Ms S entirely denied the existence of their helpful interventions, perhaps because they had not understood that the primary protection that she had needed was from the ghosts of the past. The social worker who supported Ms S had never mentioned the possible contribution of Ms S's childhood. A vital opportunity had been lost through lack of training.

I do not want to exaggerate the importance of interpreting the intrusion of the past, because, as I shall emphasize, it is only part of what therapists have to offer. But before going further, I would add that exploring the influence of the past does more than offer the possibility of a dynamic disconnection between past representations and present realities—that is, unhooking the baby from the parents' hang-ups. As Ms S demonstrated, it can ease an exaggerated sense of guilt and self-blame and it can give permission to know and to feel what may previously have been forbidden (see Bowlby, 1979).

This case involving severe childhood trauma may illustrate some points well, but happily such a dramatic re-enactment is not typical of the negative influence of the past. This usually shows in more subtle ways, not necessarily available to recall. A brief example will illustrate this.

## Case illustration 3

Daniel D was referred by his family doctor at the age of 7 months because he was excessively demanding by day and sleepless by night. He was the first child of professional parents, Mr and Mrs D, who were said to be utterly exhausted by him.

In my first meeting with the family I encountered Mrs D's great distress about her baby's impossible demands and her own sense of failure as a mother. "He won't even let me have a cup of coffee. I know I'm doing everything wrong." She was bewildered that after managing a demanding career she could not cope with a small baby.

Daniel was indeed extremely demanding. He insisted on being held in arms and fussed incessantly to get the continuous attention which his parents felt compelled to provide. Mr D felt helpless to support his wife and bound to emulate her practice of responding to Daniel's slightest need. By the end of an hour the room felt full of babies and I had to resist a strong urge to take over and impose tough limits. I summed up humorously by saying that Mr and Mrs D seemed to feel that they had given birth to a half-a-dozen babies. They laughed. Mrs D explained that she actually had been one of a dozen babies in the baby room of an Israeli kibbutz. She had no memories of the kibbutz, which her family left when she was 7 years old, but she had been determined to bring up her own baby entirely herself. Unfortunately the experience of motherhood was making her feel that she would have to find a day-nursery for Daniel if I could not help.

It seems that becoming a parent had revived Mrs D's representation of her unmet infantile need for devoted maternal care. She attributed this to Daniel, who was then felt to require the uninterrupted care that she had longed for and never had. Mrs D's expectation that Daniel always needed adult attention and could manage nothing himself seemed to have been communicated to Daniel so that he enacted Mrs D's insatiable infantile demands. Looking at it this way directed my attention to the prime importance of looking after Mrs D's needs in the present, in order to free Daniel from enacting her past. Mrs D was surprised to have her needs taken seriously. She thought that I would put the baby first, but she was relieved that I felt she could be entitled to her cup of coffee and to talk to her friends. With her husband's help she thought of various ways of reducing the stress of baby care and allowing herself some space.

In this case, the past was chiefly useful in making sense of the present. Although Mrs D could not recall her childhood, she recognized that her decision to care for Daniel herself expressed negative feelings about it. She could understand that it was difficult for her to know when Daniel had had enough attention because she had never had enough herself. I explained Daniel's need to develop his own resources and to learn to play by himself. In our sessions Mr and Mrs D practised ignoring his fussiness and were surprised to find that he could begin to amuse himself. Within a month he accepted the use of a playpen while Mrs D did her housework and drank her coffee, but his sleeping problems took much longer to solve (see Daws, 1989), requiring appointments spread over several months.

This is an example where a limited understanding of the past was supplemented by developmental guidance about the baby's needs. By resisting the impulse to take over and impose rules as the kibbutz had once done, I was able to support these parents in finding a middle way between complete indulgence and institutional care. It is also an example of the sudden emergence of representations that have lain dormant for a long time. Mrs D claimed to have had no experience in adult life of feelings of deprivation, of insatiable demands, or of incompetence and helplessness. Motherhood had brought rewards, buts its revival of the past was extremely distressing. For Mr D, parenthood was less of a shock. His father had been very dominating, and he seemed to expect to be dominated by his son, who was named after his father.

Understanding the interference of the past in the present provides both a possible explanation of the origin of infant–parent problems and a means of changing them. However, it is not the only way to intervene successfully in infant–parent relationships. Behavioural methods, too, have their successes, for changes in behaviour can bring changes in representations, just as changes in representations can bring changes in behaviour. The preliminary results of research conducted by Cramer and Stern (1990) established that infant–parent psychotherapy and a behavioural intervention were both highly effective in selected cases. The first evaluations of outcome, assessed when both these brief therapies had just ended, after an average of six weekly sessions, revealed no difference in the success of the two methods. Further follow-ups have not been published, but I can think of reasons why infant–parent psychotherapy might have a more enduring effect. It takes time to assimilate the past. Ms S provides a striking example of a parent who was still initiating changes based on her re-evaluation of her childhood long after she first recognized its relevance. Parents who have partners often support each other in exploring the past, once the therapist's intervention has raised the issue. They can help each other to reassess the influence of their backgrounds and to come to terms with them. This means mourning the parents they would have liked to have had and deciding how they wish to be different. As Main (Main, Kaplan, & Cassidy, 1985) has shown, parents who recall and acknowledge their own parents' contribution to their childhood difficulties are less likely to repeat their own parents' mistakes.

### Additional therapeutic factors: "holding" and "containment"

The overall effectiveness of both psychodynamic and behavioural methods points to two things: the extreme flexibility of adaptation within the infant–parent relationship and the amount that the two therapies have in common.

The capacity for rapid change in infant–parent relationships is a reflection of the flexibility both of the infant and of his parents. It seems that within their first two-and-a-half years or so, before internal representations become firmly established, infants retain a remarkable behavioural flexibility. Furthermore, the anxiety and turmoil attendant upon becoming parents make parents particularly accessible to issues regarding their infant. Their identification with their baby, which is part of the re-experiencing of early relationships, can bring with it a capacity to regress in order to attempt a new beginning and hopefulness about change which increases motivation. Some families are so well motivated that they can use the time and space provided by the therapist to tell their story and to work out their own solutions without the help of interpretation or developmental guidance. However, the therapist's contribution remains essential, even if it is simply to provide a "holding environment" in Winnicott's sense, and "containment" as described by Bion. It is this capacity for holding and containment that the psychodynamic and behavioural approaches have in common. Whatever the orientation of the therapist, the family know that their concerns have been heard, that they are not alone with their troubles, that they are not blamed for them, and that there is hope of change. If all goes well, the therapist is experienced as a benign parental figure who may be felt to replace a curse from a wicked fairy godmother with a blessing. The internal representation of a critical undermining parent may thus be temporarily displaced by the representation of an approving, supporting one and so allow a new pattern of interaction to be initiated. Stern has called this "the good grandmother transference" (1995, p. 186).

Holding and containment are easier to describe than to do. I have tried to draw attention to my own difficulty in this respect in order to emphasize this issue. It can be very hard to contain distress and uncertainty and to resist the urge to take sides or to intervene didactically. Experience helps. And so does knowing that these feelings and impulses are both inevitable and valuable. Recognizing them and thinking about them make them easier to contain and can also throw light on the work of infant–parent psychotherapy, as I have tried to illustrate.

Selma Fraiberg's book has inspired and influenced several generations of clinicians and researchers in infant mental health worldwide, many of whom have elaborated on and expanded her ideas, bringing the practice of parent–infant psychotherapy international recognition.

### Note

This chapter is a modified version of an earlier publication: J. Hopkins, "Infant–Parent Psychotherapy", *Journal of Child Psychotherapy,* Vol. 18, No. 1 (1992): 5–17.

# Later developments

The chapters in this section, by Paul Barrows, Louise Emanuel, and Beverley Tydeman & Janine Sternberg, describe the ongoing thinking about working with under fives, taking into account the recent burgeoning literature on parent–infant psychotherapy, neuroscience research, and attachment theory while maintaining as a central feature a psychoanalytic framework. Paul Barrows's largely theoretical chapter offers a comprehensive commentary on the model of the preceding chapters. He begins with a critique of Juliet Hopkins's chapter (chapter 3), raising the issue of "an almost magical cure" and questioning what we are actually seeking to change by our interventions. He gives a description of the current thinking with regards to parent–infant interventions, identifying three "ports of entry" into the parent-child system. His critique of research into two areas—working with parents' mental states and working with the infant's mental states—leads him to consider that neither on their own is satisfactory and that a model of parent–infant/young child intervention is the most fruitful.

He goes on to highlight the particular aspects of the Tavistock Clinic approach which give it its characteristic quality. Taking Lisa Miller's chapter as an example of a clinician working in the "recent British object relations tradition", he describes how although "the therapists are also alert to the parents' own childhood experiences as important factors . . . the focus is on the immediacy of the therapeutic encounter and the impact of here-and-now experiences". In other words, what Barrows makes clear and Emanuel elaborates in her chapter is that the situation between parents and infant/child has to unfold first in the consulting room, and only within this context can the parents' history emerge in a way that can be emotionally linked with the child in the room. "The process that effects change is the establishing of an affective link with the specifics of the parents' past that have been evoked by the interchange with this particular infant in the present." This approach is slightly different in emphasis to the classic Fraiberg model, placing a greater reliance on the apprehension of the emotional undercurrent in the here-and-now of the session to suggest relevant links to parents' past histories.

In her chapter Emanuel describes the paradox underlying a psychodynamic approach to brief work, where the technique of allowing the material to "unfold" slowly, without recourse to formal questionnaires or interview techniques, is coupled with a need quickly to select a focus from the emerging material, in order to effect some shift within a five-session psychotherapeutic model. Emanuel expands on psychoanalyst Annette Watillon's (1993) suggestion that the dramatic ways in which young children "enact" their predicament, and the family's, facilitates the speed of communication within the consulting room. She describes three "categories" of dramatic enactment that she has encountered in her therapeutic work and gives detailed clinical illustrations of each. These are broadly defined as "child-led dramatization", "internal parental drama", and "external parental drama". Emanuel highlights the range of roles and modes of intervention possible within this model.

In their chapter, Beverley Tydeman & Janine Sternberg describe the process of seeing families in a general practice and the application of the Under Fives model to this type of community setting. They illustrate their work with a case of a young girl whose separation anxieties manifested in sleep difficulties. The linking of observations in the here-and-now of the session with an awareness of cultural and family dynamics and past family history enables dramatic shifts to take place within a brief time frame. The "revolving-door" policy they describe, with families able to return for further "doses" of input as required, is a reminder of Stern's (1995) comments on the helpfulness of "serial" interventions for families with young children whose developmental trajectories are still so fluid. This theme is taken up by Dilys Daws (chapter 14) in her description of work in a local baby clinic, where sleep and separation difficulties are a major focus of the work. The pain of separation from their mother country adds a further dimension to the experience of loss of many families who are either refugees or immigrants to this country, which is elaborated on by Elizabeth Bradley in the final chapter of this book.

CHAPTER 4

# The process of change in under-fives work

*Paul Barrows*

The work described in this book is concerned with effecting changes in the relationship between parents and their infant. There is general agreement that the period of early infancy is one in which there is considerable potential for change and greater psychic flexibility than at other times, and hence it is a prime time for intervention.

In this primarily theoretical chapter, I would like to look more closely at the question of *what* it is that we are seeking to change in the kind of work illustrated elsewhere in this book, and *how* it is that we conceptualize those changes. As will be seen, this also has implications for the nature of that work, in particular whether it be brief or long term.

On the whole, previous accounts of the work of the Tavistock Clinic's Under Fives Service (e.g. Miller, 1992; Hopkins, 1992) have emphasized its brevity. It offers up to five sessions, with change often apparent within the first few sessions, later sessions being provided to consolidate those changes. At times such accounts can seem almost magical: the therapist is perhaps left in despair or puzzled—the family returns next time and all is resolved! For example:

> It was a painful interview in which I found Mrs K's rejection of Kiran hard to bear, while the extent of her depression and of her

antagonism to her husband made me feel despondent. . . . Three weeks later, Mrs K. returned with her daughters, explaining that her husband had not come because there was no need. She herself had only come to thank me and to ask what I had done. Kiran had been happy by day, was eating heartily, and was sleeping alone in her bedroom at night. [Hopkins, chapter 3, this volume]

If nothing else, such accounts can seem rather daunting for those beginning this kind of work, especially if their cases do not take quite this course!

Stern's (1995) rather broad review of parent–infant therapies, including those not adopting a psychoanalytic frame of reference, similarly proposes that they are generally and appropriately relatively brief: "usually between 3 and 12 sessions when there are no programmatic constraints." However he does suggest that we need to think in terms of a model of what he calls "serial brief treatment" rather than assuming that the initial few sessions suffice. Parents may return for additional help when problems emerge further along the developmental spectrum. These episodes of treatment then provide a kind of working through "longitudinally in time".

In marked contrast, there are the cases described by Fraiberg in her seminal paper which pioneered parent–infant therapy and in which she coined the evocative phrase "ghosts in the nursery" (Fraiberg, Adelson, & Shapiro, 1975). These cases were worked with over a lengthy period of time, often against the odds, with the therapist sometimes literally locked out of the client's home, and from a base that involved a well-resourced team, with one family having several workers, and the team having a psychoanalytic consultant in the background.

Fraiberg was, of course, working with a very deprived, high-risk, multi-problem population. However, many authors who write about brief under-fives work, citing Fraiberg's inspiration, do not draw attention to the fact that there are important differences between the kind of clients that they are working with, who can make good use of a brief intervention, and those such as Fraiberg's team helped, who might require much more intensive input. This is a crucial distinction in terms of considering the kind of input required to effect real change.

This huge contrast raises fundamental questions about the nature of the enterprise being embarked upon when we begin to work with parents and infants. In particular, it begs the whole question of what our aim is, how realistic that may be (both from a practical, resource-driven perspective as well as from a therapeutic one) and the potentially different agendas that therapist and family may bring to the clinical encounter.

## The aims of parent–infant work

If we begin by addressing the issue of exactly what our aim is in this work, by which I mean what is it that we are hoping to change, then I think that there are three main areas that can be identified, related to what Stern (1995) would call the different "ports of entry" into the "clinical system" of parents and infant. These are:

- the parents' mental state
- the infant's mental state
- the relationship between parent and infant

Different approaches privilege each of these, and I shall look in turn at the rationale, implicit or explicit, for choosing to target one or the other of these areas.

## The rationale for addressing the parents' mental state

It may well be felt to be axiomatic that the infant's emotional and psychological development will be profoundly influenced by his parents' mental state, since in most cases this provides the almost exclusive context for their earliest experiences. However, there are also now good empirical grounds for such a view. Murray (e.g. Murray & Cooper, 1997), for example, has charted the deleterious impact that the states of mind accompanying post-natal depression can have on the infant's developing mental and emotional capacities. We also know from the work of Fonagy, Steele, Moran, Steele, and Higgitt (1993) that the parents' own internal representations of attachment have a very powerful, if not determining, influence on the child's attachment status; and, from elsewhere, that that status is critical over a range of different parameters:

> Children who were judged secure with mother in infancy are found to be more cooperative, more empathic, more socially competent, more invested in learning and exploration, and more self-confident than children who were judged insecure with mother in infancy. Significant group differences have been reported at least as late as 5 and 6 years of age. [Main & Solomon, 1986, p. 96]

We might, then, reasonably anticipate that any help directed towards improving the mental state of the parents will inevitably have a beneficial impact on the infant and so justify such an approach. If, for example, we can modify the parents' internal representations, then the child's attachment status should benefit. There are, however, a number of difficulties with this rationale.

First, in so far as effecting change in the parents' internal representations is generally seen as being the province of long-term individual psychotherapy, the time scale involved is likely to be too slow to benefit the infant, particularly given what we now know about the time-sensitive nature of the developments taking place in the infant brain (e.g. Schore, 2001). As Frances Salo (Thomson-Salo et al., 1999), among others, has pointed out, "infants cannot wait".

Second, this rationale presupposes, as with the model propounded by Stern (1995), that because of the interrelatedness of the "clinical system" a change in any one element would lead to changes in all the other elements. However, this does not seem to be borne out in practice. For example, in a study by Juffer, van IJzendoorn, and Bakermans-Kranenburg (1997) that sought to promote attachment by increasing parental sensitivity to the infant, it was apparent that successfully changing the parent's behaviour, even in a very positive direction for the infant, did not necessarily impact on the parent's internal representations:

> A central hypothesis in attachment theory is that parental representations of attachment determine parents' sensitive responsiveness and that responsiveness in its turn affects the infant–parent attachment. Our case study suggests, though, that parental sensitivity and infant security can be divergent from the parent's attachment, and, moreover, that interventions may create this discrepancy. ... [This] could lead to two different developmental pathways for the child. ... The increase in parental sensitivity may be only temporary because the underlying mental representation of attachment did not change. ... The second, more positive, pathway is that the intimacy and (physical) contact with the baby would restore the parent's capacity for attachment and compassion in the long run. ... Only longitudinal research will yield information about the plausibility of the two pathways.

And they conclude:

> that it is easier to change parents' behaviour towards their child than to change the relationship that develops between children and their parents. [p. 532]

Finally, even when internal representations can be changed, there is evidence that this does not necessarily have the anticipated knock-on effect on the parent–infant relationship. "Newpin" was an innovative, community-based intervention targeted at depressed mothers which involved quite a large self-help element. Outcome research into this project, however, showed that while it did, indeed, lead to considerable improvements in the mother's personal state of mental health, it did *not* have any measurable impact on the mother–child relationship. Puckering, Evans, Maddox, Mills, and Cox (1996) concluded that programmes directed more at the adult's needs, while they may be effective in this area, do not necessarily have the desired impact on parenting:

> alleviating parents' own problems without directly addressing parenting may relieve their depression and social isolation but have little impact on the relationship of the parents and their children. Cox, Puckering, Pound and Mills (1987) showed that in a group of depressed women, their parenting did not change even when their depression improved. Similarly, studies of NEWPIN, a highly effective intervention for socially isolated and depressed women, showed that women can be helped with their own internal difficulties, but with few beneficial effects on the children (Cox, Puckering, Pound, Mills & Owen, 1990; Oakley, 1995). [Puckering et al., 1996, p. 540]

It was these findings that led Mills and Puckering to go on to develop a modified intervention called Mellow Parenting (see Puckering et al., 1996), which focused more explicitly on the parent–child relationship.

Such findings also suggest that another rationale very frequently advanced for work via the parent—namely, that if the mother feels "held" or "contained", then she may be more able to offer a similar experience to her infant—may not in fact be borne out by closer examination.

It is perhaps worth noting here that Fonagy's work (Fonagy et al., 1993) suggests that the impact of the parent's mental state on the infant is in fact mediated through the parent's capacity for what he has called "reflective self-function". This is demonstrated by the finding that in those cases where parents have had very poor early experiences (and presumably therefore have problematic internal representations) these may not necessarily be transmitted on to the next generation *if* the parent is able to reflect on them and create a coherent narrative around them that acknowledges their affective impact (a conclusion very much in line with Fraiberg's views, as cited below).

I think it might be argued that an individual could have—or develop—such a reflective capacity even while some of his or her internal representations or objects remain quite damaged. It may be, therefore, that it is in this area that the real potential of direct work with the parents lies. Rather than seeking to change the internal representations themselves, parents might be enabled to reflect upon their experiences in such a way that this capacity for reflection is enhanced—a capacity that may then, in turn, be internalized by the infant.

A recently proposed alternative to this is that the therapeutic task might be, rather, to help identify more benign internal representations and thereby allow them to assume more prominence at least in relation to the parent's relationship to this particular infant (Lieberman, Padron, Van Horn, & Harris, 2005). In this instance, it remains the case that the representations have not been modified—it is only that a broader range has become accessible potentially to be identified with.

*The rationale for addressing the infant's mental state*

Given that the prime aim of infant mental health work is the promotion of the infant's psychological well-being, it does not seem unreasonable to consider that direct work with the infant might offer one way forward. Again, Stern's argument would propose that such an approach would, in any event, have repercussions on the whole of the system. In practice, however, very little of this kind of work has been undertaken, despite the precedent set by Winnicott, whose parent–infant consultations seemed to offer just this kind of model (Winnicott, 1941).

A rare exception is the work of Thomson-Salo et al. (1999), and more recently that of Norman (2001). The former are working in a situation where the urgency of the infant's predicament is compelling, and indeed the main rationale they give for this kind of intervention is that these are situations in which the infant simply cannot wait for the patient unravelling of projections and uncovering of the ghosts in the nursery that normally form the core of parent–infant work. This approach, which does, in fact, owe much to Winnicott's example, as well as the work of paediatrician Ann Morgan (2001), involves the worker interacting directly with the infant in the parent's presence.

Salo particularly emphasizes that this approach does not necessarily have the undermining effect that many fear it might have on the mother, and which has often been the reason for eschewing this kind of intervention. On the contrary, she gives illustrations of situations where it has had precisely the opposite effect and the parents have been profoundly reassured by witnessing their infant's responsiveness. There is something similar here to the approach of Brazelton (1992), who makes use of the overt behaviour of the infant, as elicited by the paediatrician interacting directly with the infant, to introduce the parents to their infant's distinctive personality.

The examples given by Salo are compelling, and their value to the infant is obvious. It also seems very possible that the changes effected would have a beneficial knock-on effect on the parent. However, there is no empirical evidence for this as yet. Some of the findings of Juffer, van IJzendoorn, and Bakermans-Kranenburg (1997), from the intervention referred to above, would suggest, to the contrary, that improvements in the infant's state do not necessarily lead to any corresponding change in the parent:

> after four intervention sessions the mother's behaviour towards her child was rated as more sensitive than before the intervention. Also the mother–infant attachment, as observed in the Strange Situation, appeared to be more secure [*i.e. beneficial to the infant as evidenced by improved attachment status—PB*]. Nevertheless, in a second Adult Attachment Interview administered after the intervention, the mother showed again an insecure representation of attachment. [Juffer, van IJzendoorn, & Bakermans-Kranenburg, 1997, p. 540]

Field (1992) has also drawn attention to some recent interventions that have targeted the infant as their way into the system, noting that:

> Although most early interventions target the more sophisticated member of the parent–infant dyad, several recent intervention efforts have focused on improving the infant. While not saying so directly, they have tried to make the infant more like a "Gerber baby"—in order to facilitate the parents' attachment to the infant and thereby enhance their developing relationship. . . . In all cases, the interventions improved the status of the infant, and by doing so, would be expected to enhance parent–infant interactions and later attachments/relationships. [Field, 1992, p. 330]

It is worth highlighting, however, that in these examples the primary aim does, in fact, remain that of influencing the *parent's* mental representation. By improving the perceived status of the infant, allowing the parent to see the infant in a rather more positive light, it is anticipated that the parent will no longer link the real external infant to some damaged internal representation but will, rather, be able to access some more positive internal image.

## The rationale for addressing the relationship between parent and infant

It has been the case for some time that most interventions in this field have explicitly targeted the *relationship* between parent and infant. Most infant mental health clinicians would agree that the mental health needs of the infant and the parents are so inextricably interlinked that they cannot be addressed separately. As Hopkins (chapter 3) puts it:

> [Infant–parent psychotherapy relies] on the assumption that there is no such thing as individual psychopathology in infancy. This does not mean that babies do not contribute individual difficulties from their side of the relationship. It does mean that symptoms in the infant can best be treated by treating the infant–parent relationship, rather than by treating either infant or parent separately. [p. 5]

To that end, parents and infants are best seen together. As Lieberman and Pawl (1990) also note:

> Given the complexity of the mutual regulation between mother and child, neither partner may be treated either separately or directly regarding these symptoms [disturbances of attachment]. [p. 376]

In focusing on the treatment of the relationship, the aim is to identify what it is about this specific relationship that evokes conflict and problems. This is the domain of the "ghosts in the nursery" (Fraiberg, Adelson, & Shapiro, 1975) and of what Cramer (Cramer & Palacio-Espasa, 1993) refers to as "conflits de la parentalité". The primary concern is to identify the mental representations evoked in a particular interaction. However, it is also quite explicit that the intention is *not* to alter the nature of those internal representations but rather, as Hopkins (chapter 3) has described, to effect the "dynamic disconnection between past representations and present realities". Stern (1995) has similarly described this as "functionally reconnecting the representations".

In other words, the representations themselves remain unchanged but they are disconnected from the infant (in the present) and reconnected to their original source. Such a "reconnection" may be achieved relatively quickly, in some instances at least, and indeed may subsequently lead to alternative connections being made with more benign internal objects. Modifying the representations themselves would be a much longer-term undertaking.

These, then, are the three main potential targets for effecting change. As I have said, the latter is the predominant mode within current parent–infant work. I now want to turn to a consideration of the different models that have been used to account for the changes that can be brought about—that is to say, the question of *how* change is effected.

## Models of change

Within a psychoanalytic paradigm, there are two main concepts that predominate in terms of offering an explanatory framework for the process of change in parent–infant therapy.

### Containment

Perhaps the most important, or most frequently invoked, is that which draws on Bion's central notion of "containment". The following examples from papers on under-fives work are representative of how this concept is applied:

> The circle of mutual projections of the child on the parents and vice versa and the response of the child to the lack of reverie and containment and further response of the parents are re-enacted in the sessions and in the transference to the therapist. Understanding of the current dynamic relationships and links with the parents' own childhood experiences are made. *Containment, through mental digestion, transformation* (Bion, 1962b), *silent or verbalized interpretations, took place* so that insight was achieved by the parents and the child. [Pozzi, 1999, p. 70; italics added]

This account emphasizes *both* containment *and* insight, the latter being perhaps something of a more intellectual process.

Miller's description (chapter 2) stresses even more the central role, as she sees it, of containment. It is the function of offering the parent the model of a thinking object that is critical. The fact of worrying away at thinking is, in a sense, the therapeutic agent rather than any answers that this may lead to:

> I felt hopeless about my capacity to make sense of the problem and despairing about the possibility of doing anything to ameliorate it. Depression engulfed me. I felt inadequate and alone with the case. I believe that the service I performed was to identify with the anxious infant in Miss B, to receive her broadcast, and yet, despite the difficulty, to do my best to puzzle away and to keep thinking. By implication I announced myself as emotionally available. This

> is probably the single most important facet of this sort of work. . . . Once Ms B felt that the communication had been received, she was enabled to receive Ella's communication in its turn. Having been thought about, she could think. [Miller, chapter 3, this book]

While not explicitly referring to Bion, his concept of containment is clearly being invoked, coupled with the notion that through providing a containing function for the mother, the therapist enables the mother in her turn to think about and contain her infant's communications. This is also an account firmly rooted in the here-and-now of the therapeutic process, in which through the activity of the therapist the parents gain—or regain—their adult functioning, equipping them to go away and work at and resolve problems for themselves. This model generally involves a fairly explicit refusal of the role of "expert" dispensing "advice".

## "Insight": revealing the ghost in the nursery

The approach adumbrated by Fraiberg in her classic paper (Fraiberg, Adelson, & Shapiro, 1975) is somewhat different and gives more weight to the importance of conscious insight, with its emphasis on uncovering the "ghosts in the nursery". This, it must be emphasized, is not insight as an intellectual exercise—insight is only therapeutically meaningful if linked to the appropriate emotional response. However, it does, as an approach, privilege the importance of making links with the parents' own childhood past and the recall of specific memories, which may have been unconsciously evoked by the infant in the present.

There is, of course, an overlap here. For example, in the work of Miller and Pozzi that I have referred to above, the therapists are also alert to the parents' own childhood experiences as important factors. However, in conceptualizing the way in which change is brought about, the accounts differ significantly in terms of their emphasis. Pozzi and Miller are more in the recent British object relations tradition, with its focus on the immediacy of the therapeutic encounter and on the impact of here-and-now experiences, while Fraiberg is writing more from the classical Freudian tradition of reconstruction.

In Fraiberg, Adelson, and Shapiro (1975), the process that effects change is the establishing of an affective link with the specifics of the parents' past that have been evoked by the interchange with this particular infant in the present:

In each case, when our therapy has brought the parent to remember and re-experience his childhood anxiety and suffering, the ghosts depart and the afflicted parents become the protectors of their children against the repetition of their own conflicted past. [p. 196]

However, it is important to note, as Bertrand Cramer (1995) has helpfully delineated, that the conflicts evoked by the infant may not always be linked so closely to specific past objects but, rather, to aspects of the self:

> projections of past objects were called "ghosts in the nursery" by Fraiberg.... If past objects are transferred onto the infant by projection, it is fairly easy to see the interpersonal nature of the conflict. If, on the other hand, parts of the hidden self are projected, these are called *narcissistic* projections. These cases are difficult to treat in short-term therapy as the therapist has to deal with conflicts between opposing psychic parts inside the mother. [Cramer, 1995, p. 655]

In this latter situation, it is not, therefore, the elucidation of the "ghosts in the nursery" that is required but, rather, a gradual unpicking of negative projections. Again, this would be the domain of longer-term psychotherapy.

## *Discussion*

In thinking about the clinical work described in this book, it is worth bearing in mind some of the above considerations. Clearly there is no one-size-fits-all approach being recommended. In some instances, it will be entirely appropriate that the intervention is limited to a few sessions, and this will be quite sufficient to put development back on track. These are the families Fraiberg refers to as having to deal with "transient invaders" (Fraiberg, Adelson, & Shapiro, 1975), families who form a strong alliance with the therapist. The clinician may be aware of other unresolved issues in the family or in the couple's relationship, but these are not what brought the family to seek help and it is not on their agenda to address them. It is sufficient that the presenting problems have been satisfactorily resolved, and the therapist needs to hold back from opening up other areas that she has not been invited to deal with.

In other instances, however, it will be apparent that the difficulties are much more deeply rooted in the dynamics of the family. In some instances, it may indeed be the case that it is the pathology of one of the parents that dominates the picture—perhaps as in the narcissistic scenarios that Cramer draws attention to—and in such a case it may be that long-term therapy for that parent is indicated. This presents many problems since such an approach may be too slow to have an impact on the developing infant; in many instances it may simply not be available, and in many cases it will not be what brought the parent to seek help and may be strongly resisted. Moreover, however much it appears to be the case that the problem lies in one of the parents, it can never be forgotten that the parent's partner must also be playing a role here, whether by reinforcing that parent's role or by failing to mitigate it in some way.

It is my view, however, that what will prove critical is, more often than not, the nature of the relationship that the parental *couple* have, and that this will be the determining factor setting the context for the infant's psychological development and, indeed, his future mental health. It is then the therapist's task, when this seems appropriate and when both parents can attend the sessions, to try to show the couple why this is the case and thereby help them to see the value of working on that relationship, given that, for the most part, they will not have sought help with this agenda in mind, at least at a conscious level (for a discussion of some of these issues, see Ludlam, 2005).

In some institutions it will be possible to keep in mind this full range of possible therapeutic options and allow the work to develop accordingly. For many practitioners this may not be an option, and resource issues will constrain what can be offered. However, even when this is the case, there is value in being clear about the nature of the help that can be offered, in order to determine what might be most therapeutic and to ensure that professionals set themselves realistic goals rather than impossible tasks that will leave them with a sense of failure.

## Note

This chapter is a modified version of an earlier publication: P. Barrows, "Change in Parent–Infant Psychotherapy", *Journal of Child Psychotherapy,* Vol. 29, No. 3 (2003): 283–301.

CHAPTER 5

# A slow unfolding—at double speed: therapeutic interventions with parents and their young children

*Louise Emanuel*

The title refers to what may seem to be a paradox, touching on the particular technique developed in the Under Fives Service, of working psychoanalytically, but often within a brief time frame. How can there be a slow "free-associative conversation" with parents (Watillon, 1993) and a simultaneous exploration of a child's communications through behaviour, play, drawing, and interaction with parents and therapist, in what is often a *brief* therapeutic intervention? In exploring this paradox, I shall be developing Annette Watillon's (1993) suggestion that "the 'speed and spectacular nature of the therapeutic effect' in work with under fives results from the 'dramatization' of experience in the therapeutic setting". I describe how the dramatization of experience by children in the consulting room, or through parents' narratives, can be effectively used by the clinician to facilitate the unfolding of material and lead to change. As will become clear, thinking with parents about the impact of their parental functioning on the child, and vice versa, plays a central role in this work.

I have begun increasingly to recognize the dramatic quality of what unfolds in the consulting room, particularly with 2- to 5-year-olds as they often take centre stage in a child-led enactment of a crisis within the family. However, sometimes the drama takes a different form. Reflecting on families I have seen within the Under Fives Service, I found that they clustered into three different groups, each group representing a different kind of "dramatic" enactment and leading to a different kind of intervention, relating to my role as therapist, the structure of the interventions, and the "ports of entry" (Stern, 1995) to the work. These are broadly categorized, using the metaphor of "drama" for these powerful enactments as: *"child-led dramatizations"*, with the clinician in the role of "therapeutic observer/director"; *"internal parental drama"*, with the clinician in the role of "therapeutic consultant/supervisor"; and *"external parental drama"*, with the clinician in the role of "therapeutic modulator". I shall define these categories and give clinical examples, considering the technique involved in these interventions. It goes without saying that most cases involve a combination of different roles and that these are only differentiated for theoretical clarification.

### *Child-led dramatizations: therapist's observer/director role*

In child-led dramatizations, the child takes centre stage in enacting—through his play, nonverbal behaviour, and conversation—conflicts and concerns within the family, as well as his own emotional states and mental activity. The role of the therapist as "therapeutic observer" is to try to make sense of these communications, through detailed observation of the child's play and monitoring of her countertransference experience, and to assign meaning to the drama unfolding before her. The therapist takes on the role of interpreter of the child's material to the parents. Watillon states:

> The therapeutic effect is due to a "staging" of the conflict by the child himself in the form of a dramatic performance. By making his presence felt at a precise and meaningful moment while the parents are giving their account of the situation the child makes the interactional conflict manifest and allows the therapist to decode the message, to elaborate the emotions projected into him and to interpret the unconscious motivations of the various members of the cast of the "play". . . . The analyst—as theatre director—can perform a transforming function. [Watillon, 1993, pp. 1048, 1041]

The case example described below involves a little boy whose tyrannical and omnipotent behaviour at home and nursery was proving overwhelming for his parents and staff. His expressive play and behaviour in the session, with myself and his parents as observers, enabled me to help them recognize how much anxiety he was concealing beneath his imperious demeanour. This anxiety seemed to be related to a fear of dependency and an inability to tolerate feeling small or helpless. In situations of this kind, as a picture of the child's early infancy emerges, it often becomes clear that the child's anxiety about dependency may be the result of an early mismatch between mother and infant. An infant whose experience of dependency may be associated with intolerable frustration and disappointment at unmet infantile needs (this is related to the infant's temperament as well as maternal functioning) may develop "second-skin defences" (Bick, 1968) against vulnerability by becoming prematurely self-sufficient, hyperactive, and thick-skinned. An early defensive pattern develops, and the young child splits off and projects feelings of helplessness and anxiety about "not-knowing" into his parents and teachers, who feel increasingly deskilled. This emotional difficulty can interfere with a child's ability to learn and often results in an assessment of the child's cognitive ability as lower than it may actually be.

## Case illustration: child-led intervention

Mario, aged 3½ years, was referred because he was having difficulty settling into nursery, was aggressive to other children, and was disruptive at home. Although a lot of the work is done in the presence of the child, I often invite parents to attend the first session without the child, unless there is a good reason to include the whole family. I think it is important to gather in the anxieties of the parents and provide them with some containment through beginning to offer them some links to understanding, based on their description of the situation, before bringing in the children. With a child such as Mario, I often alternate family meetings, and meetings with parents on their own, particularly if issues to do with limit-setting are to be addressed, as I think it is important that parents' areas of difficulty are not further exposed in front of the child and that they are accorded some privacy to explore these further. I shall summarize the five-session intervention with the family to illustrate the unfolding process. As with most families we work with, they were told that they would be offered five sessions initially, with the option to continue the work if necessary.

In the *initial* meeting with this lively and intelligent couple, I heard about their itinerant lives over the past few years. Mother had gone to Sicily from France as an au pair, where she had met Mario's father, an accountant. They left Sicily when Mario was 9 months old, moving country several times in search of work before settling in England. They had difficulty conceiving him, so he was a special child for them, but mother had needed to return to work when he was just 3 months old, which had distressed him. Now he was difficult to manage, had prolonged tantrums if thwarted, was defiant, and sometimes attacked his mother. At other times he was clingy to her and announced his wish to "send Daddy away". He was similarly possessive of children at nursery, seeking exclusive relationships and feeling any rejection keenly. I wondered about their ideas for further babies, but they said sadly that they had not succeeded in conceiving again. Mother mentioned that Mario had recently told her she had a "baby in her tummy". I wondered whether the difficulties at nursery could stem from his shock at finding himself suddenly among so many rival siblings, all in competition for the attention of the teacher (usually a "transference" mummy figure), and they were interested in this.

I found myself concerned about his tyrannical control over them and whether their fear of incurring his wrath could have a psychological impact on their capacity to conceive another child.

They returned for their second appointment two weeks later, bringing Mario as arranged. He was an intensely expressive child, and as they described their long odyssey from Sicily, to Rome. and on to London, Mario built up brick castles, bringing them crashing down at each mention of another leave-taking and his world crashing down. They were astonished to see how Mario played out his anxieties around separation and endings once I drew their attention to the links between his play and their narrative. As we talked about the family Mario taped his father's hand to the sofa, then threw a baby rattle across the room, saying disparagingly, "That is for babies!" He taped across the vacant armchair, then smashed his way through it as if through a finishing line. My comments about his need to smash his way right inside our conversation or his Mummy and make sure his Daddy doesn't stop him resulted in further elaborations on the theme.

He became preoccupied with the door of my cupboard, acknowledging his desperate curiosity to look inside, then sealing it closed with tape. His parents watched in some amazement as I described his curiosity about things inside, "perhaps babies?" He took the small popper toy and popped the four people out of the corresponding coloured holes. He pushed the crocodile's tail forcefully into one of the empty holes, removed it, and sealed off the hole so that only three popper-figures could fit into their spaces. I talked about Mario allowing nothing to go in unless he gives his permission, and I linked this to their current family of three and to his mixed feelings about babies and other intruders. His parents smiled. I suggested to his parents that Mario might experience others as intrusive or hostile in direct proportion to his own intrusiveness and feelings of hostility; in his imagination a baby would be as possessive and demanding of his parents' exclusive attention as he feels, so he sticks himself firmly to them, to ensure he won't be displaced. They felt that this gave them some framework for thinking about Mario.

In the intervening (third) meeting with the parents on their own, I suggested that Mario's play and behaviour in the room had dramatically conveyed how much anxiety underlay his omnipotent defiance. Linking this to his possible early experiences, we explored how their own feelings of disorientation, vulnerability, and lack of support arriving in a new country may have made it more difficult for them to take on a firm parental role, feeling rather helpless themselves. That may have made it difficult for Mario to feel he had a strong container for his own overwhelming infantile feelings, which continued to erupt at home and nursery.

Their anxieties about conceiving another baby may have been transmitted to Mario, as his intrusiveness and curiosity were intensely aroused. The natural oedipal drama with Mario, reported to be most difficult on a Saturday morning when he has to adapt to a weekend at home that includes his Daddy, is intensified by this.

Conversely, I had the impression that Mario may have functioned as a "receptacle" for his parents' anxieties, as they had no family or supportive friends in London. It was easy to imagine how Mario's intellectual brightness and his tough demeanour might at times invite them to share their more adult concerns with him, give rational explanations, and expect understanding of issues that were beyond his emotional grasp. It appeared that Mario and his parents were particularly wrapped up together with each other in their strong Mediterranean identity and that in some way they idealized their son's fiery temperament as they spoke of the coldness and reserve they met in London. This may have made it difficult for them to set appropriate boundaries for a child who found it intolerable to allow them to take parental control.

They were receptive to some of these ideas, and although we touched on issues relating to their individual backgrounds, we acknowledged that discovering further links could wait. Helping to strengthen them as a united parental couple who could set firm boundaries took precedence, and the parent meetings, alternating with family meetings, gave us an opportunity to address these issues. Lieberman (2004) suggests that the priorities for addressing aspects of parental functioning when working with parents of "older" under fives may differ from those with infants; this resonates with my view in this case. Lieberman points out that although

> like infant–parent psychotherapy, child–parent psychotherapy targets the web of mutually constructed meanings between the child and the parent, it differs from infant–parent psychotherapy in emphasizing the growing child's autonomous agency during the treatment, with a concomitantly lesser emphasis on uncovering the parents' childhood conflicts or helping them reflect on their individual experience. [Lieberman, 2004, p. 99]

This is an area that may deserve further exploration.

They returned for a family meeting (the fourth session) after a long summer break to report that Mario had moved from nursery to reception class (the first year of school), but the children were still visiting the nursery twice a week to play and see the teachers. Mario was having difficulty relinquishing his "special nursery teacher" and "permitting" new nursery children to take his place. The parents mentioned that they had also moved house. As they talked, Mario was waving around a piece of tape with the four poppers attached to it, like a small kite. It looked as if the poppers were hanging precariously in mid air. I said that Mario seemed to be showing that he was in an in-between place, in between homes and classes, not quite settled anywhere. Father laughed incredulously, saying that, in fact, this was accurate—they were in transition, they hadn't yet cleaned the house for moving in, it was happening that day.

Mario had sealed a ball in a transparent plastic cylindrical container which he spun around wildly, and I talked about how all these changes could make his head spin. I talked about the ball, trapped in there, not allowed out until Mario says so. He laughed with glee and slowly began to un-stick the tape, saying: "There's wind coming"— then released the ball with great gusto. I wondered to myself whether his fantasy was of trapping a baby inside the womb, but I didn't say anything, being aware of the parents' painful difficulty in conceiving. Mother suggested he told me his news, and he said: "I'm having a baby!" I congratulated them, commenting on his particular phrasing!

Mario began writing a card for his "special" nursery teacher, as if in response to an anxiety about being displaced by the baby. He had written her name and wanted to add the word "from". He said he didn't know how to write an "r," and his mother told him. He did a perfect "r", but when she encouraged him to write it next to the "f", pairing them up to make the required word, he scribbled a silly lollipop shape, saying he couldn't do it. I suggested that he feels unsure whether he likes to be a big boy who knows about writing and has to give up the little-baby space. He's not sure about joining letters up, creating pairs, as it seems to lead to babies. Mario nodded, moodily tugging at my locked cupboards, dramatically conveying his feelings of exclusion, relating not only to the news of mother's pregnancy, but also to the fact that our agreed sessions were drawing to a close and discussions had begun about what further help would be beneficial.

A striking change occurred during the fifth session two weeks later which indicated that the formulations discussed during the parents' meetings and the elaborations of Mario's play had effected a shift. In this session, mother, who was feeling ill from her pregnancy, came on her own, saying that father had been away and that although things were better at school, Mario was "driving her crazy" at home with his anger and defiance. Mario talked about a "volcano" experiment they had done using household materials, describing the frothing detergent "lava" with passion and enabling me to talk about his overwhelming feelings that erupt in a similar way. I wondered whether father's absence had heightened Mario's oedipal feelings of omnipotent triumph as well as persecutory anxiety about his destructive powers.

He began cutting a long piece of string into small pieces, and mother stopped him. Then he settled down to covering up a toy car in layers of Plasticine, so it was completely shut in and immobilized. He glided the covered car under the table, saying it was a "submarine" and making a hole in the Plasticine for a "headlamp". I described how it has gone deep under there, looking around at what it can see.

Mother, meanwhile, described her worry that Mario can be really spiteful; he pushes and hurts other children. She recounted how Mario had deliberately crashed his trike into his friend Peter's, who had fallen heavily and been badly hurt. As we were speaking Mario was gouging the Plasticine off the car, and he said, "It was an accident." "No," repeated his mother, "I don't think so." At that moment Mario tore the last bit of Plasticine from the car, moved over to the corner of the room, sat face down, and murmured: "I didn't want Peter to win." I felt touched and said Mario seemed to feel it was too hard to be the small one and to come last, so Peter had to have the hurt, upset little-boy feelings. He said "Yes," miserably. His mother said: "It is the first time he has said that, he has always insisted it was an accident."

I commented on the car, now stripped of its outer thick layer, and said perhaps when he comes here to the clinic he has a sense that this is a place to show some of these feelings; the outer layer can be opened up to show what feelings are inside. Mario sat quietly and listened as I said that sometimes he needs to feel big, wear a big thick layer like the Plasticine, but it's different when Mum and I are here to understand and we're firm but not in a shouting mood. When it was time to leave (in contrast to the impulse to cut up the string earlier), he insisted on tying the string from the large armchair to the child's chair. I said that was showing me he needed to stay joined up with me in my mind until we met again.

I felt that mother, by not colluding with his view that this was "an accident", had created a firm but understanding parental couple with me, which provided Mario with the containment to verbalize his difficulty. Mother's ability to stand up to him, despite her exhaustion (managing to embody both maternal and paternal functions), seemed to relieve his anxiety; at least the adults did not allow the wool to be pulled over their eyes like the Plasticine over the windscreen and wheels of the car. He left clearly feeling the little boy (chair) was connected to a containing adult (armchair), tied together with string.

The situation had improved considerably within five sessions. However, bearing in mind the impending birth of the new baby, I offered further input, and the family has been seen for nine sessions. The situation may continue to improve with further alternating family and parent work. Alternatively, Mario could be considered as a possible candidate for individual child psychotherapy treatment, as he seems to have a desperate need to have his communications understood and verbalized for him and is very responsive. His parents would then be offered regular support.

I think this material illustrates Watillon's suggestion that "the primary function of the therapist is to make a space available to the family to encourage this dramatic performance, through his listening . . . subsequently by virtue of his observation and understanding of the processes taking place, he makes it possible to assign meaning to the drama unfolding before him" (Watillon, 1993, p. 1041). My role as interpreter and *therapeutic observer* in the drama is clear.

## *Internal parental drama: therapist's consultation/supervisory role*

The second category of intervention involves a more muted kind of drama, and requires a different role from the therapist. Although the child has been referred with a problem, it quickly becomes apparent that work with a parent couple who are available to thinking about the impact of their child's communications on them and on their parenting would be the most effective "port of entry" (Stern, 1995). In these cases, in the initial meeting (without the child), the parent couple both become quickly engaged in thinking about the child's difficulties and are open to making links to their own past and present difficulties. The therapist may suggest extending the exploratory work with parents on their own before introducing the children to the clinic. Instead of the child enacting his difficulties in the here-and-now of the session as we saw with Mario, in this type of work the child's difficulties emerge through the dramatic narrative of the *parents* in the here-and-now of the session. My role is to elicit and process the parents' observations and descriptions of their child's difficulties, thereby illuminating the child's internal world for them, in the light of the parents' own internal and external experience.

I perceive the role of consultant/"supervisor" as similar to that described by child psychotherapist Margaret Rustin (1998), in a paper describing her weekly fax supervision of a trainee child psychotherapist's 4-year-old intensive case. She suggests three ways in which the supervisory process can be valuable: first, the therapist needs to be *"helped to accept being hated as well as loved"* (Rustin, 1998, p. 437). This applies to parents facing difficulties in setting limits or coping with tantrums, as only when they feel supported by the therapist, or are helped to support each other, are they able to withstand the barrage of anger and hatred a small child can level at them.

Second, the therapist is vulnerable to being overwhelmed by the powerful projections of the child, "thus losing a firm grip on her own thinking capacities" (Rustin, 1998, p. 438). Parents of small children often complain of feeling immobilized in the face of their children's intense emotional outbursts or demands, expressing bewilderment at having lost a firm grip of their own parental capacities. They may display a puzzling paralysis in the consulting room when faced with a small child's defiant behaviour, and they can be greatly relieved (like the trainee psychotherapist) by being helped to understand the powerful unconscious processes of which they are recipients.

Third, Rustin suggests that an important aspect of the supervisor's role is to take the "raw data of the clinical material, reflect on it and offer to the student a *meaningful pattern of understanding*". Rustin offers as a metaphor for this process the image of a well-functioning parental couple:

> The restorative conversation between parents about a sleepless or anxious baby, in which meaning can emerge, is quite close to the experience of the supervision of a child patient as the analysis is being established. ... The exhausted mother/therapist pours out a blow-by-blow account of her breathless day. Intricate details are noted, but what to make of them? [Rustin, 1998, p. 439]

Parents often bring superb observational detail of their young children to the session. Caught up in the midst of their drama, just as the trainee therapist described by Rustin had been in relation to her intensive case, they too require a therapist who will struggle to create a "meaningful pattern of understanding" from the sometimes overwhelming raw data that they bring to sessions. One could see this as an internal drama involving the parental couple as protagonists as they work out together with the therapist an understanding of their child's difficulties.

## Case illustration: internal parental drama

In the following vignette, one of a number of cases of severe biting referred to the Under Fives Service, most of the work of understanding and transformation took place, initially, through meetings with parents, where I took on the role of therapeutic consultant/supervisor. This was the first stage of a process that eventually led to an assessment for individual treatment for the child.

Salim (aged 2 years) was referred because of the severe nature of the bites he inflicted on his parents and older sister Zenab (aged 5 years) and brother Imran (aged 8 years). The parents are originally from Pakistan. Mother is petite with long dark hair, father heavily set, and they seem to have a warm supportive relationship. I heard about how Salim hair-pulls, scratches, and "bites those he loves" so hard he draws blood. Mother made a digging movement with her nails like claws in demonstration and grimaced as if warding off an intrusive attack. I said it sounded as if Salim might be "holding on" with his teeth to keep a tight grip on them, and mother agreed, saying that she wonders whether biting is Salim's way of expressing his feelings.

These seemed to be linked to Salim having to share his mother's attention with father or siblings, or his key worker at nursery with other children.

I said it sounded as if Salim did not have the mental apparatus to deal with his feelings—perhaps of exclusion or abandonment—which quickly overwhelmed him, so he powerfully "injected" them into his parents with his sharp bites. Mother described feeling distraught when a sudden bite on her ankle shocked her with pain. She seemed to feel punctured; it was not just her skin—her sense of competence was also deflated. Their descriptions gave me a powerful sense of what it might be like to always have to remain vigilant around Salim, since his bites came without apparent warning—when a back is turned, perhaps to talk to someone else, or an arm exposed. I said Salim seemed to be making sure his parents always kept him at arm's length—at some distance. They can never allow themselves to relax into an intimate cuddle with him. And yet without warning he gets right inside them with his piercing teeth. I wondered to myself whether Salim was unconsciously communicating an early infantile experience of having been kept at arm's length, perhaps by a mother who was depressed or preoccupied during his infancy.

I heard that Salim had been an anxious baby; he had never allowed mother out of his sight, and his cry, if left for a moment, was one of utter abandonment and terror. I wondered aloud why Salim seemed to be so "thin-skinned" and anxious, and mother said she was surprised by this, as she had stayed at home with Salim much longer than she had with his siblings. She mentioned as an aside that she had had two late miscarriages prior to conceiving Salim. I explored the impact of the miscarriages on mother and heard that she had been so anxious about the subsequent pregnancy (with Salim) that she hadn't allowed herself to acknowledge she was pregnant until very late on. I suggested there was a parallel between the way in which mother had dealt with a fear of unbearable loss by distancing herself from this pregnancy and the way in which Salim seemed to keep others at a distance. Does Salim, too, avoid intimacy, as if closeness followed by separation would feel like a catastrophic loss?

Mother seemed to be brimming with emotion—father, too—as they recognized this link, and we were able to talk about the impact of the miscarriages on the whole family.

Salim's weaning had been abrupt around the time his teeth came out, when mother had been suddenly taken ill and hospitalized, but he had already begun to bite the breast. I wondered whether the dreadful cry of his infancy, which mother described, conveyed a deep terror of abandonment, which got re-evoked around the time of weaning. I said it sounded as if Salim gave them an experience of an unpredictable shock each time he bit, and I wondered whether he was conveying how he might have experienced sudden shocks and disappearances.

Mother was moved and began to describe her preoccupation and depression during Salim's infancy. I suggested that a baby's temperament also plays its part, and I described my impression, from what they had told me, of a child who still required his parents' concrete presence, who somehow had not managed to keep alive in his mind a picture of parents who will return to him after a separation. In addition, the more he bit, the more anxious he would become about having damaged his parents and the harder it would be to let them out of his sight. I suggested to them that Salim's apparent aggression could be defensive if he was feeling persecuted by constant threats of retaliation.

This had been a full and unusual first meeting because of the intensity of feelings expressed and the quality of exclusive intimacy the parents conveyed as a couple. Since I thought a further opportunity to explore some of the emotionally charged issues that had been raised might be useful, I suggested that they return for a second meeting without the children. On their return they commented on the helpfulness of the previous meeting, saying it had enabled them to think about Salim's experience. They mentioned that Salim bites his finger and toe nails off, and there was nothing they could do to stop him. I wondered whether this could really be true. It became clear that both parents felt so identified with Salim, who projected a feeling that any boundary is cruel, that it made limit-setting difficult for them. I commented that Salim always had an experience of biting at soft things that gave way or punctured—his nails, their skin—and that perhaps he needed to feel what it was like to bite against a less pliable object. They took on board the need for a firm, non-collapsible couple with some "backbone", who can keep the family safe. I spoke about Salim's need to attack and puncture the very parental capacities he most needs.

I talked about a state of mind that totally vetoes biting and gave an example of a tantrum. I suggested that the fear of a barrage of hatred from a child can intimidate parents and lead them always to give in. They would need to support each other to cope with the hatred emanating from Salim, and this, in turn, would convey to Salim that his parents are separate from him and in charge. In the same way as Rustin (1998) describes the trainee child psychotherapist needing to be "helped to accept being hated as well as loved", this is an essential experience for parents, and the reasons for the difficulty some parents experience in this area may be complex.

At this point I thought it was important to have a family meeting, as I had heard much about the rivalry between the children and had some concerns about the older siblings who were being regularly bitten by their brother. I met with the whole family on two occasions. The most striking aspect of the meetings was all the children's relentless demands for attention from the adults, each one demanding an exclusive pairing with one parent, which inevitably meant that one child was excluded. Having to wait felt intolerable to them. I was struck by the way in which physical touching—a need to be concretely connected to each other—was evident. Following on from, and alternating with, the two family meetings, I continued to work with the parents on their own. I sensed that more was to be gained from exploring with them some aspects of their own internal and external experiences as a couple but also as individuals, and how this linked to the difficulties they recounted with Salim (and, to some extent, with the older children).

On the fourth meeting the parents reported that Salim's biting had reduced considerably, although he was pinching a little. Father spoke about Salim's different bites, how they are sometimes passionate, as when Salim hugs him intensely and opens his mouth as if to devour him: "You never know whether he's going to kiss you or bite you." Drawing on my observations in the family meeting and my own response to the couple's evident closeness, I wondered aloud whether the children might feel painfully aware of being excluded from the marital relationship. Perhaps waiting is difficult for them because they fear their parents are so wrapped up with each other they may forget all about the children! They smiled in acknowledgement, and father described how Salim pushed him away in the morning, demanding Mummy. I wondered whether Salim was giving father an experience of what it felt like to be the least favourite, the one who has been excluded from the parental bedroom all night long. He agreed but wanted advice about how to handle the situation—should he give in and call mother? I talked about the importance of giving Salim time to overcome his disappointment and frustration. Perhaps father could leave, then return after a short while, thereby giving a clear message that he has not capitulated to his demands and that he has remained loving and available to him. Salim may need to see that his father has not been destroyed by the power of his rejection.

At this point we were considering whether the parents had enough understanding to take things further on their own. After a fairly brief but intense intervention, where I had taken the role primarily of "therapeutic consultant", some improvements in the referred symptom had been made. However, mother expressed concern about Salim, describing how when his "key worker" had been unexpectedly absent Salim had screamed in such terror of abandonment that his mother had had to take him home. The parents agreed with my suggestion that this seemed to be an early terror of falling apart, as if he has nothing, internally, to hold him together. This could be one way of understanding the biting, the holes he makes in others' skin being a vivid communication of his own feeling of having a punctured, faulty skin container (Bick, 1968). The lack of a symbolic capacity to hold in mind an absent object—the key worker, or his mother—seemed to be a serious area of concern, and at this point I suggested that we needed to consider an assessment for Salim to determine whether he would benefit from long-term individual child psychotherapy treatment.

Discussion

My decision to focus on meetings with the parent couple was based on my sense that they could make use of the opportunity to explore areas that they would not necessarily elaborate on in the presence of their children. Mother's miscarriages, the parents' reaction to her pregnancy with Salim, all became possible to think about in relation to his immediate symptom of biting. The cumulative effect was an increased understanding of their functioning as a parental couple. This work may continue to be an elaboration of an internal drama alongside the individual psychotherapy with the child.

As work with the parents progresses, a further exploration may be able to take place of the parents' own childhood experiences. This may clarify whether, and how, a transgenerational transmission of emotional disturbance may be influencing the couple's parenting capacities, particularly relating to separation anxieties. K. Barrows (2000), commenting on the experience of traumatic loss in parents, suggests that "When a parent has not been able to come to terms adequately with his or her own bereavements, the child feels that the parent is preoccupied by a dead internal object" (pp. 69–70). Salim created a symptom, the biting, which forced his parents to hold him away from their bodies to avoid attack or to push him away once bitten. This may have been Salim's unconscious way of communicating how he felt kept at a distance from mother during her pregnancy and then his infancy because mother's mind may have been already "*pre*-occupied" by her previous dead babies and possible earlier losses in her life. Barrows goes on to describe how "inadequate mourning could lead to an *identification* of the ego with the abandoned object" (p. 70). Salim's collapse, when the object to which he has been clinging suddenly disappears (mother into hospital at time of weaning, key worker at his nursery), has all the force of an infant feeling abandoned to die. This level of distress may warrant ongoing individual work with Salim as well as continuing work with his parents.

### *External parental drama: therapist's role as modulator*

The third form of intervention focuses on the extreme splitting and polarization that sometimes emerges between parents and its effect on the young child. Here the child does not take centre stage but, rather, has the function of highlighting the main plot, which is about the parental relationship as evidenced in the room. Often the parental couple has become polarized in its functioning and styles of discipline, and the role of the therapist is to help modulate polarized parental attitudes. In these cases one parent may embody a parody of "paternal" functioning, harsh, inflexible, punitive, and another parent may be overindulgent, unable to set boundaries. Parents of both genders can embody either function. This may be linked to the ways in which each parent has (unconsciously or consciously) chosen to respond to his or her own parental background if there has been a history of abuse, either identifying with a harsh punitive paternal figure or reacting against it, resulting in a difficulty in setting firm limits. Serious couple/marital difficulties often underlie the parenting problems and can prove intractable.

My role in this drama is as *modulator* attempting to help parents to begin to function as a containing parental couple, and to integrate the extreme positions that they have taken up or into which they may have been pushed by their child's splitting and projection. I do not agree with Lieberman (2004), who implies that it would only be "clinically indicated" for both parents to attend if "both parents are experiencing difficulties in their relationship with the child". I think that if one parent claims to be having difficulty with a child, there is a lot to understand about the parental functioning of the couple, and increasingly I try to work with both parents in the room. (See chapters 10–12.)

The following is a brief vignette illustrating the kind of drama where the extreme splitting between the parents is brought into dramatic relief.

Two-year-old Gareth was referred for severe tantrums, head-banging, and concerns because of speech delay. I was alerted to the split between these parents in the waiting room, as they were seated so far apart I couldn't identify them as a couple. Gareth ran out and set off on his own in the opposite direction from the therapy room. Father grabbed him forcibly and brought him to the room. In the room Gareth sat next to father on the couch, but mother showed him to the little chair at the table. It felt from the start as if they were pulling in opposite directions. Gareth was unsettled and restless, and he did not ask once for help to lift toys or take lids off pens. He struck me as prematurely self-sufficient, avoiding interaction with any of us. Mother spoke loudly and constantly, father sat surly and quiet, just repeating "head-banging" when I asked about his concerns.

It became apparent that their styles of discipline were extremely different. Father appeared to be much stricter, and his voice exuded a quiet controlled threat of violence—"I just raise my finger and he listens." Mother seemed much "softer" on Gareth, allowed him to rummage in her bag and tip its entire contents onto the floor of my room. She told me she "doesn't believe in routine, Gareth will have routines for the rest of his life", so he had no fixed bed time and fell asleep on the sofa. Gareth demonstrated a tantrum when I stopped him using my computer, banging his head violently against mother's legs and on the floor, becoming very distressed. To comfort him mother produced a half-empty tube of "cream", which he held and squeezed, like a soft comforting breast. Mother told me he took it to bed and woke up grasping for it; he loved soft fabrics and comforters and took them everywhere. He made baby sounds in public and hardly spoke. Father was concerned about Gareth wearing mother's shoes and handbags around the house. I said it was unlikely to be a gender-identity issue but, rather, Gareth's way of "becoming" Mummy, having total access to her. Gareth paralleled, in the split between the self-sufficient boy and the tiny baby, the split between the parents.

As well as attending nursery Gareth was being cared for by both sets of grandparents, mother, and father, all in shifts, each one imposing their own very different sets of expectations on him. I suspected that he was being driven "crazy" with worry about how he had to behave at any one time, the stress of adapting from one kind of care to another being too great for him to cope with. He was becoming hyper-vigilant, and "disorganized" in his behaviour, unable to predict from hour to hour what behaviour was expected of him. I thought his frustration and anxiety might be calmed by his parents getting together to think about how they could unite in their approach to his care. In subsequent meetings mother and father found it difficult to accept the ways in which each disciplined Gareth. This was clearly linked to their own troubled histories of abuse and abandonment—each had chosen a different response, with mother determined not to do the same, feeling that any separation or boundary would be cruel (her own history had been of sudden loss), and father by identifying with the rather menacing figures in his early life.

The parents' own internal difficulties manifested themselves in this *external drama*: the dysfunctional polarized parenting, where the extreme lack of boundaries in mother—which allowed Gareth to "merge" totally with her and where language would be perceived to be unnecessary—and the over-punitive father resulted in dysfunctional parenting that was impacting negatively on his life. Over time things shifted slightly, with father becoming a little more receptive towards Gareth and mother becoming a little more boundaried with him. Gareth's head-banging diminished although it was clear that his problems and those of the family were complex and more help would be required.

In chapter 10, Paul Barrows, having discussed the "ghosts" that haunt the nursery (Fraiberg, Adelson, & Shapiro, 1975), argues that work with the parent/couple on the "intimacy of the marital relationship" is an important and valid part of work with families with children under 5 years, given the importance of the nature of the parental relationship for the infant's psychological development. He argues that, having established the existence of "unprocessed trauma in the parent's background", work with the parental couple needs to take place in the here-and-now because "what matters from the infant's point of view is not so much *whose* ghost it is, father's or mother's, but the nature of the interaction that then ensues between the parents" (Barrows, 2003, p. 297). If longer-term work were to be undertaken with this family, assuming their availability and willingness, work on aspects of the couple relationship would be an important part of the work of the Under Fives Service clinician.

The paternal and maternal functions can manifest themselves equally in parents of both genders. In a case similar to the one above, mother was dominating and forceful, berating her husband during family sessions for his weakness and indulgence of the children, while he mildly protested that her regimes for a 4-year-old child were too strict. In this case, the parents were able to make some dramatic changes in their couple/parenting relationship; they were motivated by concerns about not only their 4-year-old son, but their 18-month-old baby, who showed signs of speech delay.

## Conclusion

In this chapter I have attempted to convey, through detailed clinical examples, how the containing setting, observational skills, and receptive state of mind of the therapist facilitate the "unfolding" of material in the consulting room, allowing for a "meaningful pattern of understanding" to emerge and change to occur within a relatively brief time-frame. However, as these examples illustrate, the brief model of intervention often serves as a form of assessment for further work, be it parent/couple, family, individual child-psychotherapy treatment, or a combination of these. I have expanded on Watillon's description of work with under fives involving a "dramatization" of conflicts by noting three different types of "dramatic enactment", each leading to a different kind of intervention relating to the therapist's role, the structure of the interventions, and the "ports of entry" (Stern, 1995) for the work. Invariably most of the interventions will involve a combination of roles and approaches, but the fundamental framework of observational skills, psychoanalytic understanding, and knowledge of infant- and child-development research remains constant.

## Note

This chapter is a modified version of an earlier publication: L. Emanuel, "A Slow Unfolding—At Double Speed: Reflections on Ways of Working with Parents and Their Young Children within the Tavistock Clinic's Under Fives Service", *Journal of Child Psychotherapy*, Vol. 32, No. 1 (2006): 66–84.

CHAPTER 6

# A sinking heart: whose problem is it? Under-fives work in the surgery of a general practitioner

*Beverley Tydeman & Janine Sternberg*

This chapter focuses on the application of the Tavistock Under Fives model to work in a community setting, a GP's surgery. Detailed case material is given from brief work undertaken with a 4-year-old girl and her extended family seen for four sessions, and we expand from this specific case to highlight key issues that arise in the application of this Under Fives model to a community context.

*The pleasures and problems of working in a GP setting*

An increased awareness of children's mental health needs and the value of early intervention has developed as part of primary care provision. Child psychotherapists have a contribution to make in supporting primary health care teams, which include GPs, health visitors, and practice nurses, alongside child psychologists and other early years professionals. The child psychotherapist's contribution to the GP service involves direct work with families with young children, as well as indirect work focused on supporting practitioners. This indirect work offers training, supervision, and consultation to help the primary care team extend their range of responses to these families. Parents will approach their GP with a number of problems for which they would never imagine needing referral to a psychological service or hospital department. The Tavistock Under Fives model is particularly well suited to a primary care context that offers help to these families, providing a "thinking space" in an easily accessible community base.

Working at the interface with primary care requires the clinician to have "a flexibility of approach and an ability to think quickly" (Tydeman & Kiernan, 2005). There is as much for the clinician to learn about primary care as there is for the primary health care team to learn about the psychotherapeutic way of thinking. The surgery milieu itself can be therapeutic for patients, as all comers have to be seen and it is an accepted place for bringing aches and pains, for being listened to and taken care of. Many consultations in GP surgeries are for mental health or social reasons—people may be lonely and deprived at various points in their lives and may present with somatic complaints, when what they need is to belong and to be understood. GPs have a few minutes to give to each patient (Balint & Norrell, 1973), and the quality of those minutes can vary enormously, from routine care that is fast and efficient to close emotional contact. In contrast, the child psychotherapist, working in a practice, will expect to spend about an hour with each family, giving the opportunity for things to unfold at a different pace.

Referrals are made by GPs, health visitors, or practice nurses, and a first appointment is offered as soon as possible; a rapid response is an essential part of the service because concerns about a very young child can feel desperate to those involved. When a baby has been vomiting too much or been unable to sleep or feed, or a toddler has not defecated for several days and the parents are at the end of their tether, the service can seem like crisis intervention. The aim is to offer an informal and responsive service. For this reason it is common for the clinician to telephone the family to make the first appointment. Apart from the practical advantages of this approach, the experience of speaking, albeit briefly, to the clinician who is offering to see them can help dispel parents' anxieties and make the service more accessible. Usually families are seen within a few weeks of making contact.

Feedback is provided to the referrers, doctors, health visitors, and others attached to the practice, usually within the practice-team meeting, to share experiences and any additional information. Confidentiality is shared by the team, and this is explained to patients at the start of the contact. Often the health visitors may decide to follow up a family who has not attended an initial appointment. The feedback also enables members of other disciplines to understand and engage in the thinking process. The team hear about the attention to detail and willingness to grapple with negative perceptions and experiences. The reflective process that takes place in the team helps each member to recognize his or her own emotional responses to the patients.

Families may return after a first set of sessions, needing some more input, perhaps for a different family member, or later in the development of the originally referred child. This pattern reflects the way families use the GP practice.

## The atmosphere of the setting

Waiting rooms are often full and noisy. The staff are under pressure, dealing with many different demands. The atmosphere is busy, rushed, intimate, and anxious. People are waiting, and they are in need; they expect to leave with something that makes them feel better. Using a medical room is unfamiliar territory for a psychotherapist more used to a neutral space. In the GP practice we often work in doctors' consulting rooms, which will have a high couch, various charts about height, weight, and safety, a device for taking blood pressure, a bin for sharps, and a computer—and all this together with a family with young children who need to be attended to. A clinician can feel less in control of the setting than in the usual consulting room. There are a limited number of toys in the room and also a supply of drawing materials. We take the view that the children are their parents' responsibility and try not to intervene with regard to what they are allowed to touch and jump on, although commenting on what we observe is part of trying to communicate our understanding of the situation. This is helpful in giving a picture of how well the parents are able to set boundaries and use their authority.

In this busy atmosphere the clinician may need to guard against the pressure to offer a premature formulation of the problem before things have had an opportunity to unfold. There may be an internal compulsion to give advice when it is asked for. This is probably similar to the pressure doctors feel to write a prescription so that the patient feels he or she has gained something from the visit.

Families are told in the first meeting that there is the possibility of up to five meetings. The first session focuses on the family's expectations, with an exploration of what they hope to gain from the service. The clinician will also explore with the children, if they are present, what they know about why they have come, making the active participation of the children clear from the start. Although there are issues that clinicians are particularly interested in—the pregnancy, delivery, and early experiences—there is no attempt to take a history in a formalized way. The family are given the opportunity to tell their story with the focus on their anxieties.

## Case example

As is often the situation for clinicians working in a GP practice, this referral was initiated by a brief letter from the GP, followed by an informal conversation. Mrs P had frequently consulted her GP about 3-year-old Seeta's eating and sleeping problems. The GP said that she found Mrs P "very puzzling, it's as though she is somehow out of touch with her child". The GP said she gets "that heart-sinking feeling" when she is with this mother, and she often doesn't know what Mrs P wants when she has come to see her with relatively insignificant complaints. At the time of her referral Mrs P was pregnant with her second child.

First session

Mrs P came alone to the first meeting. She was a tall, attractive woman, dressed in an elegant, Westernized style; heavily pregnant. She was pleasant in her manner but made it clear that she was rather puzzled as to why the GP had suggested some meetings with me. She thought perhaps it was because the GP was worried about how her daughter, Seeta, would adapt to the new baby. I was told that Seeta had been a bit spoilt as the only child and treated like a princess. Mrs P told me in a matter-of-fact way that Seeta refused to eat any food prepared by her. She would, however, take food from her father or his parents, who were living with them. Mrs P was pleased that Mr P's family had come to London to be with them after their move.

Seeta was also used to sleeping in the same bed as her paternal grandmother. She slept lying on top of her grandmother's body, causing grandmother great discomfort. Mrs P had no idea why Seeta behaved in this way but said she was sure that Seeta would adjust well as she likes the idea of another baby. I suggested that sometimes there are mixed feelings, and as well as being pleased, Seeta may possibly feel worried or cross at times—she's used to being the only one, and now she is going to have to share her mother and wait her turn. It was possible that not taking food from her mother was connected to

Seeta's worry about her mother's mind being on the new baby and not exclusively on her.

What Mrs P was keener to talk about was her experience of having had to relinquish her country of origin, her family, and her professional role. She had done an MBA in India and had loved her job before becoming pregnant. Seeta had been born in India, and they had had to move to a town in the North of England when she was 18 months, because of Mr P's job. They had recently moved to London, and she had begun working again. She found it a good arrangement that her in-laws now lived with them. She was quite sure that she had no rivalrous feelings towards her mother-in-law, explaining that she was used to children being close to their grandparents and had grown up with the expectation that she would one day be a daughter-in-law. In fact it suited her, as she was eager to return to work as soon as possible after her maternity leave.

Towards the end of the meeting Mrs P mentioned that the next baby was a son. She told me how important having a son was in her culture, and she emphasized how delighted Mr P and his family were. I wondered with her whether she had experienced any change in Seeta's behaviour after becoming pregnant, and she acknowledged that she had experienced her as more controlling since the pregnancy had become obvious. She felt that Seeta was turning away from her and towards her father when he was there, or, alternatively, towards grandmother. When it was put to her that this might be Seeta's response to the new baby, Mrs P was dubious.

I suggested that it may be useful to go on thinking about these issues, and, more specifically, about Seeta's part in them, with all the family, including Mr P. Mrs P quietly accepted this, but she felt that Mr P would be too busy at work, because he works in insurance and travels a lot.

*Discussion*

This first meeting left me with many disparate thoughts. I was confronted with a modern, professional Indian woman who had been displaced from her own culture and had newly arrived in London. What did I or the GP know about her origins and beliefs? The GP had made an assumption about the kind of mother she was—detached. How much had my thoughts been organized by this, or was I sufficiently open minded not to be judgmental? I wondered about the relevance of cultural issues on many levels and how much these might have contributed to mother's relative lack of anxiety. Her mother-in-law seemed to take a central role in running the home, which suited her. She was genuine in not feeling displaced or envious, as the involvement of her mother-in-law in the home was part of her cultural experience. Cultural patterns and family traditions—for example, regarding sleeping arrangements—need to be kept in mind and respected, while at the same time we cannot lose sight of our understanding of what all children need for healthy development.

Working across cultures requires particular care regarding meaning. The "sinking heart" (Krause, 1989) is a description of a feeling state experienced by certain Indian sub-groups that can have many meanings, both physical and psychological. The heart is seen as the regulator of life forces throughout the body, and various emotional experiences can upset the balance of the regular heartbeat, thus causing distress and upset, which can result in a visit to the GP surgery. Life events, including migration as a disappointing experience, anxiety, confusion, agitation, and sorrow can all affect the person's sense of well-being in their "heart centre".

The main task within this first session was to establish a relationship with Seeta's mother enabling her to feel sufficiently understood within her particular family and cultural context, together with trying to highlight possible aspects of her child's inner world. I felt I needed to wait and see how they interacted together in order to have a fuller picture of their relationship. I wondered whether anything in our initial discussion had interested or engaged mother enough for her to want to return.

Second session

To my surprise the second meeting was attended by Seeta, her mother, and both grandparents. Mr P's absence was explained in terms of work commitments. Seeta was a tall, thin girl with large brown eyes, dressed in tights and a pretty dress, with her long dark hair adorned with hair bows and clips. Paternal grandmother was wearing an elegant sari. Seeta spent most of the session sitting on her grandmother's lap. Both grandparents were clearly devoted to her, and family life revolved around her. Mrs P was very quiet at this meeting, allowing her parents-in-law to make it evident where the authority, at least in terms of child rearing, lay. Although Seeta was across the room from where mother was sitting much of the time, I noticed that mother looked at her warmly and, when Seeta did go over to her, welcomed her with open arms.

We explored together with the grandparents and Seeta why we were meeting. Seeta avoided eye contact with me. Her grandparents initially conveyed that they did not feel that Seeta's behaviour was cause for concern, although they spoke of her as a little underweight and wilful. We began to think together about what might be going on for Seeta. Her grandmother thought the way she slept on top of her might indicate a wish to return to being a baby inside the body, just like the baby inside her mother's tummy. As well as showing her understanding of Seeta, the grandmother was also able to communicate how physically painful this was becoming for her and how disruptive it was of her sleep.

Seeta put her thumb in her mouth and turned her head towards her mother, who stretched out her arms towards her. Seeta got off her grandmother's lap and went over to her mother, seating herself contentedly on mother's lap while Mrs P stroked her hair. I drew attention to what had just happened and how Seeta seemed to be responding to her grandmother's words. I was pleased to notice that mother clearly did have an important place within this family, and that she and Seeta had a relaxed affinity. I said to Seeta that it seemed she still had her place with her mother and she was lucky that she could move between her grandmother and her mother. Also, from what I had heard from her mother, she also had her father to turn to. I said I thought this would be especially helpful for her when her mother had the new baby also needing to sit on her lap.

Seeta remained silent throughout the contact, but she was listening. Grandmother, with her lap now free, was able to talk about the way that Seeta's "princess" position within the family would need to be limited with the arrival of the new baby. Grandfather was a quiet but benign presence who said that his wife had really been in pain with her back and she needed Seeta to be a bit more independent; maybe she could sleep next to "Ama" (the Indian word they used for grandmother, though they used the English word "Mum" for mother). I wondered with them whether Seeta was feeling worried about her own position and that this had made her behave in a more princess-like and controlling way. I suggested that the sleep and feeding problems may imply that she was behaving in a "baby-like" way, perhaps because of anxieties about losing her place as the "one and only baby". I said grandmother's intuitive comment seemed to indicate that Seeta was trying to be the baby, but she was also going to be the big sister. By the tone of my voice I tried to convey to Seeta that we understood that she might be experiencing fears of loss and that it made sense that she wanted to hold on to things.

I commented that Seeta's responses to the anticipated new baby were very ordinary and not pathological at all. The expansion of the family unit creates opportunities as well as bringing adjustment difficulties. Becoming a big sister could give Seeta the opportunity to find in herself capacities that will promote her emotional development: she might be able to lie next to grandmother rather than on top of her, having internalized enough of a sense of how loved and valued she is within the family. She had not lost her mother; in this session she had found her. We agreed on one more meeting before the birth and a final one afterwards.

*Discussion*

This extract highlights how a clinician uses observation to gain a clearer picture of what is going on. Commenting in the here-and-now on what had happened in the room when Seeta moved from "Ama's" (grandmother's) lap to her Mum's may have helped the family make some space for the changes ahead by linking mind and body, showing the possible meaning of behaviour. This seemed to be a positive move that became the focus of the session.

The focus of the work emerged as the link between the description of Seeta's symptoms and mother's pregnancy gradually became clear. Under other circumstances, with the opportunity for longer work, one might have wanted to attend to mother's style of mothering or differences within the couple about parenting, or to look in more depth with mother and her parents-in-law about the possible tensions created by living as an extended family. The focus in these sessions was on finding meaning in Seeta's behaviour by suggesting its possible link to her feelings about the new baby. She had a sense that things would never be the same again for her and was naturally fearful about this, especially at night. The particular circumstances of Seeta being able to turn to her grandmother in such a way would not have been available to a child living in a nuclear family, who would then have found other ways of dealing with the same conflicts.

In the first session, enabling Mrs P to convey her experience of becoming a mother, leaving her own family and country of origin, and her struggle to encompass both maternal and professional roles gave her space to think about this in the context of her own childhood, which would be quite different from that of her own children who would be growing up in London. This is probably what brought her back to the surgery with her child and in-laws. Realizing what a central place she had in her child's emotional life might have helped her to focus more on Seeta's emotional experience and step back from feeling rejected by her daughter who had been refusing to take food from her.

The open manner in which I addressed Seeta's possible feelings of loss and displacement may have resonated with the family's own feelings of displacement in London and enabled them to feel some empathy with her. Grandmother had felt free enough to express herself and her complaint, helping to move Seeta along and to find her place on her mother's lap.

Third session

Mrs P and Seeta attended this meeting. She explained that her husband would have liked to come but the demands of business kept him away, and that he was in fact a very involved father; she did not give the impression that she felt unsupported in her parenting. Mindful of her father's absence I explored what differentiation there was between mother's and father's activities with Seeta, encouraging her to tell me about special things she did with her father, to which she responded readily. Mrs P joined in, offering a reminder of her own special time when they read books together.

I heard from Mrs P about what a good son her husband is to his parents. They also have a daughter living in Goa who recently got married. Mrs P said that it was possible that her parents-in-law may have to leave and go to help her with her first baby; she was sad about this. I spoke about all the comings and goings and how hard that was for all of them. Mother spoke more about what it had been like when she first came over to England and how much time they had spent at airports flying backwards and forwards with Seeta who had been unwell, having to take lots of antibiotics. She had been unsettled and clingy, as well as being very bossy and not letting her mother out of her sight. Despite this, she is doted on by all of them.

Seeta stood close to mother's chair, touching her arm with her body. She did not attempt to clamber onto mother's by now very heavily pregnant lap. Mrs P joked that perhaps Seeta had now forgiven her for having another baby and was quite looking forward to being a big sister. Although the concept of rivalry was still unacceptable in this family, perhaps having done some thinking about it had prepared them for the mixed feelings that lay ahead. Seeta smiled at me when her mother was taking pride in reporting her progress. I was told that she had now ceased to sleep on top of her grandmother, lying in the bed close to her instead.

We acknowledged that this was our penultimate meeting, with the last to take place after the baby's birth. At this point it seemed as if progress had been made, but there was uncertainty as to whether this could be sustained at the time of and after the baby's birth. Seeta still seemed shy in my presence, staying close to her mother, but she was able to make more eye contact with me, and she looked at and fingered the farm animals I had put out, although she did not play with them.

*Discussion*

It was apparent that the relationship between the parents was one that left mother feeling supported. The father in her mind was a good and helpful man. Anticipating the departure of her in-laws, Mrs P was thoughtful about their possible move back to India to help with the arrival of their own daughter's first baby. Her parents-in-law had come to live with them and settled in London when Seeta was 2 years old. They were retired and dependent on their children, but also it was accepted that extended families support their children around the time of childbirth. Some Western families may have to use the professional network, particularly health visitors and GPs, as a quasi-extended family. Seeta had been able to stop sleeping on top of her grandmother, a move that may have been linked to what had taken place in the previous session.

Fourth and last session

This took place when Raju, the new baby, was 8 weeks old. The grandparents accompanied Mrs P and Seeta again. Raju appeared to be a contented baby. I was told that he had taken well to the bottle; mother explained that she preferred not to breastfeed. Raju was in a pram, and when he woke towards the end of the time, Mrs P was quick to lift him out and comfort him by rocking him gently in her arms. While she did so, Seeta went to her "Ama", who took Seeta's doll out of her bag. Seeta took this, held it against her chest, and rocked it. She looked taller, more grown up, and clearly full of pride when telling me her baby brother's name. I was told that Seeta had started playgroup. She was still restless at night. Mother looked exhausted, but exhilarated. Everyone exuded pride and a sense of achievement.

We began by noting that this would be the last meeting. All seemed relaxed with that idea. After admiring the baby, and hearing how the family were getting on, I was told by the grandfather that they were being called upon by their daughter to return to India to help with her first child, due to be born in a few months' time. Although they would keep a place within their son's London home, they would now have to divide their time and energies. I acknowledged their sense of loss (as well as gain) in not being an ongoing part of Seeta and Raju's daily life. Mrs P joined in, acknowledging what she, too, would lose. She said that she would be returning to work after twelve weeks' maternity leave.

Grandmother said that she felt in much better health, without so much physical pain, because Seeta was now sleeping in a small bed in the grandparents' room. She felt herself to be more able to refuse some of Seeta's demands, knowing that she was able to bear and cope with minor disappointments. Her heart was stronger and so was Seeta's. Mother commented on the way that Seeta seemed much more able to show her affection despite still being "Daddy's girl". I shared with the family my sense that there seemed to be no need for continuing contact with me. They had wanted to show me Raju and how well they were doing, but they had a sense of having moved on. As I frequently do in my work at the surgery, I reminded them that they would be welcome to return if they wanted to in the future.

*Discussion*

The predominant communication in this last meeting was the sense of pleasure and pride for all of them. The family had grown now to include a healthy baby son. The delivery had gone well, and Mrs P seemed to have found more confidence in her own mothering and was able to express herself in a way that had not been possible when I first met her. She spoke of being upset at losing the support and practical help of her in-laws but of not being prepared to put her professional life on hold while she took care of her two young children. She would have to get in hired help. She was not comfortable with breastfeeding, and it suited all of them to have sleeping arrangements that might seem unusual in Western families.

She was relieved and genuinely pleased that Seeta had such a strong tie to her grandmother and was concerned about how she would respond to the grandparents' return to India. Although she had been unsure why she had been referred in the first place, she seemed to realize that this was not a "vote of no confidence" in her capacities as a mother; on the contrary, she had flourished through taking up her maternal role more actively. The work had been less active with Seeta, who was very shy and hard to engage, but she had moved on too. Four meetings of under-fives work, spread out over a few months, had been all that was necessary to free things up for this family. The GP who had referred the case was pleased at the change in her relationship with mother, as well as in the reduction of appointments that they sought for minor physical complaints.

I had wondered why the GP had initially felt a "sinking-heart" sensation in the presence of this mother, which led to her making the referral. This leads us to the question of whose problem it is when a child is referred. It may have been that it was the GP's uncertainty about how to help this mother and her daughter. It is possible that it may have been a communication of Mrs P's own state of mind that the GP was picking up. Perhaps she was communicating in her frequent visits to the surgery some sense of heaviness, being pregnant with another child in a foreign city, far from home.

## Things move fast

The way that the dynamics had shifted within this family after only a few meetings is a familiar pattern. Often the child's "symptoms" represent a conflict in the relationships within the family. The brevity of the contact creates the opportunity to focus on realistic goals that are achievable. In Seeta's case the whole system seemed to have been freed up to move on. Seeta had become something of a tyrant, using her grandparents to gratify her in a way her mother could or would not. It also seems likely that father had joined with his parents in indulging Seeta, possibly seeking to compensate for the warmth and physical affection that her mother was finding difficult to give her.

It was disappointing that Seeta's father did not attend any of our meetings. It is not unusual for fathers not to come, with child-rearing often being seen as predominantly, if not exclusively, the mother's concern. This was not the case in Seeta's family, where the mother had a picture in her mind of father as making a significant contribution—in fact, one that allowed her to take a back seat. If anything, she seemed initially to be the one who had been marginalized from the child rearing. Through the sessions she seemed to find a more active position, which gave her pleasure.

While mindful of the number of families who do not have a resident father, the presence in mind of a helpful paternal figure is essential. It is not the child's biological father, or even necessarily another male presence, that is critical but, rather, the internal partner in the mother's mind and how this is conveyed to the child. Wherever possible both partners are encouraged to come to appointments from the beginning, acknowledging the importance of both of them. Sometimes the work facilitates the father to feel able to take a more potent role in family life. This creates a situation of shared parenthood, a partnership in which the child can be thought about from two different but complementary perspectives. In Seeta's family this perspective was broadened to include the grandparental view, and, with each member having their allotted role, multiple perspectives could be tolerated.

## *Finding the focus*

Brief work is both compact and complicated. The clinician needs a flexibility of approach, a lightness of touch, using the minimum necessary to get a family over the present difficulty. Awareness of the brief nature of the intervention means finding a few points of focus clustering around a central theme. This involves not exploring other issues that are raised by the family which might be usefully explored in longer-term work but do not relate to the mutually chosen central focus. It is necessary to find the focus and agree on it with the family, and it may take a while for this issue to emerge. As well as close observation of the family's behaviour and communications in the here-and-now of the session, detailed reports of incidents give a flavour of what has made specific events so painful, providing an indication of where the problems may reside, and how they might be resolved. Frequently the under-fives clinician encourages the parent to reflect on the child's birth, the early months, and any events in the adults' lives at those times that might have impacted on the family's emotional well-being.

After the second or third session the central theme will usually have been clarified, and a sense begins to emerge of whether the family will be able to make use of this approach. The family often makes an intense connection to the service following the sharing of intimate details of family life with the clinician. The end is kept in mind from the beginning, with the clinician often referring to it, so that the family members are all aware of how much time remains. Endings are necessary and are often an opportunity for reflection; by showing how useful they can be, without minimizing the pain associated with them, the clinician gives the family a picture that can then be adapted usefully to situations involving many goodbyes and moving on to new phases of life and growth. Many of the issues that families bring to an under-fives service revolve around the problems caused when change is only seen in terms of loss and not also in terms of opportunity for new experiences.

## *Conclusion*

The clinician's task is to think about the meaning of the child's behaviour, or "symptom", in the present—what this child does and why, and how this makes the parents feel or react. What the child does is likely to be influenced by the unconscious expectations of the parents as well as by the child's own temperament. In the work with the parents, those expectations are made conscious by making links between different aspects of their narrative which they had not previously put together or by making links between the parent's narrative and the child's play in the room.

Through the questions asked, parents are encouraged to think about why and when particular behaviour occurs. Often the very act of thinking in this way is a surprise, and parents derive considerable pleasure from the understanding it brings. When approaching the under-fives clinician, families are in a state of heightened emotional arousal and find it hard to think for themselves. They need some thinking to be done on their behalf.

The primary care milieu in itself serves a therapeutic purpose. The psychotherapeutic presence helps all the workers who are under such pressure to be more fully themselves in their work (Balint, 1993; Elder, 1996), having an increased ability to access their own thoughtfulness and sensitivity. As Daws (2005) states, "A psychotherapist can perhaps back the primary care team in continuing to recognize the importance of the emotional and psychosomatic aspects of their work, and in keeping going over years of dealing with the cumulative experience of seeing patients with undefined needs" (p. 36). In this way we believe that the clinician's presence helps both the patients and the staff, as the sense of a sinking heart is diminished when it can be thought about and understood.

*Note*

The work described was carried out by Beverley Tydeman; the discussion of the work is by both authors.

# PART II

# COMMON THEMES IN WORK WITH UNDER FIVES

# Challenging and disruptive behaviour

This section, in common with the book as a whole, reflects a universal preoccupation of children, parents, and professionals alike: that of how to cope with mental pain. Who is to have the mental pain? Can it be got rid of into someone else by the unconscious mechanism of projection, and does that alleviate the problem? Tantrums and disruptive behaviour are by their very nature expressions of a child's need to evacuate unmanageable emotional experiences. The therapist's capacity to absorb the child's projections and understand his communications are exemplified in the clinical work described in this section.

The chapters that follow address some of the behaviour problems in young children which most commonly lead to referral to Under Fives Services: tantrums, and disruptive and aggressive behaviour, at home or in nursery and day-care settings. Using a psychoanalytic framework the authors describe how experiences in early infancy can lead to the development of infantile defences that may, over time, evolve into patterns of challenging behaviour; they also describe how parents and professionals alike can be helped to reflect on these in a therapeutic way. Invariably, there is some overlap in the themes elaborated in this section. The underlying reasons for disruptive behaviour often relate to anxiety about catastrophic separation and loss. There is a close link with the last section of the book, which focuses on work with families where separation anxiety, coping with loss, change, and bereavement, underlie common problems in young children, such as sleeping or eating difficulties.

Controlling, omnipotent behaviour is often resorted to as a defence against feelings of helplessness and dependence. "Temper tantrums" by their very nature imply a collapse of the child's capacity to cope, a collapse that Lisa Miller refers to as a "miniature breakdown". These outbursts of screaming, kicking, or head-banging appear to be a powerful mechanism for evacuating or getting rid of intolerable feelings that cannot be thought about. The authors describe the therapeutic effect of "puzzling away at" (Miller) and trying to understand the meaning of these outbursts, in order to work out "what the matter can be", as well as absorbing and containing children's and parents' distress. Clinical interventions focus on understanding the children's communications as well as the emotional obstacles that can prevent parents from asserting their authority and setting firm boundaries with their children. The underlying technique of trying to put words to children's often nonverbal communications of distress, fear, excitement, or anxiety is described by Miller as the "naming of experience"—naming what "the matter can be". This can facilitate the shift away from evacuation and towards symbol formation as a means of psychic survival.

Lisa Miller, in chapter 7, introduces the notion that although we all have a wish to ensure a perfectly harmonious, conflict-free relationship with our infant or young child, this may not necessarily be beneficial. By trying to avert conflict or to deny the existence of painful feelings relating to separation or loss, parents may deprive a child of the experience of someone (parent, carer, therapist) who can tolerate uncomfortable feelings and be attuned to her baby's affective states (see also Hopkins, 1996). Miller describes how a parent's "smiling composure" in the face of her baby's distress can be perceived by the baby as a "rejection" or refusal to "receive" his communications. Faced with what he experiences as "an impenetrable barrier", a baby may "redouble" his efforts to get through to his parent in the hope that his feelings will be registered. In chapter 8, Emanuel has argued similarly that a baby may attempt to elicit a response from a depressed mother with increased force, screaming, kicking, or head-banging in order to have an impact on her. The child internalizes this early pattern of relating, which can be reflected later in difficulties in concentrating or paying attention for any length of time. The child may also transfer to other situations his early experience of needing to "force" his way into another's mind, leading to disruptive behaviour in settings where this may no longer apply—for example, with an attentive nursery nurse.

An important aspect of Miller's chapter is her thinking about the difficulties faced by professionals who are at the receiving end of often overwhelming emotional experiences. such as staff on special care baby units. It is difficult to remain "attached to babies or to parents" while needing to administer intrusive interventions or facing the possibility of a baby dying. Offering support in thinking about their experience may enable staff to remain emotionally in touch with their patients, despite the arrangements on the ward, which, as Menzies (1960) has described, are set up to help staff avoid anxiety and mental pain.

Miller also alludes to the ways in which organizational dynamics within childcare agencies may contribute to the further deprivation of already neglected or abused children. When professionals avert their eyes from the extent of "murderous threats" and anger emanating from families by overemphasizing "anything positive" reported about a family, confusing "soothing" with "collusion", they may be unconsciously employing the same defences against thinking used by these very troubled families. "These defences, including unconscious attacks on linking, can interfere with the professionals' capacity to think clearly or make use of outside help with their overwhelming caseloads, thereby replicating these children's original experience of neglect" (Emanuel, 2002a). Support for social workers and their managers can contribute to their capacity to reflect on the ways in which they may be pulled in and pressured to collude with a denial of severity of violence.

All three chapters in this section deal with violent, controlling, or out-of-control behaviour in young children, and sometimes in their parents. The omnipotent control and tyranny of children who are disruptive and aggressive is often a reflection of their identification with an intimidating or controlling parent. It may be difficult for a mother to hold on to the idea that her child is a dependent little boy if his behaviour and appearance remind her of his abusive father. Domestic violence, neglect, and abuse form the background of many babies and small children's lives, and Miller, in her last example, addresses the difficulty of confronting the severe damage caused to children exposed to violence in the home.

Miller also stresses the "addictive" quality of violence, illustrating how, in the chronic absence of a "friendly adult", severely deprived children hold themselves together by generating excitement linked to danger and risk-taking. These children, who seem to have very little hope of relying on supportive internal or external figures in their lives, are likely to require long-term interventions and the involvement of multidisciplinary agencies.

Cathy Urwin (chapter 9) gives a clear exposition of young children's struggles to develop a sense of self, and how stepping into the shoes of an adult by imagining themselves to be omnipotent and in control is a common defence resorted to by little boys struggling in this way. She suggests that the intensity of these children's tantrums is linked to their "reaction to challenges to . . . omnipotent identification", an intolerance of the helpless, dependent part of the personality. When thwarted by a parent or any adult setting a firm boundary, the child's omnipotence is punctured, resulting in a need to evacuate awareness of "littleness" and feelings of vulnerability. In tantrums of a more "ordinary" kind, children discover that they have "wills" that can come up against the "wills" of others (Sully, 1895, quoted by Urwin). This is linked to a sense of agency and ego strength, with one ego "pitted against" another, and is part of a normal developmental process. This is contrasted with those tantrums whose intensity and magnitude give the impression that they result from primitive terrors of annihilation and can result in extreme states of fragmentation as a result of excessive splitting off and evacuation of unwanted parts of the self. These tantrums are concerning to parents who may seek help because a child's tantrums seem "different" to the "normal" kind (as described by Miller).

Lisa Miller's exploration of the difference between the terms "anger" and "rage" seems to suggest that while the term "anger" describes an emotion that has been thought about, processed, and named, "rage" refers to an unprocessed collection of intolerable sensations, a combination of frustrated, envious, and murderous impulses, over which a child has no control and with which he can do nothing except evacuate. Helping children to shift away from uncontrollable outbursts of rage towards an ability to express feelings of anger verbally or through symbolic play is often the underlying aim of the therapeutic work on offer.

CHAPTER 7

# Anger between children and parents: how can we help?

*Lisa Miller*

This is a chapter about angry people. In the caring professions we are confronted by people who are distressed and vulnerable. Consequently the question of negative feelings—anger, hatred, aggression, and hostility—affects all of us in our work, as an inevitable feature of our professional lives. We hear about and witness scenes of antagonism in families which we know must do damage to small children. Either this is upsetting or it makes us angry in turn; some response in us is inescapable. People who work with families where there are babies and small children lay themselves open to the experience of powerful and primitive anxieties. Families—and I recognize that a family can take many shapes, from one single parent and an infant to a complex grouping—that contain an infant or small child are in a labile emotional state, because babies, toddlers, and children do not consume their own smoke. Their distress has to be dealt with by the adults around them; they have not yet learnt to manage their feelings independently, and consequently they ask their parents to bear some of their feelings for them.

If a baby is in pain it will cry, and that cry will disturb people who hear it. A parent will feel worried: for example, are these cries a response to pain in the mouth associated with teething? Are they more complex than that, with an admixture of anxiety related to growing sharp things in your mouth and having an urge to bite? Is the baby not teething at all, but unhappy or ill in some other way? No situation could be more ordinary, and yet the parent of this baby is subjected to a barrage of anxiety. How parents respond depends upon their resources at the moment: will this prove to be one of the numberless crises of infancy, which are soon surmounted and forgotten, or will it be too much for the parent to bear? Will the health visitor or the GP, the day-care worker, or the social worker be facing a mother in tears, overwhelmed by anxiety of her own which has been ignited by her baby's? Or an angry mother, persecuted and irritable? And what will the worker feel? It might be an occasion where the worker is well able to absorb the distress, where it seems understandable that the mother gets upset, and where the worker is able to combine sympathy with thoughtfulness and experience, to explore the situation to help the mother to think about it and leave things in a more manageable state. Then the mother feels better, the baby feels better, and the worker feels satisfied. Or perhaps it will not be like that at all. Perhaps the worker, despite all good intentions, will start feeling exasperated, thinking secretly, "Why can't she see there's nothing wrong with the child?" or, "If I had a mother fussing like that I'd be yelling too." Perhaps the worker will feel superior, along the lines of, "I could look after that baby much better." Or again, it may be anger that enters into the worker—anger with the mother who seems to be mismanaging things, anger with the father for not being supportive, anger with the Council for not providing satisfactory housing, anger with society that has put such pressures on this mother; possibly even anger with the baby for crying relentlessly and inexplicably.

We have in our mind's eye a worker struggling to contain his or her feelings, which are unwelcome ones. We, all of us, have some tendency to shy away from difficult feelings and a corresponding belief—albeit unconscious—in the possible existence of perfect parents, always patient, always available, never resentful—in a relationship between parent and child where friction is absent, where smoothness and harmony are paramount—where conflict and unpleasant emotions are avoided. But in our work with under fives, and in infant observation, we have ample chance to see that life from the start is not free of troubles, and sometimes we even see people who are trying to spare their babies pain but who are actually failing to give these babies the help they need to deal with pain and conflict.

For instance, it is common and understandable to see people hoping that weaning can be accomplished without problems, or that toilet-training can be dealt with without ups and downs. Often people think that if they postpone weaning or training the baby will wean itself, train itself. No need for anger or sadness or for doubt about doing the right thing: no need for all the powerful feelings that, as common sense tells us, may well rise to the surface. We see parents bobbing and weaving—doing everything they can to make sure the baby doesn't get upset. Where is the line between the necessary wish to protect a young child from unnecessary and damaging bad experiences, and the inability to tolerate the notion that not only does your child get cross with you, but also you get cross with it?

Here I should like to glance back at the imaginary worker who may or may not be feeling full of sympathy for the mother with the teething baby. We have in this an example of a worker in conflict. Much of her professional training and conscious motivation lead her to feel that as a helper she should be patient, available, and not resentful.

Here she is, inwardly flooded with unacceptable feelings—feelings, we have postulated, of anger, rivalry, and scorn. How is this to be understood? Can we use this experience of an uncomfortable quandary to further our thinking? Instead of feeling that we *should* be the expert, that we *shouldn't* get cross, it may be possible to utilize our emotional responses in the service of greater understanding and consequent lessening of discomfort—our own discomfort as well as the client's.

Before I develop this idea, I should like to describe briefly a case where I think difficult feelings were avoided, with consequent trouble later. A young woman came to the Tavistock Clinic's Under Fives Service with concerns about her little boy, Anthony, who was about 2 years old. The concerns included anxiety about his tantrums, but there seemed to be an all-pervasive sense of desperation, which I felt I began to understand a little when I heard Anthony's history. He had been an extremely premature baby, one of those who are nowadays miraculously saved. His mother described the long weeks of hospitalization in the special-care baby unit. One thing particularly interested me. Mrs A said that she herself had been regarded by the staff on the unit as the ideal mother. (Perhaps I should say that I have, of course, no idea what the staff actually thought, but certainly this is what the mother experienced and carried away with her.) She had always done exactly what they required of her. She threw herself into looking after her little boy with the greatest ardour, modelling herself on the nursing staff themselves. She was said to be just as good as a nurse and mastered all the techniques necessary for the care of the premature newborn. Never despairing, always present, always doing her best, she drew warm praise and approbation from all around her, and when Anthony was discharged she had a triumphant send-off. Ever since then, however, she had felt herself gradually more troubled and depressed and finally told me that she was radically worried about her son's progress and development.

My view is that this woman had tried to be an ideal mother. However, in one sense she had not felt like this little boy's mother at all. She had found her own way of protecting herself from the full awfulness of her position: every mother of a premature baby, fearing for the baby's life and viability, must be in turmoil about the baby she has inadvertently failed to hold on to, who is now vulnerable, unhappy, and subject to all kinds of medical procedures. Instead of feeling any degree of anger, guilt, resentment, this mother became the perfect patient. However, by acting this part, she also deprived herself of the staff's comfort and understanding. She behaved as though she didn't need it.

As I talked to her it became clear that she was feeling not like a perfect mother at all, but the very opposite: she was deeply convinced of her inadequacy, afraid she had injured Anthony, and always susceptible to the idea that he was reproaching her and hated her. Indeed, he *was* an angry child. He tyrannized over her; he wanted her full attention all the time; he felt outraged if he was required to endure any sort of minor frustration. Mrs A had been trying to maintain the image of herself as the person who did everything right for her baby, unable to see that help when things go wrong is one of the essential experiences every baby and child needs.

Real help, help that feels like help, is not based on denial of need. Nobody makes us feel better by saying, "There's nothing the matter with you", when there is. For people to feel that their distress is received, they have to make an impact on their listeners. Sometimes the listener can take it in her stride, can note and understand the other's distress without being thrown off balance; however, particularly in the case where aggression and anger are uppermost, we can be faced with difficult feelings in ourselves. For instance, if Mrs A had not been an "ideal patient's mother", she might have caused more trouble on the unit. She might have been much more critical if she had not been so eager to identify herself as one of an ideal team. She might have been depressed, she might have been demanding, she might have complained angrily; she might, in short, have been a worry to everyone.

We have to ask ourselves why Mrs A was so particularly susceptible to fear of her own anger, and why she seemed to feel that it was out of the question for the nursing and medical staff to put up with it. We need at least to consider the possibility that perhaps the nursing and medical staff were *not* up to it. Studies have been made of the emotional pressure put upon the staff who care for these premature babies. As they contend with issues of life and death—and these babies do die at times—what happens to the emotions aroused in the staff? I think there is plenty of evidence to suggest that under adverse conditions, with too few staff, with too little support from each other, with insufficient time for discussion and mutual thoughtfulness about cases, the nursing and medical staff have often to resort to finding ways of not experiencing their own feelings. They find ways of not becoming attached to babies or to parents. For example, without realizing what they are doing they may interrupt the continuity of their work—a continuity that could lead to thinking about a baby, which could lead to feeling attached, which could lead to suffering from hope and disappointment, which could lead to grief and rage if the baby's fight for life is lost. By interrupting the continuity of their work I mean simple things—one nurse starts a procedure, another finishes it. A different nurse feeds a baby each time. Or, indeed, there are other ways to protect oneself from pain.

We have no way of knowing to what extent the hard-pressed staff at the special-care baby unit where Anthony was placed were in this state, but we know that Mrs A behaved as though they could not be expected to put up with her unless she gave no trouble. This indicates to me that inside herself she carried around the deep-seated idea of people who cannot bear trouble; also, that she was lacking in the conviction that someone would bear with her if she was distressed, would be resilient enough to tolerate her anger, and would put up with it if she refused to be comforted. Here it seems to me we have an essential component of "good-enough" mothering, to turn to Winnicott for his famous phrase. The good-enough mother or father or carer has the capacity to put up with it when things cannot be put right—not merely to do their best to alleviate distress, but to grasp the nettle of imperfectability.

Mrs A seemed to have a demanding mother inside her, a mother who wanted not just the very best she could give, but better than that.

The result was that Mrs A lost touch with her real feelings. She became idealized by the staff as the perfect patient, and she wanted to go on idealizing herself when she got home. Of course, Anthony was not an other-worldly child; he was a baby with unhappy experiences inside him, starting from the moment when he began to be turned out of his mother's inside before he was ready.

Consequently, as soon as he felt sufficiently gathered-together, he began to show signs of distress. Mrs A tried to maintain the position of patience, cheerfulness, total availability which she saw as a prerequisite of being a good mother. All the time, though, she was also struggling to avoid experiencing her frightening negative feelings: her anger with Anthony for being less than perfect (for idealization cuts both ways), her anger with the world around her for failing to help her more. The result of this was that she could not help Anthony with his baby feelings. There is an ordinary—indeed, universal—process that is like this. The baby feels afraid. He cries, and at the same time his cries emit fear. His mother acts like a receiving station for broadcasts; she feels the fear, she registers it, she says to herself, consciously or unconsciously: "This baby's frightened." And in that knowledge she comforts him. He feels that his message has been received and his fear departs.

What happened when Anthony, back from hospital, emitted these feelings of fear? My contention, for the sake of illustration, is that Mrs A could not pick this up, deal with it unconsciously, and just say, "Oh, poor thing." Nor did she in a more vulnerable fashion receive the message, get the feeling of fear, and yet battle on—feeling frightened but putting up with feeling frightened and continuing to try to comfort him and understand the problem. I think that Mrs A attempted to behave like her unrealistic idea of a perfect nurse. Her "perfect-nurse" self, unflappable, imperturbable, tried with smiling composure to attend to Anthony's needs, judging them to be mainly physical. Anthony felt obscurely but powerfully that his communication was being rejected, and he redoubled his efforts to convey his fear. Mrs A redoubled her efforts to repulse them, impelled by a dread of being overwhelmed by fear. Anthony got the idea of a closed door, an impenetrable barrier; he did the equivalent of hurling himself against it, howling with fear. We might speculate that Mrs A was a parent whose childhood and infancy had been marked by a lack of tolerance for negative feelings in general, and who subsequently found it impossible not to fend off negative feelings from a baby, for fear these feelings would reactivate an intolerable infantile vulnerability in herself.

I should like to turn more specifically to anger and to make a working distinction for the sake of my argument between anger and rage. A young mother, Mrs J, came to the clinic with her small son, Jonathan, concerned about the child's development. It transpired that her partner, the boy's father, had been killed in a workplace accident. She was only too clear that she was angry with her late partner's firm. Her conviction that they had been both negligent and heartless was fiery and bitter, and she pursued them as far as she could for recompense and revenge. Jonathan, as well as being quite slow to learn, was subject to fits of meaningless rebelliousness. For example, asked to put his anorak on, or to go to school, he would cry, "No! no! no!" He would shriek, cry, bite his mother and kick her, flinging himself on the ground in an extreme tantrum. This I would call rage.

A tantrum is what children suffer when their whole system of managing their feelings collapses. Indeed, it sometimes seems helpful to say that they are suffering a miniature nervous breakdown—a breakdown that lasts five or ten minutes and from which they recover as best as they can. The normal system we adopt for managing our feelings, whether we are children or adults, is called thought. We understand the meaning of the emotional sensation that comes over us: we see it in context and we are able, without deliberating consciously over it, to give it a name. We grasp it as part of a logical system: A therefore B, consequently maybe C or D? Part of the work of bringing up a child is the emotional education that we perform without being aware of it. We help children to think about what is happening to them both outwardly and inwardly, and we do this by thought, action, and words of our own. I am talking about numberless tiny unremarked events just as much as about the times when things are actually talked over. Every time a parent correctly grasps the nature of a baby's feelings, these feelings, having been communicated, gain solidity and meaning. Sometimes a parent is consciously aware of doing this and remarks on it: "Oh, you are *cross*, aren't you?" or "I think that frightened him", or "Oh, how lovely, isn't it?" Perhaps more often, in those early months, where the physical intimacy of feeding and changing and handling a little baby is matched by mental intimacy, infantile communications are registered and responded to wordlessly or simply through a response—a hungry cry gets a feed; a dirty nappy gets changed.

As a child grows older, he acquires from different sources the capacity to know and to name feelings and to understand what causes them. It can be a great relief to acquire a way to think about what is troubling you. I remember seeing it a long time ago when I was working in an infant school with small groups of deprived children. I had a group of three children who vied painfully for my attention, and I recall the process whereby they began to understand what was happening to them. On one occasion I said to a little girl who was pulling at me angrily, "I think you might be a bit jealous because I was looking after somebody else just then," and she looked straight at me and said, "Jealous," in an obviously thoughtful way. I thought that the penny had dropped, and after weeks of my trying to sort these three rivalrous children out, this was the fruit of the work. This child had been one who had grabbed me, climbed up me, bitten my watch (so that the one I wore then had a dent in it for ever), who during several sessions had had what anyone would call a *tantrum* and I would amplify by calling a breakdown of her system of thought. She, gradually and sporadically, began to see what was the matter with her. This did not at once make her less angry, jealous, envious, and rivalrous, nor easily allow her to deal with the feelings that sprang from her very real deprivation in a too-large, under-resourced, disadvantaged family. It just introduced her to the idea that if you know what's going on, and why, you feel less panicky and desperate. This involves linking what you are feeling with what's actually happening to you, and progressing beyond a simple causal link ("I'm cross and upset because she was playing with Mark and I feel left out") to increasingly more sophisticated capacities—for example, trying to think what the matter could be when inner feelings do not apparently match outer events. How we reconcile conflict, paradox, and ambivalence involves complex emotional work.

To return to Jonathan's mother, Ms J, whose partner had died in an accident. Her system of thought was equal to the task of experiencing fury, impotent desperation, and revenge as related to the manufacturing firm that had employed Jonathan's father. But there was something else in her and her boy, which was expressed by Jonathan's bouts of rage. Jonathan's tantrums seemed meaningless and random. They were not linked to the job in hand; they could happen when he was asked to do something he could be expected to like doing, or at least not mind. His mother, by her own account, was remarkably patient with him.

A disquieting characteristic of these tantrums was that they were not modifying, altering, or fading away even though Jonathan was growing past the age when you would expect the immature ego of the toddler to be unable to support a storm of emotion from within. It was as though the tantrums functioned as a massive evacuation or rage:

rage functioned here as it often does, as a phenomenon that washes out all complicated or contrary emotions. Thus any chance of perceiving and experiencing the elements of emotional distress is lost. In this case it would be reasonable to think that among the components of Jonathan's distress would be irrational anger at his father for dying, irrational anger at his mother for somehow letting it happen, grief at his father's loss, anxiety for his mother and himself left to struggle alone, guilt for the times he had felt dislike and resentment towards his father, and an appalling sense of helplessness in the face of disaster. Rage was the force that enabled every painful thought to be rushed out of his mind before it crystallized. Every time life seemed to issue him an imperative—"You *must* go to school", "You *have* to wear your coat"—Jonathan was threatened with sensing his own smallness, vulnerability, and powerlessness, or, indeed, threatened by the potential inevitability of having to think his own thoughts. Thus he resorted again and again to opening his mind and his mouth and letting it all out. His distress was evacuated—but with such force that it temporarily left him completely and became unavailable for subsequent thinking over.

This is a useful case for us to consider, even though it has to be simplified for our purposes, because it seemed that while Jonathan's misery was indeed all his own, it was being added to by his mother's. She was unconsciously projecting into him much of her unrelieved anguish. This mechanism of projection, familiar to us all, is worth dwelling on since it can help us in thinking about anger between children and parents and the way these clients can inspire anger in us too. Jonathan and his mother were offered a series of meetings at the Tavistock by myself and a colleague from another discipline. Ms J wanted to know what was wrong with Jonathan. However, of course, it would have been no good to reel off a list of possible problems and to expect this to do the trick. In these sorts of discussions we are moving off into uncharted waters every time. We have ideas about the possible areas of emotional difficulty that might occur, but to pre-empt enquiry, doubt, and uncertainly short-circuits understanding and leads cases to blow up. As the meetings went on, Ms J got more restive until it became clear that she was becoming angry with us. Her discontent was palpable. Finally she came right out with it: we were useless, we had no appreciation of what she was going through, we were professionally incompetent and offered her nothing in the way of advice or support, nothing to help her feel better. Actually, she thought we were making things worse. Along with all these words came a sense of dislike, perhaps hatred, certainly contempt for us as well as a boiling anger below the surface. She said she was thinking of putting in a complaint about us.

You will have noticed how similar Ms J's feelings about us were to her feelings about her late partner's manufacturing firm. I hope I do not make it sound easy if I say that my colleague and I, with some anxiety and considerable discussion between sessions, managed to hang on, carry on talking, and try to understand. Gradually things moved a little. We stopped hearing so much about Jonathan's tantrums. To cut a long story short, it became clear, in a way that will be familiar to all of us who have thought about bereavement, that she was profoundly angry with the dead man himself. How could he have been so careless of his life? She was also afraid of getting unmanageably angry with her child, whose very existence threatened to put her in touch with her own vulnerability.

The point I wish to pick up is the one I mentioned of projection. It seemed as though Jonathan was being asked to bear a double burden, beyond the capacity of a little boy in his first year at school. His mother had shied away from receiving Jonathan's emotional burden, which in many ways was like her own. When he tried to project his distress into her, to let her feel how disturbed he was, she (metaphorically speaking) batted it back to him. Sometimes she did this by being infuriatingly patient; sometimes she did it with angry reproaches. The effect had been to leave Jonathan on each occasion with a doubled load of anger and the additional burden of feeling that nobody understood him, nobody supported him, that there was nothing to make him feel better. You will notice that these were exactly the feelings that emerged in his mother. When she had projected these feelings into us (making us feel useless, lacking in understanding, not up to the job) and had the experience of our not collapsing, she felt marginally better and her thinking moved on. She felt that someone was trying to look after her and consequently felt better able to look after her son.

Before we leave the question of projection, and the function of the worker as a survivor of projections, I shall mention another case where the father was absent, this time involving a divorce case. Mrs C, the mother of several little girls, came to see us in the middle of a bitterly contested suit. One of my colleagues decided to see her on her own and had a difficult first meeting, mainly because of the feelings Mrs C aroused in my colleague. Mrs C reeled off a long string of complaints, which revealed that she came from a privileged section of society. She couldn't find a reliable nanny; she didn't know how she would afford the school fees—complaints that made my colleague inwardly indignant. A young working mother herself, she found herself having no time for this woman, who struck her as feeling that the world owed her a living. In contrast, my colleague, Dr X, felt that she herself had plenty to put up with but didn't make this unattractive fuss about it. She mentally registered the client as a snob and a time-waster, but felt that since she had planned a series of appointments including the children she was professionally bound to put up with it and carry on.

Only afterwards did she start to digest the meeting and to realize that Mrs C carried around within herself some deeply unhelpful critical figures—characters in the inner theatre of her conscious and unconscious mind who kept on feeding into her dreams, memories, and imaginings ideas of her as hopeless. It was as though inside herself she was always feeling, "You pathetic creature, look how useless you are!" as though smug, superior people were sitting in judgment on her, proclaiming her inferior and worthless. All this was projected unconsciously into Dr X, who then, in trying to get to grips with this unwelcome message (who wants to feel superior and disdainful towards a patient or client?), began to find a way of thinking about it. The temptation had been to *act*: to say, "Well, it doesn't look as if I can help you much", or in some less unprofessional way to bring the contact to a close. This would have been to allow Dr X's anger to turn into rage and to eject the unwelcome client along with the unwelcome feelings.

Anger—certainly the extremes of it—carries this idea of getting rid of something, "Get out! Go away!", whether this applies to a person, a situation, a feeling, or a thought. The important thing is to resist some of the temptation to enact this and to try to keep mental activity afloat. I want to turn now to violence in the family, starting by considering again Ms J and Jonathan. What was Ms J defending herself against? Why could she not absorb, feel, recognize, name Jonathan's distress? Why did she have to return it to him unmitigated or amplified? I believe she was defending herself against the possibility that she herself might have a tantrum. I called a tantrum a nervous breakdown in miniature; I think that Ms J was afraid that her whole system of behaving—as a sensible person, an ordinary good-enough parent—would break down if she were to partake of that infantile rage suffered by Jonathan. She doubted her capacity to keep it under control if once she tasted it. If she felt herself getting angry—not angry with people outside the family, but angry with Jonathan and his dead father—who knows how it might end?

Infantile feelings are primitive and omnipotent. The buried infantile urge in the face of distress says, "If you don't like it, get rid of it." You cannot with impunity apply this to your own son. This impulse turns out to be a murderous one. Somebody in Ms J's position stands to discover not only feelings of burning resentment and hatred towards her dead partner but also antagonistic ones towards her child. These, of course, are the two main people of her life. It touches on one of the core questions of emotional life: the question of ambivalence. What do we do when we find that the person who is the object of our love is also the object of hate? In ordinary life the extremity and polarity of some of our infantile feelings stay well below the surface. Only under pressure do they begin to bob up into our conscious awareness.

One of the features of infantile anger or rage is its inability to distinguish between violent feelings and violent action. The baby, suffused with panic and anger, not only yells but also kicks and thrashes around. We are familiar with what happens when a toddler or even an older child is under the sway of this kind of emotion: violent action ensues. And when adults are under the same infantile influence the result is the same. Ms J was afraid that she might start to batter Jonathan, not only emotionally but physically. Many of our clients have already reached this stage, where a breakdown in adult thinking capacity has occurred and "jaw jaw" has given way to "war war". This is not a fanciful reference: when Churchill said this—that jaw-jaw was better than war-war—he was thinking of international relations, but relations inside the family or between the family and society can break down similarly. The rules of diplomatic negotiation between countries are designed as a framework to contain conflicts of interest; in just the same way the rules of ordinary behaviour are designed to keep people talking—around the kitchen table rather than around the conference table, but in the service of keeping open the channels of communication and not resorting to declaring war. In cases where domestic violence is a feature, murderous impulses are at play, and when we involve ourselves with them we involve ourselves with alarming behaviour, which cannot fail to disturb us.

When I say "domestic violence" I include cases that would be familiar to the police, but I also include cases where something less publicly abusive is occurring, cases where nevertheless abuse of children can result in damage that will be carried on into the next generation. How can we keep our systems of thinking alive and not resort to thoughtlessness and denial? I was involved with a sad family. Both parents were in prison for serious offences but were due to return to the community. In view of this the local authority wanted an assessment made of their three children, in order to make plans for the children's future, who were currently living with different members of their extended family. Should an attempt at rehabilitation be tried? And, if so, with which parent, for the parents were not only incarcerated but also locked in dispute and separated. The account of the children's family life to date was disheartening. They (7-year-old Steven, 6-year-old Darren, and 3-year-old Lorraine) had witnessed numerous scenes of violence and had on many occasions been the victims of neglect in the past; for instance, being found toddling late at night down the main road. Social services' input had been extensive.

The children had been placed with members of the father's extended family, one of considerable range and complexity, and the workers involved from social services felt that they needed a fresh look at this situation. A colleague and I offered them, in the first place, a consultation. A catalogue of severe problems emerged: drug-dealing, drug-taking, theft, domestic violence between the parents, concerns about the children's present placements with aunt and grandmother. Yet all the time there seemed to be an undertow pulling the professionals back from facing how bad things were. The children were described as idealizing their father, waiting for him to come back to them. People said he was charming. "He'll charm the socks off you," said a social worker. Yet this man, who appeared to have charmed or otherwise influenced even the magistrates he had appeared before, was the same man who could not protect his children on the most basic level when they were in his care. Our discussion seemed to be going round in a circle, when my colleague said, "It seems hard to remember that we're dealing with a delinquent family", and there was a conscious sense of relief in the room. Our discussion started to turn on the fact that this father could be threatening in the extreme; we began to think of the bully who lay behind the charmer, waiting to see if charm failed—if charm didn't work, the threat of violence moved into the open. We thought more about the professionals' impulse to pacify him and other family members, and about the difficult distinction to make between soothing someone and colluding with them.

During the course of our subsequent assessment of the three children there were ample opportunities to observe how difficult it was really to confront two things: first, the murderous threats emanating from a family whose anger, antagonism, and violence lay continuously seething beneath the surface. Second, it was hard to confront how damaged these small children were; we shrink from thinking what existence feels like to children who have are terrified and neglected. "Unimaginable, unthinkable," we say. At a child-protection meeting I attended, I noticed how strongly anything positive was emphasized. The school nurse, for example, became eloquent as she stressed how well appointments relating to Steven's glasses had been kept. It was as though she were hoping against hope to find here some responsible, careful person to set against the bald facts that our very presence at such a meeting spoke.

My colleague and I met the children with their carers, and then she (a senior psychologist) met them individually twice each for psychological assessment. Finally, she and I saw all three children together. Nothing had prepared us for the fact that these three siblings would be unable to stay in a room together with two friendly adults, who were not strangers. With all the information at my disposal I was still naïve. The children could not last out more than a few minutes without extreme anxiety resulting in aggressive, rivalrous, and disorganized behaviour. Lorraine, the 3-year-old, sucking endlessly on a dummy, emptied the small toys out, finding herself unable to think how to play with them, and left them on the floor to crunch them underfoot. All the children showed us graphically how dangerous life seemed to them; they wanted to climb onto unsafe things or up on the window sill. Steven could not stop trying to run out of the room to the coffee machine, whose gush of hot water he found vastly exciting; he could not keep away from it; he behaved like an addict. Both boys wrestled with us or each other. At moments one would try to "save" us, and both revealed some anxiety about our strength and durability when they asked questions of us such as: "Are you old?" and, "What's that thing on your face?" (meaning a mole).

These children were dramatizing by their behaviour scenes of uncontained infantile anxiety where the slightest feeling of discomfort (nervousness, shall we say) has to be got rid of, slammed out, expelled. What started in infancy as an ordinary projection of distress—the baby's communication of unhappiness—has become angry and aggressive. When distress met lack of response, it turned panicky and became the vehement beating on a closed door which I described earlier, and, as the response was still insufficient, a destructive and revengeful wish was added—from distress, to panic, to destructiveness.

These children were the inheritors of generations of deprivation and anger. They have not only had to contend with their own unmet needs, but they have also been subjected to a bombardment from the adults around them, people who for much of the time have been adult in name only, people who have been unable to reflect upon their own experiences of feeling victimized and vulnerable but who pass on these feelings to their children rather than experience them themselves. Children brought up in a violent household are asked to endure excess of terror. It is too much for them to do, to grasp the dreadful truth—that they, small and dependent, are in the hands of people who are far from being in command of themselves. Instead of feeling like witnesses, they feel like participants; they feel that they are joining in and that they are destructive people too. Violence can be addictive; it can come to seem a sign of life. Steven knew the risk of the hot water in the coffee machine, that it could scald him, and he also knew we were telling him he must not go there, but he was drawn towards it. It seemed something to organize his fragmented self so that he didn't feel all over the place; it acted like a magnet to his scattered feelings. Instead of being attracted by the attention of a friendly adult in a straightforward way, Steve felt the attraction of the forbidden machine. When he was removed from it, he was furious with the person, essentially helpful, who seemed bad to him.

We, whose work is in the emotional field as well as in the practical, find ourselves the objects of conflicting feelings from people who are chronically or temporarily unable to manage the question of ambivalence, of recognizing that we human beings often hate what we love and what is good for us. On the one hand, people regard us with hope, knowing they have troubles, looking for someone who will put up with their troubled selves and bear with their difficulties. This may lead to their finding some resources within themselves, resources to begin to discern what is wrong, to learn from what has happened, and to plan for the future. On the other hand, the very act of forming a relationship—trying to make a useful working alliance—brings up confused, conflictual feelings. The helpful person is also resisted and disliked.

Professionals find themselves swamped by unconscious projections from their clients which affect their powers to work and to think. We find ourselves feeling stupid, helpless, blind to the obvious, or full of uncomfortable responses tinged with contempt, anger, or rejection. But if we persevere and try to keep thinking, observe ourselves as well as our clients, and realize what is happening, we may find ourselves able to do more than we thought we could. Indeed, the better we understand what is being communicated to us, the more effective and interesting our work has a chance of being.

CHAPTER 8

# Disruptive and distressed toddlers: the impact of undetected maternal depression on infants and young children

*Louise Emanuel*

In this chapter I describe how the process of undertaking clinical work with toddlers referred because of disruptive behaviour and sleep difficulties revealed patterns of interaction between mother and child that suggested, retrospectively, that the mothers had suffered from undiagnosed post-natal depression during the period of their children's infancy. These hypotheses were subsequently confirmed by the mothers during our discussions. Clinical work was undertaken in a community health centre, targeting families who were unlikely to find their way to a child and adolescent mental health service.

The recognition that a mismatch in attunement between mother and baby during infancy resulting from post-natal depression (or possibly contributing to maternal depression) is associated with impairments in infant cognitive and emotional development (Murray & Cooper, 1997) highlights the need for early diagnosis and intervention for mothers, within the adult mental health services, and for parents and their infants, within child and family mental health services. I first discuss the impact a mother's post-natal depression may have on her infant's development and then illustrate through clinical examples how patterns of relating between parent and toddler, which may have become entrenched since infancy, began to change through the relatively brief interventions offered within an under-fives community service.

## The effect of maternal depression on infant development

Maternal depression during pregnancy may have an impact on the developing foetus. It has been postulated that a depressed mother may transmit her mood to the foetus in the tone of her voice, which will be "flatter, its rhythm slower and pitch lower than the voice of a non-depressed mother" (Maiello, 1997) and that this could have a negative effect on the foetus.

Research has shown that, from birth, infants engage socially with their caretakers and are sensitive to the quality of their communication (Kennell, Voos, & Klaus, 1979). In the first 24 hours after birth infants respond to the sound of their mother's voice above anyone else's. By 6 weeks they gaze and smile at their mother's face in preference to others and are sensitive to the timing and nature of her response. Post-natal depression, which may result in a disruption of this mutual process, has its onset at a critical time in the developing relationship between mother and baby, when the infant is very tuned in to the most subtle nuances of feeling and expression communicated between mother and child. Studies by Lynne Murray (1988) of deliberately contrived disruptions to normal infant–mother interactions (the "still-face" and "mistiming" studies) show how a lack of attuned responsiveness in mother can lead to a reaction of protest and withdrawal in the baby within a very short space of time.

If a parent is suffering from post-natal depression, it can be difficult to "focus on the baby's experience", and her responses to the baby in social interactions will be compromised. On the one hand the mother's preoccupation with her own feelings may cause her "to miss infant cues and appear withdrawn ... on the other hand depression is sometimes associated with intrusive and even hostile play, when the mother may fail to recognize the baby's discomfort and persist in trying to gain the baby's attention, possibly poking the baby roughly or being otherwise over-stimulating" (Murray, Cooper, & Hipwell, 2003, p. 72).

In addition, Murray, Cooper, and Hipwell (2003) suggest that depressed mothers are more likely than those who are well to give up breastfeeding early and, according to Seeley (Seeley, Murray, & Cooper, 1996, quoted by Murray, , Cooper, & Hipwell, 2003, p. 72), are more likely to report difficulties "managing their infant's crying and demands". The mother may have a perception of the infant as a "drain and hindrance to her" (Cramer & Stern 1990, p. 254) and may be struggling to adapt to a new identity as a parent.

The longer-term impact of post-natal depression was demonstrated in a study by Murray (1988) that indicated that toddlers whose mothers had been depressed post-natally were less securely attached at 18 months, as measured by the Ainsworth Strange Situation test (Ainsworth, Blehar, Waters, & Wall, 1978), than 18-month-olds with non-depressed mothers even if the mother's depression had abated by this time. There was also a significant impact on some aspects of the infant's cognitive development, notably poor performance on object-permanence tasks (Hay, 1997, p. 91, quoting Murray's Cambridgeshire study). These deficits themselves can be characterized as a form of "dysregulated attention" (Hay, 1997, p. 98). Murray's study also suggests links between a depressed mother's speech, which is less infant-focused (and more mother-focused), and the infant's cognitive abilities (Hay, 1997, p. 100).

The infant's contribution to maternal depression can also be significant. Murray and Cooper (1997) describe the "role of infant and maternal factors in post-partum depression" (pp. 111–135), arguing in the Cambridge study that poor motor functioning and neonatal irritability "significantly increased the risk of the mother's becoming depressed". My experience of infant observation and clinical interventions would support this finding.

Not all mothers who are depressed will have these kinds of interaction difficulties. It is possible that an easily gratified baby can serve to cheer up a mildly depressed mother and defuse a potentially anxious situation. However, in its more extreme form, this can lead to idealization of the child as "perfect", so that the child is not seen for who he really is, with both positive and negative feelings. It can lead to over-dependency of the mother on her child, a reversal of the caregiver's role, with the child feeling at some level a sense of responsibility for cheering up mother and bringing an element of liveliness into the relationship. However, some vulnerable mothers are thrown into a state of depression by their very attempts to focus on their child, who may be particularly demanding and easily frustrated in temperament. To such mothers, the life and death communications of small babies are terrifying and unbearable. Mothers may "switch off" so they do not have to notice the intensity of their baby's communications. "Some mothers cannot notice their babies' signals because they remind them of their own unmet needs as babies and noticing is too painful to bear" (Daws, 1996, p. 14).

*The infant's defences against maternal depression: a psychoanalytic approach*

A mother who is post-natally depressed over a period of time may mistime her signals to her baby, and her baby may contribute to this misattunement (Murray & Cooper, 1997). As a result, the baby will unconsciously develop defensive forms of behaviour to deal with excessively long periods of inattention or inconsistent unpredictable responses.

*Bion's concept of container–contained*

Infants have a limited mental capacity to deal with overwhelming sensory experiences of, for example, distress, excitement, terror, hunger, loneliness, or intense pleasure, which they may experience as persecutory or even life-threatening. Consequently they need their parents to bear a large part of their feelings for them. If a baby is in pain or distress, he attempts, in phantasy, to evacuate these unpleasant sensations, together with bodily excretions, crying, and excessive kinetic activity. If his distress is taken in and absorbed by an attentive parent, who is able to receive the infant's communications and reflect on them without becoming overwhelmed by anxiety herself, the infant has an experience of feeling that his communications have been understood.

This process of "containment" is achieved when the parent is able to attend closely to the infant, in a state of "reverie" (Bion, 1962a, 1962b). When the parent has made sense of the infant's communication in her own mind, she is then able to respond appropriately to the infant and tend to his needs—for example, change him, comfort him, feed him, and so forth—and the infant has had an experience of a mother who can think about, understand, and process his feelings. The infant gradually becomes less overwhelmed by his upset feelings, learning through experience of a thoughtful parent how to make sense of his own experiences—that is, to think for himself. A thoughtful attentive parent provides the model for the infant's developing capacity to think about his own feelings.

*Lack of containment: its impact on learning and thinking*

What happens when the mother cannot perform this function of containment and "reverie" for the baby? The baby's only recourse is to intensify his efforts to evacuate the persecutory sensations that threaten to overwhelm him, to attempt with greater force to gain entry to the mother's mind so that his communications can be received and understood. In response to a mother who may be unavailable or inconsistently available to her baby's communications, the baby may attempt to gain access to her mind with increased force and hostility, perhaps screaming, kicking, scratching, or even at times banging his head against her as if to gain entry in this manner.

The baby may unconsciously experience a depressed mother's inability to receive and contain his feelings as a lack of willingness to do so, or hostility towards him. If his states of persecution are not received by the parent and do not find a "home" in the mother's mind, they rebound off the unavailable parent figure and return unmodified to the infant, whose state of persecution is intensified. A vicious cycle can be set up as the baby pushes back his feelings into mother with increasing force and hostility, attempting to elicit a response. This is often the source of the disruptive attention-seeking behaviour labelled Attention Deficit Hyperactivity Disorder (ADHD). It is possible to trace the origins of such behaviour to the early weeks and months of the infant's life. The early pattern of inattentiveness which the child internalizes is reflected later in difficulties in concentrating or paying attention for any length of time and can have detrimental effects on a child's ability to learn at school.

In some circumstances, and depending on his temperament, the infant may give up on trying to "get through" to the mother and may become a bit like a depressed mother himself. In the classroom one can later see an inert, seemingly empty unresponsive child, whom teachers describe as difficult to "get through to". The baby may have internalized a model of a parent figure who is unreceptive to the communications of others, and identifies with this internal model. This often leads teachers to believe that a child operating these "no-entry" (Williams, 1997) defences has less intelligence than might actually be the case.

An alternative response to a deficit in attention resulting from maternal depression is the infant's unconscious turning away from states of dependency by becoming precociously self-sufficient and controlling, dealing with unmet needs by appearing to require little comfort or gratification from adults. These babies sit up unaided very early; they do not mould themselves into their mothers' laps but tend to develop their own muscular strength, standing on well-developed legs while very young and occasionally walking by 6 or 7 months. Although perceived as super-advanced, their controlling manner and apparent lack of vulnerability may be seen as a way of coping with disappointment at unmet early needs by refusing to allow themselves to feel any need or any sense of loss or disappointment at what they lacked.

The psychoanalyst Esther Bick (1968) described infants developing muscular "second-skin defences" as a way of holding themselves together in the absence of maternal containment. This type of "second-skin" defence in their babies may increase the strain on depressed mothers who, already suffering from a lack of self-esteem, may become the recipients of the baby's feelings of vulnerability and helplessness, which have been split off and projected into her. In this way the baby remains out of touch with these unbearable feelings of loss or disappointment, and mothers are at the mercy not only of their own feelings of inadequacy, but of their baby's projections, which increase their burden of depression and sense of helplessness. Babies in this state can make a mother feel even more useless and inadequate because they give the untrue impression that they don't really need her.

These early primitive unconscious defences can pose problems for learning, too, as children who cannot bear to be in touch with feelings of dependency may have difficulty coping with the fact that the teacher (like a mother) may have something to offer them that they do not have themselves. These children cannot bear to let themselves know that they do not have all the knowledge and answers within themselves but may have to rely on an adult, a teacher, to show or give them something. This makes them feel small and anxious, stirring up all the helpless unbearable feelings of infancy, when neediness had led to frustration instead of fulfilment. It is often at moments when new tasks or information are given that children like this either become disruptive or "disappear" into a daydream, where they can fantasize being in control of all resources, relying on no one.

A depressed mother may sometimes respond in a very restricted way to the baby's varied communications, not differentiating between them—for example, feeding the baby in many circumstances for comfort, where the message from baby could be a need for a different kind of contact or action. The baby then never learns to differentiate clearly his own different feeling states as he has not had the experience of mother doing that for him. This can result in a restricted, rigid kind of thinking. The older child in the classroom may be unable to discriminate between what is important to take in and what is not and may struggle to allow his imagination full creative sway. He may deal with all learning situations in exactly the same way, which becomes a limiting factor for learning and thinking (R. Emanuel, 1998).

## Clinical vignettes

I would like to give some examples of parents and children I have seen at the local health clinic. They were referred for a range of problems, but in each case it emerged, through the children's material and parents' recollections, that the mother had suffered from post-natal depression after the child's birth. I was struck by the fact that none of these mothers had received treatment for post-natal depression when their children were infants, although most of these families would have been attending this or a similar health centre since the time their babies were infants. Many of the predictive factors for post-natal depression—previous miscarriages, loss of the mother's mother early in her life, unsupportive or absent fathers—were present in these cases.

I attended the local health centre once weekly, from my base at a CAMHS unit, to offer support and discussion meetings with the health visitors and to see some of the families they felt needed more specialist input than they could offer, but who would be unlikely to travel to the CAMHS unit. I offered up to five sessions with families, with the possibility of further work, and often saw families jointly with the referring health visitor. Although the families described below were seen by me on my own, I held regular feedback meetings with the health visitors to discuss the interventions.

Timmy and Douglas, both 3 years old, were children of mothers who appear, in retrospect, to have suffered from post-natal depression. The children's disruptive behaviour could be seen as a response to early patterns of mother–infant interaction where the infant has had difficulty "getting through to" a preoccupied mother and has needed to "broadcast" his distress (Miller, chapters 2 and 7) loudly in order to gain a response.

### Timmy

Timmy's father had left the family two months after his birth, and mother's new partner, with whom Timmy had a good relationship, was in prison. Mother had experienced some levels of violence from both partners. In the first meeting with mother, Timmy, and baby Susan (6 weeks old), mother told me she hadn't wanted Timmy and without her own mother's help in the early months would not have coped. However, her relationship with her mother had deteriorated, and she was unsupported by close extended family. The family was referred because Timmy was physically attacking mother and appeared to be out of her control. In this meeting baby Susan slept throughout, and in subsequent sessions she slept or stared blankly ahead of her while Timmy rampaged around the room. Mother confirmed that Susan slept a great deal at home. Timmy's mother was so fraught, dealing with Timmy's demands and clearing up his mess, that she seemed to forget the baby's existence for long periods. It became clear that mother felt so intimidated by Timmy who had taken charge at home, and was so frightened by his violent tantrums and attacks, that she would do anything to placate him. She seemed to be literally flattened by him, as if she had no sense of authority at home, and it took her a while to realize how little she was able to give to her "good" and "undemanding" baby. I made some comments to this effect.

At the following (second) meeting, mother complained that she had had a sleepless night, as the children, in turns, had kept her up through the night. Neither child had been able to sleep. I suggested that perhaps Timmy was feeling anxious and frightened because of his daytime behaviour and attacks, and baby Susan was healthily protesting, determined to find some individual attention from Mum for herself. We discussed the importance of Timmy having an experience of sharing his Mummy, and feeling that she can keep a space in her mind for both her children. Mum reported the following time that both children were settling much better at night.

In this (third) meeting, mother conveyed how overwhelmed she felt by Timmy's fierce temper tantrums. As I watched Timmy flying into an uncontrollable rage, lunging at his mother, attacking and biting her, it made me think of an infant whose unprocessed projections have not been contained, and who tries with increasing force to push his way into his mother's mind and find a place in her for his unbearable feelings. I could see how the violence of his feelings escalated as his anger provoked *her* to respond angrily. She was unable to reflect on his communications of rage, and a vicious cycle of destructiveness unfolded before me. Yet mother commented that Timmy was much calmer in the room when the two of us were together. I felt he was responding to the containment of firmly set boundaries, as well as to his mother and myself thinking and working together as a couple to take charge and not allow him full control. This was all the more poignant because of the absence of a father figure in his life.

Mother told me that Timmy had started walking at 6 months, and was "completely self-sufficient", apparently needing no one. As she talked, Timmy was trying to get out of the room, and mother stopped him, with my help. Furious, he stood on a box and transformed himself into a tough boxer, yelling "No! No!" and curling his small hands into threatening boxers' fists. To Mum, feeling so rejected and inadequate, it was as if he were six feet tall, much bigger and stronger than her. A moment later he tumbled from the box and fell, and a look of panic flashed on his face. We talked about his rather pathetic attempts to become tough, the superman. He felt a need to get rid of the needy dependent baby part of himself which might have had quite a bad time as an infant. Mother agreed, saying he must have felt her to be a disappointment, as she had not been available to him and able to satisfy his demands as baby. Now he needed to ensure that he would always be in control and to get rid of his feelings of helplessness into mother.

In our fourth meeting Timmy had a violent tantrum, exploding with rage, biting his mother and flinging the toys at me like missiles. Overwhelmed with anger, mother hit him. He flinched, as if anticipating the blow, then sat on his own, crying as if his heart would break. This time he was showing us a different side of Timmy, not the tough, threatening boxer man but a distressed, upset, crying baby, who needed to be held by a mother who would contain and think about his upset baby feelings. Earlier in the meeting he had been making baby sounds, babbling and trying on the baby doll's hat, looking towards us as if he now knew we would notice and comment on this. Now, as he sat crying, I wondered aloud what mother would normally do in this situation at home. She said, "He's not a very cuddly child, he'd just push me away if I tried to hold him." We can see how inadequate and rejected mother felt and how easy it was to push those feelings back into the baby, expecting him to cope with them, especially if mother felt unsupported herself.

With encouragement, mother made a space for him on her lap, rather tentatively. As he sobbed and I passed him a tissue, he shook his head, refusing it, saying through his tears, "I haven't finished crying yet." I think this was the pain and upset about all sorts of losses and worries that Timmy had to face when, for a moment, he was able to bear to be a little boy on his mother's lap, being comforted by her. Once he cried, as he remarked, he might not be able to stop crying. His defences, once breached, left him exposed to a great deal of mental pain, which would require containment by his mother and by me in the sessions. Fortunately the family were able to make use of the brief work (eight sessions in all) sufficiently for mother to feel able to recognize the more vulnerable side of Timmy and to respond to him as a toddler, rather than the tough "man" (possibly the violent father) of her imagination. Timmy's aggressive attacks reduced, and mother became able to give more appropriate attention to the baby. The health visitor, who kept in close contact with the family, reported that the improvements had been sustained six months after the sessions ended.

## Douglas

Douglas, too, was having apparently uncontrollable tantrums, and the parents in my meeting with them (without Douglas) gave me a picture of an "absolute monster", saying that their extended family called him "psycho Douglas" or "Douglas the nutter". He was hyperactive, verbally and physically attacked his mother, and had once smashed his bedroom door off its hinges in a fit of rage. His sleep was disrupted by nightmares. I shall describe my initial meetings with the parents, without Douglas, where we explored some of their difficulties in parenting him.

Although father was present in the family, he felt unable to cope with his wife's irritation and bad moods when he came home from work, and the relationship was under threat. Father was unable at this time to provide containment and support to his wife and to help her exert her authority over Douglas. In fact, he seemed to relish the split that was developing between them, where Douglas would obey him but ride roughshod over his mother. Like Timmy, Douglas coped with possible feelings of disappointment in his early infancy by becoming prematurely grown up, watching adult TV programmes with mother in the upstairs bedroom, while father watched sports programmes in the living room. It seemed as if Douglas had become mother's little companion, and in his omnipotent state of mind he may have felt as if he had taken his father's place as her "husband". Mother confirmed that he would not permit her to call him a little boy and that he was very jealous when she and her partner showed affection towards each other.

Douglas had developed a passion for motorbikes and took a motorbike to bed with him instead of a cuddly toy. He seemed to identify with a rather tough father figure, strengthening himself with defensive armour to protect him from the terrifying dangers of the night. We might understand Douglas's night-time fears in the light of his omnipotent phantasy that he has replaced his father as mother's partner, and his resulting persecutory anxiety about retaliatory attacks.

His mother described how, when she took Douglas to nursery, he would go running in without a backward glance and rush to grab a tricycle. Once on the hard bike, it seemed, he could distance himself from any softer, more worried feelings about separating from his parents, as if he had internalized a notion that helplessness and weakness are contemptible and that one needs to be tough to survive. This may be a response to experiences of frustration and disappointment in infancy, when he might not have found an adequate containing maternal object for his projections of anxiety or terror, as well as an internalization of father's rather tough, "survivor's" attitude, which became more understandable when I heard about his own childhood experience.

When his parents talked to me about his cruelty to their pet cat, whom he kicked about like a football, I felt concerned. I suggested that since there were no younger children or babies at home, the small cat could stand for not only a rival baby, towards whom he might feel quite murderous, but also the vulnerable baby part of himself. I wondered aloud whether they had thoughts about having another baby. Mother implied that Douglas was too much of a handful and she wouldn't want to aggravate the situation. It appeared that Douglas was actually managing to prevent the appearance of more babies in the household. I spoke about the way Douglas was creating an angry split between his parents to ensure they would not be in a loving state to create a baby who might displace him and how this sense of control and power could increase his anxiety and fuel his disruptive attacks. The more persecuted he became, the more he persecuted them, and a vicious cycle ensued.

This was confirmed when they described Douglas's severe phobia of flies and bees, and his hatred of their buzzing noise, which sometimes prevented him going into the garden. I talked about a worry that seemed to be buzzing around inside him, tormenting him, which penetrated through the tough armour. It might be a worry about something small, like a baby (or a fly), which could come and attack him back, in retaliation for all the damage he felt he might have done to mother or mother's unborn babies, for all his own violent and aggressive outbursts towards his parents. Both parents struggled to recognize how Douglas's anxieties would increase if he felt they were unable to prevent him attacking and abusing his mother and obstructing their functioning as a combined parental couple.

The parents seemed to feel helped by this discussion and told me about their "horrendous pregnancy, labour and birth" and the "poor welcome" they felt Douglas had received into the world. Mother had felt dreadful during her pregnancy, and her depression had manifested itself in irritability. Father recounted how, after an anxious prolonged labour, the paediatrician had thrust the baby roughly towards him, saying brusquely: "Here's your baby." Mother had become increasingly fraught and depressed when they returned home from the hospital. Although she had been planning to breastfeed, she was so "shattered" by the birth that she resorted to bottle-feeding. Douglas would never fall asleep under any of the circumstances in which babies normally feel lulled to sleep, such as in the car or pushchair, not until he was safely in his own solid bed. I talked about a baby who sounded as if he were always in a state of alert vigilance and how, from early on, he might have absorbed feelings of tension and panic in those around him, which made it difficult for him to feel quite safe about letting go and drifting off to sleep.

The parents' extreme reactions and feelings of being badly treated at this vulnerable time did not quite match up with my knowledge of normal practice in obstetrics units. It was not until the following meeting (second), when I heard about their own backgrounds, that I could understand how much of their own feelings of rejection (particularly father's feelings about his own poor welcome into his family) had been projected into the setting of their son's birth and confused with it.

Mother had lost her own mother from a lingering illness, at 16 years, and her depression was linked to feelings of deep loss and regret that her mother was not present to witness Douglas's birth and to "dote" on him. Father described with some bravado having been brought up in a children's home. One by one his siblings had been sent for to return to their natural parents, but he was the last to be taken back and, by then adolescent, he had stayed for two hours before leaving in anger. We could see why father might have found it difficult to provide mother with support and containment during her depressed period, having no internal model of support or containment as a child. Perhaps he had had an expectation of being mothered by his wife in their marriage, and this was shattered by the new baby's demands.

The parents told me about Douglas's obsession with batteries, and his father described how Douglas smashed cars to take the batteries out, as he wanted to see how those battery-operated toys work. I said it seemed as if Douglas himself was like a battery, who got charged up and ran and ran until he collapsed. I wondered aloud whether he had been an infant who may have felt from early on that it was his role to bring mother to life, to charge her up, so to speak, with his lively activity. Mother sadly agreed that this might have been so. I commented on Douglas's curiosity to see how things worked from the inside. Did he have some unconscious desire to get in behind the depressed mother's eyes and see inside her mind (and body), as if to see what could be preoccupying her and filling her up with other thoughts, when he felt her mind was not on him? Perhaps he imagined that other babies were filling her up inside, in the same way as batteries fill up an empty space inside a toy.

I suggested that the image of Douglas wrenching the batteries out of his toys symbolized the effect that his disruptive behaviour was having on his mother. He seemed to be extracting from her, and destroying, all the good qualities that make a Mummy work properly, just as when one pulls a battery out of a toy it stops functioning. He "pulled" out of her the capacity to set firm limits and be authoritative as a parent (taking on a paternal function), leaving her feeling flattened and useless, like a flat battery. In this case, father did not have the resources of his own to recharge her.

Douglas's parents returned to their next meeting (third), telling me how much calmer he had been, and mother said she had found herself able to think more about Douglas's outbursts of rage and to process them for him, putting words to his feelings rather than simply screaming back at him. I had the impression they felt I had helped them to recharge their batteries a little, with hope, and had helped them replenish their dwindling stock of resources by providing some maternal care and containment for them as parents, and as a couple, as well as giving a space to the needy child within them both.

Father told me movingly how at the children's home he would sit for hours dismantling then putting together clocks to make them work again. Douglas, similarly, would sit for hours, building Lego houses and garages, in an apparent attempt, I thought, to restore his parental objects. They clearly felt motivated to put together their family again after the trauma of Douglas's birth and the difficult feelings it had stirred up in them.

The parents attended, together with Douglas, for a further three sessions and made great improvements, delightedly reporting that family friends had commented that he was a "changed child". Now that some work had been done with his parents, Douglas was able to use the sessions to explore, through his play, issues to do with being big and little, with boundaries and limits. He built an enclosure with the toy fences and showed great interest in the gate, insisting that all animals entered and exited through it. This was in contrast to his violent smashing down of his bedroom door at home. They all listened with interest as I talked about Douglas's interest in the right way of getting in and out of the enclosure, about who is allowed to go where, and when. They described Douglas being "obsessed" with building roofed constructions, brick edifices that were all enclosed. I reminded them of how we had spoken previously about Douglas's experiences in infancy, when his feelings of anger, frustration, and distress might have overwhelmed him, leading to violent outbursts at home. Perhaps Douglas might still feel a need at times to put a lid on these powerful destructive feelings in a rather repressive way, which then simmered away inside. As I spoke, some animals burst out of Douglas's fence enclosure, which was filled to capacity, and father accompanied this with "Smash! Crash!", indicating an explosion. Father then talked about his own explosive rages and how he recognized this trait in Douglas.

As their final session progressed I mistakenly referred to him as "Dougie". He said, "I'm not Dougie, I'm Douglas Smith." I said he felt he was a big boy and I mustn't say his name as if he were little. There was heartfelt agreement from everyone. Douglas climbed on top of a tall filing cabinet, and I talked about him feeling he was the king, in charge, like a Daddy. He said: "I'm not a daddy, but I will be one day." I said, "Yes, he's thinking about where he fits in, he's not a baby, he's becoming a big boy and one day he'll be a big man, a daddy, like his Daddy—he is going to grow up." Anne Alvarez, in her book *Live Company* (1992), talks about the developmental importance of allowing a child to express his "anticipatory identification" with an admired figure, to imaginatively conjecture what sort of grown up he will be. Douglas was becoming increasingly able to do this in a safer and more thoughtful atmosphere, with parents who recognized that there were still difficulties to work through and who were continuing to try to puzzle over the meaning of his behaviour without becoming overwhelmed with feelings of despair.

## *Conclusion*

Neither of these families had been referred with a specific concern that the mothers might have been suffering from post-natal depression since the birth of their children. The main focus of the referrals had been the disruptive toddlers whose behaviour had become difficult to manage. Using the Tavistock Clinic model of brief psychoanalytic work, I grew to understand through discussion with the mothers, and through following the children's play and communications, that the resulting difficulties in the relationship between mother and child, as well as the child's internal problems, might have originated in a disruption of the early mother–infant relationship as a result of the mothers' suffering from post-natal depression.

I hope these examples have highlighted the need for early detection and intervention in mothers most at risk of post-natal depression. The impact on children of a disturbed mother–infant relationship caused by post-natal depression, at a critical period of infancy, is considerable, and it can adversely affect a child's emotional, cognitive, and social development. However, on a more hopeful note, from my experience with these cases short-term, focused work with families where mothers have suffered from post-natal depression can be effective in pointing the way to recovery of their capacities to recharge their own batteries.

*Note*

This chapter is a modified version of an earlier publication: L. Emanuel, "The Effects of Postnatal Depression on a Child", *Psychoanalytic Psychotherapy in South Africa*, Vol. 7, No. 1 (1999): 50–67.

CHAPTER 9

# Where the wild things are: tantrums and behaviour problems in two under-fives boys

*Cathy Urwin*

In his children's classic, *Where the Wild Things Are,* Sendak (1963) describes how one day a small boy called Max donned his wolf suit and "made mischief". His mother called him a "wild thing"; he threatened to eat her up and was sent to bed without any supper. In his imagination, Max's room became transformed into a jungle and then the open sea as he sailed away to "where the Wild Things are". Though they roared, gnashed their teeth, rolled their eyes, and showed their claws, Max tamed the Wild Things by staring into their eyes. He became their King, and all sorts of rumpus followed. Eventually Max tired of this. He sent these creatures to bed without supper. Then Max was lonely and "wanted to be where someone loved him best of all". From far away, he smelled good things to eat. So he gave up being King, got back into his boat, and sailed back across the world. In his room, his supper was waiting for him, still hot.

As Raphael-Leff (1989) has noted, this story captures astutely some of the psychological challenges of parenting children under the age of 5 years. Judging from the illustrations, Max had been tormenting the dog, making holes in the walls, and shouting back at his mother. Behaviour problems at home and at school are among the most common reasons for referring under fives to CAMHS. The referred child is often described as a "Jekyll and Hyde", delightful one minute and a monster the next. Alarm in parents and referrers may be exacerbated by public concern and media attention given to the question of the origins of violence and delinquency. Television programmes about ADHD and the interventions of a "super nanny" stress that it is urgent to intervene early for the family's benefit as well as for the child's. CAMHS referrals will generally implicitly if not explicitly highlight the risk of parents lashing out or harming the child, in reaction to their powerlessness and loss of control. These referrals commonly, but certainly not exclusively, tend to be of boys.

Given the high anxiety behind these referrals, any effective service must aim to respond as soon as possible. What does a psychoanalytic view of development offer, and what are the particular advantages of psychodynamic under-fives counselling?

Psychoanalytic approaches are distinctive in recognizing that such apparently unpalatable emotions as possessiveness, jealousy, and the aggressive and destructive behaviour that may express them contribute to the robustness of the developing personality if the child can master rather than be mastered by these states. Effective parenting can help with their integration. Temper tantrums, so common in 2- to 3-year-olds in Western culture at least, have long been identified as reflecting young children discovering that they have "wills" that can come up against the "wills" of others (Sully, 1895). Neuroscience now points to the development of new neural pathways during this time and to systems contributing to the differentiation of a clearer sense of the self (Schore, 2004). However, psychoanalytic thinking also stresses that, at this age, children are still working through the aftermath of weaning and separating from parents. Although separation and increased autonomy bring advantages, giving up the privileges of being a baby is painful, bringing the emotions and anxieties of coping with loss and being on one's own. These include an increased awareness of rivalry, of the mother's attention to the father, and the ever-present (to the child) possibility of being displaced by a new baby. These unpleasant feelings provoke the child to feel hostile towards the loved parents, which in turn provokes further emotional conflict.

Klein (1935) describes how children struggle with their ambivalent feelings towards their parents, overcoming their hostility and envy enough to recognize their parent's need for freedom to engage in separate relationships (including the couple relationship, which of necessity implies their exclusion). This itself helps to bring increased separation and separateness. In this state of mind, which Klein (1935) calls the "depressive position", children become especially concerned about the negative effects of their aggressive thoughts and actions on others. This vigilance also strengthens the child's grasp of the difference between what is happening in imagination and in external reality (Segal, 1973). Along with a new-found concern over putting things right, for Klein (1935) as for Winnicott (1963), the wish to please parents out of admiration, love, and concern rather than out of fear enables children to internalize a less harsh and punitive superego and promotes a recognition of realistic adult values. A new sense of parents as a couple working together, with the father backing up the mother's authority providing a so-called paternal function, is part of this process (Emanuel, 2002b).

However, this cannot occur before the parents have recognized that the independent and responsible behaviour they require depends on acknowledging their children as people in their own right, with their own likes, dislikes, and feelings, including disagreeable ones. They, too, are required to become more separate. On the child's side, becoming more separate is linked to the developmental challenges of discovering and consolidating identity and coming to terms with their own limitations. An important aspect of this will be discovering what it means to be a boy or a girl within his or her particular family.

The development of identity and a sense of self are crucial to the separation process and are closely linked to characteristic ways in which young children manage the emotional pain associated with becoming more independent. These include using defences like going "manic", as when young children keep themselves going without sleep, denying their vulnerability, the need for rest, and hence a need for separateness. This is associated with the characteristic omnipotence of thought and action, which young children achieve through identifying with or modelling themselves upon adult figures. By becoming Mummy or Daddy, young children can believe that they are as all-powerful as they imagine adults to be, therefore cutting across a distinction between adult and child worlds and dispensing with the need to recognize feeling small, vulnerable, and still dependent on others for guidance and protection

The challenge for parents is to support their children's wish to be more grown up without colluding in the denial of vulnerability and dependency, including dependence on learning from others. However, imagining one is superlative cannot last forever. Tantrums in small children often involve their frustration at not being allowed what they want, when they are unable to imagine alternatives beyond the immediate situation and are then unable to control the tumult of emotions that follows. They may also reflect the failure of omnipotent identification, either as it collapses or as adults successfully challenge it. As Miller (2004) points out, because adults will appear huge, children will make themselves huge, leading to inflation. The collapse of this identification will be alarming, if not terrifying. The child's anger, expressed in the tantrum, keeps the anxiety at bay, holding the child together in the face of fears of disintegration through acting as a kind of skin—an example of the "second-skin" defence described by Bick (1968).

Something of this process may be indicated in Sendak's story, in Max's "donning his wolf suit", stepping into an identification with a monstrous state of mind, as he is carried away by his mischief-making. The theme of reparation is also central. Max first found a way of reducing anxiety, here by mastering his terror of being taken over by his angry feelings by projecting them into the Wild Things, and then by banishing them. Once anxiety is reduced in this way, Max can miss his mother, opening the door to remorse and eventually reparation.

As Max's mother appears to have done, riding out the storm is integral to parenting young children successfully. In some circumstances, this will be more difficult. According to Bion (1962a, 1962b) effective parenting depends on an empathic process whereby motivated parents can identify with and respond to emotional experience communicated by their infants or young children. Parents' capacity to bear their infants' communications, as they muse over, puzzle about, and try to understand their infants' feelings and what their behaviour means, contributes to the process whereby eventually the child acquires, through identification with a thinking parent rather than an inflated one, something of the capacity to keep a sense of proportion and to reflect on consequences before acting. Perhaps Max's mother was working things through in this way. Infants' feelings of fear or rage, for example, are extremely powerful and can rapidly evoke similar states of mind in the parents, temporarily overwhelming them. In extreme situations, the intensity of the emotion can revive in the parents' minds abusive or traumatic aspects of their own childhoods. Fraiberg, Adelson, and Shapiro (1975) have described these as "ghosts in the nursery". Confusing their children's situations with their own may sometimes lead parents to re-enact abusive experiences. For the children, repeated experiences of this kind will create fear and avoidant behaviour, culminating in disordered patterns of attachment (Main & Solomon, 1990) and/or what Bion (1962a, 1962b) described as the installation of an extremely savage and judgmental superego, as the children receive the unconscious communication from parents that their strong emotions are intolerable. This amplifies the child's sense of guilt. Both Klein (1934) and Winnicott (1956) have noted how challenging and antisocial behaviour can be aimed at reducing the intensity of this internal torment through provoking punishment in the external world, which would at least be time-limited and negotiable.

Children's presenting difficulties can be understood in relation to these kinds of developing processes, affecting the therapist's approach. For example, parents of children presenting with age-typical tantrums may be helped, in relatively few sessions, to recognize a need for consistent limits and firmer boundaries. As the issues generally hinge on managing separation, reflecting on changes in the roles of parents as their children develop may also be part of this work.

More persistent unmanageable behaviour may indicate a wider pattern of developmental difficulty. Under-fives counselling is a form of family intervention that involves parents as well as psychotherapists in understanding and reflecting on the meaning of their children's play, through which they are attempting to work through developmental dilemmas. The work sometimes includes identifying and working with unfinished business from parents' own childhoods, as the play is produced in a context in which both the therapist and the parents may be open to the communication of intense emotion and anxiety. The therapist may observe, through monitoring her own feelings, any increase in the emotional temperature in the room. As the child's behaviour indicates increased anxiety, anxiety in the parent may escalate sharply. This may indicate an overlap between what the child is struggling to master and areas unresolved for one or both parents. For example, a child frightened of the consequences of his aggressive feelings may meet in the mother increasing alarm if, consciously or unconsciously, she is reminded of domestic violence in her own childhood. This alarm, communicated back to the child, will intensify rather than reduce the child's fear of the dangerousness of his feelings.

On the other hand, if this escalating anxiety can be held and processed, and the child is enabled to symbolize the experience in play, the parent will have had an experience in which unthinkable anxiety and emotional pain can be made manageable as something that can be thought about. This provides an experience of emotional communication at a deep level. The parent can perceive and enjoy relating to the child as a child rather than as a monster to be feared. Furthermore, as parents are likely to be highly motivated and receptive at this time, the method can also be an agent of change for them as well as for their children.

This chapter describes work with two children referred for unmanageable behaviour. The first case illustrates how explosive tantrums can be entwined with difficulties with separation and separateness, associated with the collapse of omnipotence, as described above, alarming to the child because his sense of his own self disappeared. This presentation was closely linked to the mother's earlier depression that followed the birth of a younger child. In the second case, familial circumstances appeared to have affected the containment of anxiety in the child's infancy. In the sessions, once anxiety was contained, we were able to observe that symbolizing his aggressive feelings and his terrors rather than acting them out was associated with a reduction in the disturbed and unmanageable behaviour, while developments in his drawing indicated stronger boundaries and a clearer concept of himself.

Timothy

Timothy was referred at age 4 years by his GP for destructive behaviour, aggression, and his refusal to accept the word "no". Timothy had a 2-year-old brother, Stephen, and another brother, Daniel, aged 7 years.

In this brief-work model, I normally offer the first two or three appointments a week or fortnight apart. Thereafter, assuming the parents' anxiety has lessened and they feel more in control, appointments are usually more widely spaced. I invite the parents to choose the time for subsequent appointments. This confirms their sense of progress and helps them pace the separation that will come with the ending of our work.

In this case the whole family attended the first appointment. Timothy's father, Mr P, had taken time off work. He was not able to do so for the five subsequent appointments, but nevertheless he remained involved. At the first appointment I learned that Timothy's mother, Ms P, had become pregnant with Stephen when Timothy was only 9 months old. For a short period she had breastfed Timothy and Stephen simultaneously. There was little support from the extended family. Mr P took time off work for the first three months after Stephen's birth, when Ms P had felt depressed and isolated. Timothy was close to his father. Ms P felt that he missed him when he went back to work.

Timothy still slept with his parents and had not yet slept through the night without waking his mother, suggesting anxieties about separation. Nevertheless, he could also appear fiercely independent. For example, in the morning he would insist on getting dressed himself and getting his own breakfast. This was extremely time-consuming. If his mother tried to move him on, Timothy would protest persistently and violently with a terrifying intensity. She felt that Timothy's tantrums were different from the tantrums that Daniel had had. The parents were concerned with how he would cope with the first year of school in six months time.

The way Timothy insisted on being very grown up suggested omnipotence and that he was strongly identified with his father. Perhaps he was taking his place to support his mother out of concern for her, and/or to deal with his own pain at his father's absence; by becoming his father he would not miss him. His tantrums appeared to be a reaction to challenges to this omnipotent identification. In the session Timothy was reasonably contained as his parents thoughtfully answered my questions and made observations. At the end of the session, they agreed that we had described different aspects of Timothy. On the one hand, Timothy wanted to be very grown up; on the other, he wanted more time as a baby.

While this gave them a framework for understanding Timothy's feelings, in the next session we were able to observe how roles moved around within the family. It became clear that there was very little space for the *boy* Timothy aside from his identification either with his father or with his baby brother. In the first session he had particularly liked a "Billy-in-the-Barrel" toy, consisting of coloured nesting barrels that fit inside each other like Russian dolls, the last one having a figure of a boy fixed inside. Now, he got on his mother's lap with this toy, as if he were the youngest child or the baby. He showed his mother how he remembered the toy, taking the barrels apart to find the boy hidden inside. Notably, he referred to the figure as "underneath" not "inside". In the meantime, Stephen picked up a man doll and called it "Daddy", as if *he* were now marking his father's absence.

I pointed out that Timothy was on his mother's lap today as Stephen had been last time, while the baby was exploring as if he were the "big boy". Ms P smiled and said that she now thought that Timothy's problems were mostly to do with wanting her attention, having missed out when Stephen was born.

Ms P intuitively recognized that Timothy's interest in finding the Billy inside the Billy-in-the-Barrel reflected his need to rediscover his own infantile self, lost in his identification with his baby brother. She recognized that sometimes Timothy needed help with feeling taken over by Stephen. I suggested that he might also need help to discover his age-appropriate self. I drew attention to a box of bricks with a picture of a boy on the outside. I said, "I wonder what could be inside." "Bricks!" Timothy said enthusiastically. I added, "I wonder what they can make." "I can make a plane," he said, and got down from his mother's lap. Timothy's identification with the boy on the box of bricks mobilized his more potent "big-boy" side so that he could get off his mother's lap, using the image of the plane to bridge the separation.

Difficulties with separation stood out clearly in discussing sleeping. Ms P reported that some things were better at home. Mr P was being firmer with Timothy and backing her up. But Timothy was still up and down throughout the night so that, even though he was now in a separate bed, in the end his father had to go in with him. Timothy moved further away from us during this discussion, hiding inside his jacket as if he believed we could not see him. Nevertheless he was listening. He brought over a box of toy animals, picked up a sheep, and said it was "sad". Asked why it was sad, Timothy said, "Because it is sleeping."

To explore the link between "sleeping" and being "sad", I put a doll family and a doll's-house bed on the table. Timothy chose a man-doll for himself and had a boy-doll as the father. The baby-doll was tossed away. I asked what happened when these two went to bed. Timothy stood up as he tried to make the Daddy—that is, the boy-doll—taller by standing it on the man-doll's shoulders, then trying to fit the small doll inside the larger one. Then Timothy himself tried to make himself taller by stretching himself up inside his jacket. It appeared that Timothy believed either that he was the Daddy or that he had to become the Daddy in order to separate and/or to restore some sense of order in the family. He became more anxious and said that "Daddy has to go off to work now," giving the boy-doll a car to take him off to the doll's house.

Ms P was struck by the way that Timothy had assigned father and son roles the wrong way round. She also asked why Timothy referred to the sleeping sheep as "sad" and could not explain this. I suggested that, when their parents are sleeping, for the children this is a separation. This can be painful. It might account for Timothy feeling he has to wake the parents throughout the night. Ms P said that Timothy needed reassurance that his parents loved him, even though he knew this to be true. I said that perhaps Timothy is uncertain about the consequences of his angry feelings—for example, when he has a tantrum. Ms P gave an example of a battle earlier that day over a pizza, which initially Timothy would not eat. Timothy did end up eating it, but she was left feeling guilty and depressed. I congratulated her on getting through to Timothy, queried whether Timothy was making his mother feel guilty on his behalf, and stressed that it was confusing to Timothy to feel he was all-powerful and unstoppable. It was, again, important that his father backed her up.

We discussed how at times Timothy might really actually believe that he *was* the grown-up father. Ms P acknowledged that there had been times when she treated Timothy as more grown up than he was, when they were alone with the baby when he was young. It was important to enable Timothy to recognize and accept his identity as the *boy* Timothy within the family.

In his identification with the father's role, Timothy was relying on what Bick (1968) described as a "second-skin" defence against fears of disintegration and loss of the self. This was illustrated in his hiding inside his jacket to move from place to place, trying to get one doll's body inside the other, and confusing the words "underneath" and "inside". Whereas Daniel's tantrums, like those of the typical 2- or 3-year-old, were probably associated with frustration in relation to external events, Timothy's tantrums were associated with being trapped inside this identification and the fear of complete devastation should this defence be challenged or collapse.

Appreciating the distinction between Timothy "being" his father and receiving father's support, at the next appointment four weeks later, after the Easter holiday, Ms P felt that things were, again, a bit better. Timothy had told her that he loved her, and there had been much less violence. In the session, Timothy appeared more outgoing and interactive. He told me about a visit of one of his father's friends, who had come on a motorbike, had taken off his motor-bike gear, and had "just ordinary clothes underneath!"

The possibility that this interest in what was underneath indicated that he was beginning to leave behind a second-skin defence in favour of a fuller recognition and enjoyment of himself as a little boy was supported three weeks later. In the room Timothy went straight for the Billy-in-the-Barrel toy, taking it apart and announcing, "There he is! He was just hiding!" By this time Timothy was sleeping well. Ms P felt that his behaviour was not as good as last time. However, she recognized that Timothy was more aware of family relationships and of the adult–child hierarchy. She thought that Timothy's tantrums were now more like the ones Daniel had when he was young and much less alarming.

After one more appointment, Timothy started school. With careful thought from the teachers, Timothy settled well. Timothy had maintained his progress at a review appointment two months later and eight months after our first meeting. His mother felt confident enough to end the work.

Kesley

Like Timothy, Kesley felt displaced by a younger sibling and experienced difficulties with establishing a personal boundary. Kesley was possibly a constitutionally vulnerable infant at a time when his parents had to deal with losses of their own. My working hypothesis was that these factors had contributed to a history of difficulties in containing anxiety, leaving Kesley prey to the savage, primitive superego that Bion (1962a, 1962b) described and as mentioned in the introduction. That is, Kesley's unmanageable behaviour was in part driven by immense anxiety stirred up by guilt, of which he had too much rather than too little. A major aspect of this work was recasting the meaning of Kesley's behaviour for the parents and the school.

Kesley's mother, Ms L, is white British. His father, Mr L, is black British from a Jamaican family. His school referred him at age 4 years after he had been sent home the previous week for hitting a teacher with a chair. His younger sister, Jasmine, was 20 months old. Mr L worked as a driver and was away a couple of nights a week. He was unable to attend appointments. Ms L and the children attended five sessions, followed by a further block of five sessions and a follow-up review.

In contrast to the monster portrayed at referral, at the first appointment Kesley presented as a thin-skinned child, extremely sensitive to criticism. I found it was important for both Kesley and Ms L that I put things in a positive light. I learned that Kesley was a much-wanted baby. A first child had been stillborn, and Ms L had had a threatened miscarriage with Kesley. There were no such concerns about the pregnancy with Jasmine, a lively baby who was kept firmly in the buggy for the first appointment. Ms L was plainly worried about things getting out of hand.

Kesley appreciated my making a space for him by finding him a chair, but he needed help to play. He was interested in a pop-up toy with four wooden pegs with faces on them. He made the pegs shoot out sharply, startlingly aggressive. Unusually for small children, he was not at all amused by the Billy-in-the-Barrel nesting beakers. I had the impression of a child terrified of criticism and of what might come out.

Ms L explained that Kesley was confused about why he was not at school and whether he had done something wrong. He found it difficult to cope with school rules. On holiday he really loved it when they could go to her mother's in the country, where he could just run wild. I said it was good to have times when the family could enjoy being together. As Ms L relaxed, Kesley became more at ease. Ms L's concern was that Kesley got very wound up. Reprimanding him made things worse. Kesley became increasingly restless as we talked about him, pulling down a bag of bricks, as if someone were after him, and seizing toys plainly designed for much younger children. "The baby has got one of these," he would say, as if this made it particularly desirable. Alternatively, he would focus on things that were out of bounds, such as the power plugs. The behaviour was not easy to contain. To avoid a battle, I tolerated it as long as he did not risk hurting himself.

Ms L described Kesley as a "good" baby who slept a lot of the time. During that time Mr L's brother had died unexpectedly. Mr L had been very upset. Ms L thought that Kesley had changed when he was about 2 years old, when she would have been pregnant with Jasmine. At school, he had settled into the nursery class initially, but his teacher left to go on maternity leave. He then had another teacher when he changed classes the following term.

I commented on the losses in the family, and on how much change Kesley had had at school. Ms L observed that this was over the time when she had had Jasmine and that this must have been difficult for him. During this rather reflective discussion, Kesley came and sat at the table.

Ms L told me that they were using a sticker system at school to encourage him to settle to his work. I said I thought this was a good idea. Kesley needed to know he could get things right and that people would be pleased with him. At present he heard "No" a great deal. I thought that Kesley was a *sensitive* child. His mother agreed. He liked to come for a cuddle in the morning. He was concerned about his father when he got in late, asked if he was tired, and would rub his sore back. Mr L would say when he was going and when he was coming back. I agreed that it was important that Kesley knew what was going to happen. I said that I thought that Kesley found separations difficult.

They might make him very angry. At this point, feeling understood, Kesley brought me the barrel toy that he had previously rejected and asked me to show him how to open it.

Kesley found it hard to leave at the end of the session. He insisted he wanted to draw. He overturned the table, trashing the toys. Recognizing that he felt constantly criticized, I said how much Kesley really wanted to draw and to show me what he could do. This helped. He gave me back the paper and said he would draw the following week.

Unfortunately, the family cancelled the next appointment because Jasmine was ill. I heard from the school that Kesley had been worryingly difficult. When the family attended the following week, Kesley was pleased to see me. He wanted the baby out of the pushchair, but his mother did not allow this. Kesley pulled at the cupboard doors and went for the light switches, and the crocodile was very aggressive. A baby lion got dropped behind the cupboard.

Nevertheless Kesley had had a good day at school. His mother reported that things had gone well during the first week but went downhill after that. I noted that this was also after the missed appointment. Kesley started to switch the light switch on and off. "Don't do that, Kesley"; his mother threatened a slap. Kesley darted across the room, knocked over a baby chair, and made as if to throw it, and things went from bad to worse.

I thought that Kesley knew he had transgressed the limits in my room, perhaps because of the missing appointment. The problem was that, rather than lacking guilt feelings, he was tormented by them. Kesley was raising the ante by being wild in order to get the slap or the sanction that would release him from this pressure. His mother's escalating anger and anxiety intensified Kesley's, as he identified with her. I said that I thought that, once things tipped over, Kesley did not know how to restore the situation so that he could regain positive attention and approval. Ms L was happy for me to meet with the school, where I explained this line of thinking, and the idea that Kesley needed getting-back-in-touch strategies as well as praise for success.

By the following week, Ms L could report a good week at school and at home. His parents would take Kesley's Action Man toy away from him when he was in trouble, telling him he could have it back when he was a "nice boy". In this way Kesley could receive positive results for putting something right. In the session Kesley was settled enough to spend a little time making marks. He could not draw anything resembling a person, suggesting some difficulty with holding on to and putting a boundary around his self. Interested in what was happening between Ms L and me, at one point he gave his mother the tiger and me the crocodile, telling us, excitedly, to "fight each other, go on!" I thought that Kesley was looking for a position from which he could observe his own thinking and anxiety, as opposed to immediately identifying with the angry monster-parent, as he had done in the previous session. The material also possibly suggested Kesley's anxiety about the sexual relationship between the parental couple and what it might produce.

Two weeks later, at a school meeting, Kesley's teacher reported many improvements. Kesley was responding well to a reward system. When he was interested, he was learning rapidly. By this time, in his sessions, the fact that he was thinking about replacement babies became very evident. Where in the first session Kesley had been reluctant to investigate the inside of anything, he now enjoyed playing "hide-and-seek", hiding a toy rabbit under his jumper, making himself fat, and telling us he was going to have a baby.

For the first time, Ms L let me know that Kesley was still finding it difficult to sleep in his own bed. She was not concerned enough to insist on this yet. I thought it likely that Kesley would have been stirred up by his parents' sexual activity. I also thought that Kesley resisted the night-time separation because he was too frightened of his hostility towards his baby sister to allow his parents to come together in his mind because of the thoughts of a new baby that that would generate. This anxiety was made more intense because his mother could not help him with it; a baby had already been lost in the family, and she had nearly lost Kesley. Interestingly, for the first time the baby was awake throughout this session. At the following one, she was let out of her pushchair. Ms L was clearly more confident that things could be managed between them.

However, all was not resolved immediately. At the next session, Kesley arrived whooping "I'm NOT in the mood!" The end of term loomed, and Kesley was to have a new teacher next term. Kesley said that he did not like her and that he did not like me either. He threw a toy across the room. His mother warned him. Kesley threw something else for good measure and began to trash the room.

Kesley illustrated very clearly how, in his terror of being taken over by his feelings, the teacher or parent or therapist became even more frightening as he projected his feelings into them and then identified with them again, becoming even more monstrous as he could find no way out. I addressed the fact that I would be away over the holiday period and commented how, when Kesley approached a holiday at school and his therapy, he got the idea that he was not wanted. Then he would get into even more trouble by being the "throwing-out monster" himself.

By this point in our work, Ms L was able to register the impact of what I was saying to Kesley, be contained by it, and make a contribution herself that would reduce Kesley's anxiety. She said in a reflective tone that Cathy would be coming back. Kesley had had the new teacher before; it was someone he actually liked. Kesley calmed down and cooperated with his mother's suggestion that he put the lids on the pens and "sit quiet for five minutes". She was getting him to do this at home. Mother was more accepting of Kesley's struggle to manage his intense emotions. When he said sorry, she gave him credit for meaning it at the time; although it would not stop him getting in trouble again, she would let the matter drop. Like Max's mother and Max in Sendak's story, Ms L would give Kesley his supper, and they could start afresh for the rest of the evening.

The sense that Ms L was more in charge was confirmed after the summer holiday. At their first appointment Kesley struck me as more contained. His play nevertheless showed some disorientation following the break. For example, he tried to make a tower of nesting beakers beginning with the smallest on the bottom and the biggest on top and wondered why it fell over. "Why does this tiger not have children?" he asked, picking up a toy tiger. I wondered if it was a man tiger or a lady tiger. Kesley said it was a boy tiger and made the female (according to him) crocodile savage the tiger. I commented to Kesley how I thought he was very angry with me for my long absence over the holiday period.

After this, Kesley came and sat beside me and worked with me to sort out a set of Russian dolls, quickly developing a strategy for getting the dolls to fit inside each other. I commented on his concentration. His mother said that she thought that Kesley was more grown up. He was now interested in books. He had chosen one himself from the school library. It was about a new baby in the family.

Kesley became uncontained at this point, getting on the chair by the desk, pulling at my desk lamp. "Get down, Kesley, don't start!" Ms L interjected. "Sorry, I'm sorry," Kesley squeaked. I felt that, as before, Kesley seemed compelled to do something forbidden in order to obtain the reprimand from an external agency that would release him from a terrible internal accuser. I said that Kesley was very angry with me and thought I was very bad. Kesley tripped over me on purpose and howled, rubbing himself as if blood were going to pour out of him. He began a picture, which consisted of patches of colour with no clear boundary around them. We had a glimpse, and then the picture was ripped in half.

Despite this distressing and distressed behaviour, Kesley also tried to create a little calm. At one point while his mother was talking to me, I saw him take down a forbidden object, check himself, then put it back. He also began to tidy the toys towards the end of the session. Ms L explained that, although Kesley was still frightened of the dark, she was beginning to transfer him into his own bed when he was asleep. He was accepting this. Kesley came and sat beside me to do the pop-up toy, pointing out that the pegs had faces on one side and not on the other. Although anxious about the mouths on these faces, he was clearly distinguishing front and back. His mother said that she was less worried about him. A factor contributing to this may have been our bearing the "wild" behaviour in the room together, attempting to process the anxiety and be receptive to the underlying meaning. Ms L was rewarded by seeing Kesley becoming calmer and more receptive.

Kesley's question "Why does this tiger not have babies?" may have been an expression of his age-appropriate curiosity about who can become mummies and who cannot, and why this option is not available to boys. But I think it may also have been a reference to the lost baby in his mother's mind who, in phantasy, he may have replaced. At the following session, Kesley drew a simple, tadpole figure, with a boundary around it, which he said was himself. Three weeks later he drew a worm with legs and a smiley face. A month after this he drew a face with eyes, ears, mouth, and a long body. Finally, shortly after his fifth birthday, with his sister very actively present, he drew a picture representing two children and a parent. This suggested an identification with a mother who was able to contain the feelings of both her children. Kesley was settled well in school and at home and was now sleeping in his own bed.

## *Discussion*

Freud's (1900a) first published exploration of the Oedipus complex came in a discussion of the timeless effects of great tragedies such as *Oedipus Rex*. He argues that these plays do not move us by creating their effects *de novo* but, rather, because they resonate with experiences, wishes, and phantasies that we have already had, even if these have been suppressed or we have not become aware of them.

Similarly, Sendak's children's classic, referred to at the beginning of this chapter, appeals to children and their parents through capturing common if not universal aspects of young children's emotional and social development at an age when omnipotence and magical thinking are at their height. The story resonates with children's own experiences of excitement as they discover new powers to challenge limits set by adults and sometimes to overturn them, and also the terror that the monster desires and phantasies will overwhelm them totally and that the damage will be irrevocable. The story appeals perhaps equally strongly to parents through mobilizing their own infantile phantasies and their fear that their view of their children as monsters will remain forever.

In this chapter I have described how under-fives counselling can contain parents' anxieties about their children's aggression by providing a context in which "wild thoughts" can be domesticated, given a home, and made sense of, as described by Bion (1997). The two cases illustrate how temper outbursts and behaviour problems can be driven by quite different kinds of anxieties or emotional experiences, depending on developmental level and dominant defences. In the first case, temper outbursts were a reaction to the collapse of omnipotence or a second-skin defence and the resulting loss of a sense of identity. The work helped the child to manage separateness from his mother and to move more freely between infant and growing-boy aspects of himself, facilitating integration. The second case illustrates wild behaviour as a consequence of identifying with a violent and intensely intrusive persecutor or savage superego. Play and symbol formation were particularly important to his beginning to think about his emotional experience as opposed to reacting to it, and in giving him a clearer sense of himself.

In both cases, the work enabled the parents to come in touch with their capacities to set and hold to reasonable limits, to enjoy their children, and to respond with humour, pacing their demands and giving their children space to get back in touch. The immediate benefits for family life are clear. We may also speculate that long-term effects may follow from enhancing symbol formation in the children through a process that has actively involved their parents, who have been introduced to new possibilities for communication at a deep level.

# The parent couple and oedipal issues

In this section, the focus is on the quality of the relationship between the parental couple and how this may impact on their young children's development, including the capacity to cope with oedipal feelings towards their parents. As can be seen throughout the book, oedipal feelings of exclusion from the parental couple and difficulties coping with the reality of a parent relationship from which they are of necessity excluded underlie many problems in young children, including separation anxiety and sleeping and behaviour difficulties.

Work with parents is a crucial part of an under-fives service. It has become increasingly clear that there is a delicate interface between their functioning as parents and their couple relationship that clinicians often need to address if progress within the family is to be made. This has implications for the training of early years clinicians, who may require some additional training in couple psychotherapy. It also has implications for those we select to see within the family. For example, Lieberman (2004) when describing her treatment parameters in child–parent psychotherapy suggests that "both parents may participate when clinically indicated, *such as when both parents are experiencing difficulties in their relationship with the child*" (p. 110, my italics). This is not a view shared by the authors in this book, as it has become increasingly evident to us that if *one* parent claims to be having difficulty with a child, there is a lot to understand about the functioning of the *parental couple*. This leads us to try increasingly to work with both parents in the room when possible. Addressing the concept of the "parental couple" in single-parent families is an important feature of this section.

Paul Barrows, in chapter 10, takes the concept of Fraiberg's "ghosts in the nursery" further by describing the value of exploring the "ghosts" in the pasts of both mother and father, the transgenerational transmission of patterns of relating, and indicating how these have a profound influence on the quality of the parent/couple relationship, which, he claims, "should be at the heart of our work". He raises an important and controversial point regarding the question of whether, developmentally, an infant begins life by "relating to many different people rather than just to one, the mother." He suggests that from birth "the infant is already having to deal with numerous relationships and . . . it is above all the nature of the *parental couple* the infant encounters that will be paramount for the infant's future mental health."

His clinical examples, in which he explores the "ghosts" of both parents' pasts through parent and family interventions, highlight the complexity of the work and need for flexibility of approach.

Barrows makes an interesting link between psychoanalytic and attachment theory in his description of Freud's and Klein's concepts of the development of the superego, suggesting that the "superego" of the grandparents, which has been unmodified by the parents, is the "body responsible for the transgenerational transmission of 'judgements of value'". He links the idea of this "unassimilated 'foreign body'"—which has been handed on to parents and is once again being handed on to their children in an "unprocessed form"—to the concept of "disorganized attachment" and its connection to unprocessed trauma in the parents' background. This is pertinent in many cases seen in the Under Fives Service, where domestic violence is a major feature in the parental relationship and is often associated with the abuse or emotional neglect of children. Children faced with a frightening or frightened parent figure (as described by Main & Hesse, 1990) become "disorganized" in their responses, faced with conflicting impulses to flee a frightening figure or turn to one and the same figure for comfort.

Louise Emanuel, in chapter 11, develops the theme of Barrows's chapter, focusing particularly on clinical interventions in families with single parents where young children have been referred with behaviour problems. Clinical illustrations describe how the children often feel uncontained in situations where the mother may be excessively preoccupied by the absence or unreliability of the father, thereby being unavailable to receive the communications of her children. One of the aims of the interventions is to help single parents to internalize both a "paternal" and a "maternal" function, in order to provide for their children the functions of a containing internal combined parental couple.

The particular difficulties in negotiating the oedipal situation faced by children of single parents or unstable partnerships are explored. Many referring problems in the under-fives age group may stem from underlying oedipal wishes and fears and the persecutory anxieties that accompany them. The clinical examples in Emanuel's and Gurion's chapters highlight the importance for the clinician of attending to the nonverbal and verbal communications of young children in the presence of their parents, while simultaneously monitoring countertransference responses to the material, in order to provide an effective intervention.

Chapter 12, by Michi Gurion, takes as its premise the initial dyadic union between infant and caregiver and the very gradual and arduous task of moving away from the exclusive relationship with mother, towards interacting with others. This contrasts with Barrows's view discussed earlier, indicating the infant's readiness to engage with both parents (and the parent couple) from birth. Gurion describes in detail a three-session intervention with a family where a small child's feelings of exclusion and oedipal rivalry were causing disruption within a family, particularly at night. The account is structured in such a way as to highlight the therapist's countertransference responses to the material and the use she makes of them, together with her close observation of the family interactions, in order to process the experience in the consulting room.

The question raised by Barrows and implicit in all three chapters is whether different approaches to work with families with young children and infants can be equally effective or whether one particular "port of entry" (Stern, 1995)—for example, work with parent couples—can be claimed to be more effective than others, for certain kinds of presenting difficulties. The jury is still out on these questions, and hopefully the clinical and theoretical ideas presented in this section will provide further material for consideration.

CHAPTER 10

# Locating the ghost in the nursery: the importance of the parental couple

*Paul Barrows*

Most of the authors represented in this book, and indeed many of the clinicians working in the Tavistock Clinic's Under Fives Service, have been very influenced by developments within the Kleinian tradition of "object relations" theory. Within that paradigm, more recent thinking has tended to emphasize that it is the nature of the parental couple that the infant and young child internalizes that is central to successful psychological development. It is this couple, and its creativity or otherwise, that forms the core of the personality and, not surprisingly, is particularly influential in determining the kind of parent that the child will become in his turn.

It follows from this that in working with parents, infants, and young children, particular attention needs to be paid to the couple and to their relationship. In much of the literature on parent–infant work, however, this aspect has been rather lacking. As I have argued elsewhere (Barrows, 1999b), those working clinically with the under fives have all too often privileged the role of the mother's "ghosts" (Fraiberg, Adelson, & Shapiro, 1975) at the expense of those the father brings to the nursery (although Fraiberg herself was very attentive to the father's importance). This has been to the detriment of our potential therapeutic impact. This neglect has applied to researchers and developmental psychologists as well as to clinicians: most research papers still tend to be about *mother–infant* interactions.

However, while it is essential in my view to ensure that fathers are not left out, it would, of course, be equally mistaken to focus our attention too exclusively on the father–infant or father–child dyad. Rather, my central proposition is that fathers (and mothers) are important primarily *as part of a parental couple,* and it is that couple and their relationship that should be at the heart of our work.

Several recent researchers have been seeking to redress the balance in this direction and to give due weight to the importance of the father's contribution to the family system. Fivaz-Depeursinge and Corboz-Warnery's book *The Primary Triangle* (1999) is a particularly notable example, as is the related work of von Klitzing (von Klitzing, Simoni, Amsler, & Burgin, 1999; von Klitzing, Simoni, & Burgin, 1999) and the Cowans (Cowan & Cowan, 2001, 2002). McHale has a slightly different emphasis in his important work on co-parenting (McHale & Cowan, 1996; McHale & Fivaz-Depeursinge, 1999). Clinicians, too, are increasingly seeking to involve fathers in the work of parent–infant therapy.

This shift of emphasis seems essential because the fact is that infants simply do not grow up—unless in the most pathological of situations—in dyads. From the beginning they are part of a much broader social matrix. As Corboz-Warnery, Fivaz-Depeursinge, Bettens, and Favez (1993) note: "Although the contributions of each partner in the triad are important, describing them is not sufficient to convey the full context of the infant's development. It is also necessary to '*move beyond these additive approaches to capture the ways in which the family operates as a small group*' (Parke, 1990, p. 182)" (p. 299).

In some ways it is surprisingly difficult to assess whether this idea (i.e. that infants begin life by relating to many different people, rather than just to one, the mother, followed by a gradual extension of their circle) is particularly controversial. To my mind, it seems self-evident, and indeed, as much as twenty years ago, the French analyst Colette Chiland (1982) was able to write:

> The concept of a purely dyadic relationship between infant and mother is now as unacceptable as the concept of a stage of normal autism. [p. 377]

And yet in the same book that brought this quote to my attention (*The Importance of Fathers*: Trowell & Etchegoyen, 2002) another contributor wrote:

> Developmentally, interactions with an external mother precede those with any other object, thus the mother is the first object to emerge in the inner world. The father is the second. [Fakhry Davids, 2002, p. 83]

It is this point with which I would take issue. I would suggest that, in fact, from birth the infant is already having to deal with numerous relationships. Furthermore, within this complex network, it is above all the nature of the *parental couple* the infant encounters that will be paramount for the infant's future mental health. This holds true even for those infants who are raised in single-parent families. I would agree with Target and Fonagy that:

> The physical availability of the father may be neither sufficient nor necessary for triangulation to evolve. What does seem critical is *a situation within which the child can envisage a relationship between two other, emotionally significant figures.* [Target & Fonagy, 2002, p. 57, emphasis added]

In other words, even if the father is not actually present, the infant still has to encounter what is, in effect, an oedipal situation as soon as the mother entertains thoughts of an emotionally significant other. More specifically, the infant will be particularly affected by the nature of the parental couple that his single parent has in mind. This is discussed in more detail in Emanuel's chapter in this section.

As mentioned above, the primacy of the parental couple as a factor in emotional development has been adumbrated particularly by contemporary British object relations theorists. They hold that a central feature of psychic development, and a measure of mental health, is the way in which the child manages to negotiate his relationship to the parental couple. It is the child's ability to allow the parents to come together in a creative and procreative relationship, through tolerating the pains of the oedipal situation, that lays the foundation for his own future identity as a parent. It is through identification with such a parental couple that he will become a good-enough parent in turn, as well as developing the capacity to be creative in other spheres. As Britton has put it:

> In normal development the perception by the child of the parents' coming together independently of him unites his psychic world. [Britton, 2002, p. 116]

Thus the oedipal situation does not necessarily have only a tragic outcome. In fact, the presence of a united couple is deeply reassuring for the infant and lays the foundation for his future emotional well-being. Conversely, a couple living in disharmony can often give a child a false sense of power, confirming his omnipotent phantasy of being able to split the couple by triumphing over one parent and taking possession of the other.

A brief vignette from work with a child patient illustrates the kind of situation that can arise when this process goes awry.

> *Case vignette*
>
> Sarah was referred with encopresis and was initially seen with her parents in the Clinic's Under Fives Service, which offers brief work, but she was subsequently offered long-term individual child psychotherapy.
>
> At the stage in the therapy from which this material is drawn, 4-year-old Sarah could not seem to bear the reality of her position in relation to the oedipal couple. When, in her session, she was playing with two baby dolls, she said she wondered how they were made. I took up her curiosity about how real babies were made. She asserted that Mummies have babies, and I agreed, pointing out that this was something Mummies can do and children can't, or, rather, I corrected, something that Mummies *and Daddies* can do. She insisted that Daddies did not have babies, nor took any part in making them, then added that babies have babies. She then claimed to have a 5-year-old brother (her actual brother is much younger) and that she could look after him much better than I could.

We can see here how not only is the role of the father completely done away with but, following on from a fleeting recognition of the mother's role, this too seems to be promptly diluted by the assertion that babies have babies too. It was Sarah's inability to tolerate the recognition of the true nature of the parental couple that led to her presenting difficulties. In her mind, she sought to assume control over her parents and their parental function. This control was also then extended to her faeces, which she sought to control by retaining them—her encopresis manifesting when this control necessarily broke down.

However, my work with a number of encopretic children at that time suggested that it was not only the child's intolerance of the nature of the tie between the parents that was at the root of the difficulties, but also that the real external parents were not presenting the child with enough of an experience of a well-functioning parental couple to enable their child to learn to tolerate and accommodate to that reality (for a fuller discussion, see Barrows, 1996). This lack of containment may result in a child internalizing a "leaky" container and can manifest in urinary or faecal incontinence.

Further support for the idea that the couple's relationship is of central importance also comes from a number of research findings in several different areas. Some of these I have referred to in my earlier paper (Barrows, 1999b), but I would also draw attention to two further recent findings.

The first is that of an initial report of an ESRC (Economic and Social Research Council) research project at Bristol University that set out to investigate "The Transition to Fatherhood in Young Men". Looking at the factors that affect whether these young fathers continue to have ongoing involvement with their children, they noted that it was not family or individual factors that were predictive of the men's involvement at follow-up, but

> Rather, the most important factor at this stage . . . appeared to be the quality of the relationship between the couple themselves. [Quinton, Pollock, & Golding, 2002, p. 16]

The other is the work of Cowan and Cowan (2001), who have reported an equally telling conclusion from longitudinal studies they have been conducting in Berkeley on the factors affecting couples' transition to parenthood and subsequently the toddlers' adjustment to starting in kindergarten. It is clear from their work that it is the quality of the *couple's* functioning that is the most critical factor, and their preventive intervention programme consequently involves a group-based programme for couples. They also note how important the father's role can be and how the direction of this influence is critically affected by the nature and "fit" of the attachment style of each partner. The most striking influence is in those situations where "the man ha[s] a secure working model of attachment based on his description of relationships with his parents", when "his interaction with his partner tended to be productive regardless of her attachment pattern . . ." (p. 72). Interestingly, this did not hold good the other way round: "men with insecure models of attachment whose partners had secure working models . . . represented the most negative and volatile combination" (p. 72). They conclude: "We cannot emphasize enough how important the fathers are to the success of family relationships and to their children's development."

But perhaps even more telling was another finding. Within the group programme, the leaders of some of the groups were instructed to focus on the couple's relationship *as a couple*, whereas in the other groups, the emphasis was more on *parenting* as such. This involved only a slight shift in emphasis on the part of the therapists—but the outcome where the emphasis was on the couple was better: the couple's relationship improved *and* so too did their parenting (Cowan & Cowan, 2002).

The centrality of the role of the parental couple has important implications for us as clinicians. I shall give an example of some recent work to illustrate my point and then try to spell out what this means in terms of where we should be looking for the "ghosts in the nursery", linking this with some thoughts about the nature of the changes that may take place in the course of our work with fathers, mothers, and families.

## Clinical example

John, aged 2½ years, was referred for aggressive behaviour, including attacking his mother and younger sister, swearing, and tantrums. The referring health visitor described a difficult family background: the mother, Mrs A, had a history of depression dating back prior to any pregnancies; she had been depressed following John's birth and then acutely depressed when pregnant with the sister, but refused the psychiatric admission that was offered. The father was also apparently depressed. The health visitor had offered a lot of help and positive encouragement, but felt she was not making progress.

When I first met them as a family (although they did not bring the sister), John behaved in an exemplary fashion, being quiet, polite, and constructive in his play. His mother, however, gave a catalogue of his awful behaviour completely at odds with his presentation in the room. She attributed this to the fact that his sister wasn't there. Father, meanwhile, sought to promote a more positive view: he reminded the mother of what a good report John had received from his day-care worker—he was her "star child". Mother agreed, but she quickly went on to say that she had then learnt that this worker was equally positive about all the children.

I arranged to see the couple for some sessions on their own, and a very sad picture emerged. On the mother's side there was a history of domestic violence, and she could recall her father attacking her mother, although apparently the children were never victims themselves. Her mother is still with her father and is still at times attacked by him, although she tends to deny this. Her brother is also violent and irresponsible and has stolen from her (for which he was attacked by her father). These grandparents live nearby and look after the children, though Mr A is not happy about the fact that the grandparents use foul language in front of the children. Mrs A acknowledges that she herself has a very short fuse and will become fiercely angry, though not actually violent, and she has described how overwhelming her bouts of depression have been. She was scathing about some of the "help" she had received for this, particularly her most recent episode of attendance at an outpatient psychiatric facility, where she had met someone different on each occasion. Indeed, a condition of attending our own service had been that she should see the same person each time. Clearly there were enough ghosts from the mother's side for it not to be surprising that she found it difficult to deal with what might be the quite ordinary boisterousness and bossiness of a 2-year-old. And indeed, the referral did make it appear that this was predominantly a difficulty between mother and son, with the father trying, though not very effectively, to improve the situation.

Mr A was very intimidated by his wife's angry outbursts and felt that in the past she had made his life unbearable. Things were somewhat better now between them, perhaps at the cost of John now being the focus for mother's outbursts, and this made father wonder how this must feel for John, given how he had experienced her attacks. Over a few sessions father's own story unfolded. Paternal grandfather had wanted to be in the emergency services, but his wife had been concerned about the dangers involved and so he had become a lorry driver instead. Tragically, on one of his first jobs, some girders being unloaded had slipped and crushed his head, leaving him severely injured and prone to epileptic seizures. Despite these difficulties Mr A had very fond memories of his father, who had died from a seizure when Mr A was aged 12. Thereafter he had felt put upon by his mother, who had made him feel guilty whenever he went out with his friends, but he had gone along with her demands, which also involved being very helpful around the house. However she had subsequently remarried and the step-father had thrown him out of the house. He therefore now had no contact with his mother.

In addition to this, relations with his brother were also very strained: this brother had lived with them for some time when he was unemployed but, since leaving, had had little to do with them. He was seen as favouring a cousin and taking little interest in Mr A's own children.

It was a source of great sadness to Mr A that he was therefore unable to provide his own children with any kind of extended family, and he felt strongly that he had let them down. It became clear that he had a warm image in mind of what family life should be like, and that he felt he was failing to provide this. He gave a poignant account of how, before a family outing to a nearby attraction, his wife had become so exasperated with John that she had sent Mr A and the two children off without her, but then half an hour later had phoned on her mobile phone to see where they were, by which time it had been too late to go back for her.

Mr A conveyed clearly his depression, sense of isolation, and feeling that he had many unresolved issues. He was having acupuncture to try to help with this but, like his wife, felt let down by GPs and other professionals, who were seen as having done nothing to help. When his wife had a course of weekly counselling for a year, he made a point of being present for every session, supposedly to make sure that his wife told the counsellor everything that she should. It was apparent, though, that he felt *his* needs were just as great as hers. It was also very striking that while Mr A appeared quite pale and not very tough, he was in fact a devoted teacher of martial arts.

Discussion

I would like to make a few points based on the material that had emerged up to this time. I think it would have been quite easy, at the beginning, to approach this case as largely centred around a conflictual relationship between mother and son. In this context, a major factor would be the background of domestic violence in mother's family of origin. Is this male child perhaps seen by mother through the lens of an internal representation of a violent father (or, indeed, brother) such that an ordinary expression of anger by John is felt by mother to be catastrophic and responded to accordingly? An additional contributory factor would be the mother's periods of depression, which would have meant that she was not available at an emotional level to contain her son's more aggressive feelings and help him to manage them.

Of course, all of this remains true, but I believe it is only half of the story. I would suggest that the final outcome, in terms of John's actual experience, is in fact determined by the *interaction* that takes place between mother and father. For example, Mr A appears unable to protect John from his wife's angry outbursts—just as he seems unable to protect himself from them. The reasons behind this would seem to lie in the ghosts within his own nursery. There is some evidence that Mr A struggles to deal with his own aggression in a way that leaves him prone to becoming a victim. For example, *he* was put upon by his mother as a child in a way that was not true for his siblings; I also learnt subsequently that he seemed to have been involved in a rather masochistic relationship with one of his martial arts teachers. This situation is then again recreated in his relationship with his wife, a relationship in which he feels pushed around and intimidated. His own aggression, which is not apparent in the sessions except in so far as it is referred to in his martial arts activities, can then be readily located in his wife, who—for her own reasons—is a very suitable target for such a projection.

In the interaction that is thereby generated, both parties then find themselves taking up more and more polarized positions. This became much clearer in a session that took place a little later.

I had commented on Mr A's tendency to always play the role of peacemaker, trying to make sure everyone is okay (he had typically begun the session with several enquiries about how I was getting on and if I was all right). We talked about how he also does this at home in an attempt to smooth things over between John and his wife, partly out of anxiety about the aggressive feelings being expressed but also because of his concern for his son and his wish to provide a family life akin to his internal image of what family life should be like. When he takes on this peacemaker role, though, Mrs A seems to experience her husband as failing to deal with John's angry feelings, and, of course, to some extent she is right. This then raises mother's anxiety about John's feelings getting out of control and prompts her to become more harsh and punitive, which in turn pushes father to work even harder at trying to calm things down in an attempt to avoid both John and his wife's feelings getting out of control—and so on.

To some extent, what this couple share, albeit for quite different reasons, is a lack: the lack of an internal representation of a father who can be firm and yet tolerant of, and able to acknowledge, aggressive feelings. *Mrs* A's father was himself unable to manage such feelings and acted them out; *Mr* A's father had been in a fragile and damaged state, and there was reason to suppose he had had his own difficulties in this area and had been somewhat dominated by his wife.

While the role played by this lack highlights the importance of one aspect of the father's function, what I would particularly wish to emphasize is that it is the *interaction* between the two parents that is most critical. It is the product of that interaction that determines the emotional atmosphere into which the infant is born.

However, it must also be acknowledged that when parents present with difficulties involving their infant or young child, they rarely do so in the expectation of needing to address issues in their marital relationship. Frequently, as in this case, it can prove too painful or threatening to begin to look at those issues, and in fact Mr and Mrs A broke off their sessions with me. The health visitor later reported continuing improvement with John's behaviour but also that many of the underlying tensions remained.

## Implications for locating the ghost

Fraiberg's classic paper (Fraiberg, Adelson, & Shapiro, 1975), to which I have referred in my title, defines the task of the infant mental health clinician. It is to elucidate the nature of the "ghost" that is haunting the infant's nursery, to trace its origin in the parent's own childhood experiences, and to enable the parents to recover the affects belonging to that experience to allow them to become the protectors of their children. According to this argument, it is the transference on to the infant of a figure from the parental past that distorts their representation of their child and hence their capacity to function as parents.

The therapeutic task is, therefore, to effect, in Hopkins's (1992) words, a "dynamic disconnection between past representations and present realities", freeing the parent to see the infant as an individual in its own right. But what exactly is the nature of this "past representation" or "ghost"? And where is it located?

Let me begin with a comment from Freud on the transgenerational transmission of patterns of relating. He wrote that,

> As a rule parents . . . follow the precepts of their own super-egos in educating children. . . . Thus *a child's superego is in fact constructed on the model not of its parents but of its parents' super-ego*; the contents which fill it are the same and it becomes the vehicle of tradition and of all the time-resisting judgements of value which have propagated themselves in this manner from generation to generation. [Freud, 1933a, pp. 98–99, emphasis added]

It seems to me that in thus separating out "the parents" and the "parents' superego" Freud makes it clear that the superego is to be seen as something of a separate construct, not exactly a part of the parents' self. It is an internal representation of the parents' parents, or, in object relations terminology, it is a particular kind of "internal object". Crucially, though, it is one that remains untouched by new experiences and so remains unmodified. It is responsible for the kind of experience we may all recognize when, despite all our conscious intentions not to do so, we find ourselves, in the heat of the moment, identifying with it and replaying scenarios from our own childhood. In seeking to account for its unchanging nature and hence its persisting influence across the generations, I think that an idea introduced by Paula Heimann, a colleague of Melanie Klein, is helpful. In one of her papers (Heimann, 1942) she coined the term "assimilation" to describe a process whereby internal representations might become absorbed into the ego. She wrote of:

> a process which I like to call the "assimilation" of the internal objects, by which the subject acquires and absorbs those qualities of his internal parents which are suitable and adequate to him. As Goethe says:
> > What you inherited from your fathers,
> > You must acquire yourself in order to possess it.
> [Heimann, 1942, p. 42]

Thus objects that *have* been assimilated become a part of the self, and, through a process of what could be called "introjective identification", the qualities of the object become integrated. When this occurs it means that those qualities can be owned and acknowledged, and this in turn allows them to be tested against external reality. This kind of "reality testing" allows the personality to continue to develop and to be shaped by new experiences. When, on the other hand, this process of assimilation does not take place, then the objects that have been internalized remain unassimilated and unintegrated and do not change in the light of experience.

Thus, while some internal objects *are* assimilated and become a part of the ego, others are not and they remain as "foreign bodies". The superego, as described in Freud's formulation, would seem to be just such an unassimilated "foreign body" that remains unmodified and hence is the body responsible for the transgenerational transmission of "judgements of value".

In parent–infant work, I think we are often presented with a situation in which it seems particularly clear that an "unassimilated object" is making its presence felt across the generations. This "foreign body" is akin to Fraiberg's "ghost in the nursery". It represents some aspect of the parent and his or her history that has not been integrated. Precisely because it has not been integrated, there is an inherent tendency for it to find expression and embodiment somewhere, as an alternative to the attendant conflicts having to be dealt with intra-psychically. Often it is projected into or onto the infant.

There may be a variety of reasons to account for its non-integration. It may be, as Heimann suggested, that this is because of the individual's hostile projections into that object, projections that are then denied. This would lead to the kind of situation that Cramer (1995) refers to, whereby the core of the difficulty lies not so much in a conflict specifically related to parenthood but in the projection by the parent of a part of the self into the child. In these situations only longer-term individual therapy has the possibility of addressing the problem and effecting the kind of change that would lead to a withdrawing of those projections. I have a lot of sympathy with this point of view, although even here I think we still have to take into account what the role of a partner might be in either mitigating or colluding with that process.

On the other hand, it may equally be that there is something inherently indigestible or traumatic about the nature of the object that prevents this process of integration from taking place. As is implied in Freud's description, it is likely that this is something that the *parents* have themselves been unable to digest and may have been handed on to them by their parents and, in any event, is being handed on to their children in this unprocessed form. Main and Hesse's (1990) work on "disorganized attachment" is particularly relevant here. In the paper in which they discuss the link they found between disorganized attachment in the infant and frightened and/or frightening behaviour in the parents, they note that the latter was a product of unprocessed trauma in the parent's background, usually involving *"unresolved loss of attachment figures"*.

Kate Barrows (2000) has made a very similar point. The following account comes from a chapter in which she discusses Seamus Dean's novel *Reading in the Dark*, in which the mother is haunted by a ghost from her past that appears on the stairs of the house. She writes:

> I suggest that when the parent has not been able to come to terms adequately with his or her bereavements, the child may experience the parent as *pre*-occupied by a dead internal object. This may be represented by a shadow or ghost, a concrete phantasy with which

the child comes to identify and which impedes his development as an individual in his own right, with a life and personality of his own. The presence of the ghost means that there is no room for the lively ambivalence which is essential to separation and emotional growth. The child then identifies not with the object *per se* but with the object's un-mourned internal object; thus an incapacity to mourn can lead to generations shadowed by loss. Freud (1917e [1915]) described how inadequate mourning could lead to "a pathological identification with the abandoned object" (p. 70). Thus the shadow of the object fell upon the ego . . ." In the scenarios which I shall describe, it could be said that it is the shadow of the object's *internal* object which falls upon the ego. [p. 70]

More precisely, it is clear that this refers to the object's *unassimilated* internal object.

Putting this together, I think we can formulate the situation that we are presented with when consulted by parents as follows. The presenting "symptom" or problem that is apparently located in the infant alerts us to the fact that there may well be an unassimilated internal object exerting a powerful dynamic force on the current situation, an object that may be located in either of the parents or, indeed, in both. This object has, for whatever reason, been evoked by some specific circumstance or characteristic related to this particular infant in this particular family. Without intervention this "foreign body"—an element of the parents' superego—is what the child will identify with and then internalize as his superego, which again will remain unassimilated, "propagated . . . in this manner from generation to generation" (Freud, 1933a).

If this formulation is correct, I believe it has important implications for the way in which we intervene, since putting an end to this transgenerational transmission will require an approach that will enable the object in question to be assimilated by the parents, preferably before it has become established in the infant's psyche.

There are three important consequences that follow on from this thesis. The first is that long-term, sustained change is most likely to be achieved if and when we can engage with the nature of this "foreign body" or "ghost". That is to say, we need to attempt to make it conscious and explicit and to enable the parents to come to terms with it—to assimilate it. This is what Fraiberg and her colleagues managed to achieve so movingly in the clinical accounts she gives in her classic paper. This process of "assimilation" is partly achieved by enabling the parents to develop a coherent narrative of their own early experiences or, in Fonagy's terms, to develop their capacity for "reflective self-function" (Fonagy et al., 1993). I appreciate that this view may be somewhat at odds with those who argue that many different approaches can be equally effective, and I think that this is an area we need to continue to debate.

The second consequence has to do with the locus of our intervention. When parents present with a problematic infant, I would suggest that the "foreign body" has been projected on to that infant. The new-born infant is a prime target for this, with all the consequences that have been described for the infant's own psychic development. It is also the case that this projection will probably have strongly influenced the generation of the symptoms that have led to the request for a consultation.

When this situation presents clinically, it is, of course, quite possible that the "foreign body" will be projected on to the therapist, and a process of containment may well ensue as the therapist receives and thinks about this unconscious communication. In the short term this may be sufficient to relieve the infant of the projection and may lead to a rapid improvement in the presenting problem. However, it is unlikely to produce any long-term change in the nature of the foreign body itself. If, in addition, the therapist is able to make links with the parents' own childhood experiences, then it is to be expected that improvements will be longer lasting. The "foreign body" will be more permanently detached from the infant in question. Again, though, it seems unlikely that this will alter the internal representations that were being evoked *per se*.

When the child is thus relieved of the burden of the projection of parental ghosts, we may well consider that, as infant mental health clinicians, we have done as much as we can realistically expect to do. However, the problem does not, of course, simply vanish. The "foreign body" remains present in the psyche, and if it is no longer manifest in the relationship with the infant it is likely to re-emerge elsewhere (or perhaps at a later date in response to some new crisis).

It is my impression that in practice it is most likely to be in the intimacy of the marital relationship that the foreign body will re-emerge. Indeed, I would generally assume that it will to some extent have made its presence felt there anyway, but that this may take on a renewed emphasis either when the child ceases to provide a focus, or when some theme has been particularly aroused by the child's presence. I think we must therefore regularly expect that parent–infant work will reveal (or may indeed seem to create) difficulties in that relationship.

There is a particular point that I wish to stress here—namely, that when it *is* possible to take this work further, what matters from the child's point of view is not so much *whose* ghost it is, father's or mother's, but the nature of the interaction that then ensues between the parents. In benign cases one parent may be able to offset or counteract the influence of the other parent's "ghost"; in other situations, however, they may play into each other's difficulties in such a way that the parents take up more and more polarized positions, preventing them from working and thinking together about how to resolve a particular issue.

The third consequence has to do with the nature of our role as therapists. There are at least two aspects to this. First—and perhaps most obviously in those situations where the father seems to have difficulty exercising a paternal function—we have to ensure that we do not become too active, thereby taking over his role, but work with the couple to allow him to assume (or resume) an appropriate place in the family. This may, of course, be a particular issue for a male therapist, but I think it can equally apply to a female therapist where it is the paternal *function* of the therapist that matters rather than his or her biological sex. The therapist needs to embody within his or her approach some kind of balance between maternal and paternal functions.

Second, it allows us to conceptualize our role as therapists in a way that I find particularly helpful. This could be described as the therapist providing what Britton (1989) has called a "third position". He writes about the "successful" outcome of negotiating the oedipal situation as follows:

> A third position then comes into existence from which object relationships can be observed. Given this we can also envisage *being* observed. This provides us with a capacity for seeing ourselves in interaction with others and for entertaining another point of view while retaining our own, for reflecting on ourselves whilst being ourselves. [Britton, 1989, p. 87]

For us as therapists this means finding a position from which we are able to observe what is taking place between the parents, without intruding upon it, while also being emotionally engaged with what is taking place. In so far as we can achieve this, and the parents can identify with this "observing" function, they may in turn become better able to reflect upon their own relationship and ultimately gain a capacity for reflective function that will serve them in the future. Daws has written more about this in a 1999 paper in *Psychoanalytic Inquiry*, and Morgan (2001) at the Tavistock Marital Studies Institute has also described something similar in referring to the "couple state of mind" with which therapists need to approach a consultation.

I am aware that this raises issues to do with the gender of the therapist and the choice of whether couples are best seen by two therapists, but space does not allow me to develop this theme. What I hope to have shown, though, is why I think it is essential for us, as infant mental health clinicians, to endeavour to work whenever possible with both parents. I believe this to be crucial not only to address the specific kind of marital interactions that I have described but, in a more global way, because I believe that the long-term mental health of the infant will be profoundly determined by the nature of the parental couple that he encounters and then internalizes. It is within the couple's relationship that we need to look for the detailed way in which the ghosts in the nursery act out their tattered scripts. And it is with the complexity of these triangular—at the very least—relationships that we need to be working. This is a daunting task because it is so much more complex than work with the dyad, but it is, of course, just such a complex web of relationships that infants are born into and are influenced by.

However, I am also very aware that when parents consult us about their infant's difficulties, they may be very far from entertaining any idea that those difficulties are linked to their own relationship as a couple and that consequently we, as clinicians, do not necessarily have the remit to explore those issues. This is something that needs to be negotiated in each case, and I would argue that it is part of the clinician's task to try to show the parents why it is not only the father's role that is important but, even more, their combined role *as parents* that is fundamental to shaping their infant's future mental health.

### Note

This chapter is a modified version of an earlier publication: P. Barrows, "Fathers and Families: Locating the Ghost in the Nursery", *Infant Mental Health Journal*, Vol. 25, No. 5 (2004): 408–423.

*CHAPTER 11*

# Father "there and not there": the concept of a "united couple" in families with unstable partnerships

*Louise Emanuel*

This chapter is based on clinical work carried out as part of the Tavistock Clinic's Under Fives Service. As the brief nature of this work implies, it is necessary to focus on a few selected aspects of the problem, and addressing some areas of difficulty in the parental relationship can often provide relief to children and reduce their symptoms.

Nearly all of the work of the Under Fives Service is done in the presence of one or both parents, either with the child or on their own. Often the focus is on helping the parents to gain the insight and strength to function together as a benign parental couple, despite sometimes conscious or unconscious attempts by the child to split the couple. Work may also centre on helping a "single" parent understand her child's need for her to exercise both paternal and maternal functions: to maintain in her mind, and to cultivate in the child's mind, the notion of a well-functioning parental couple. Underlying this approach to work with parents and children is the idea that each parent embodies within him/herself both a paternal and a maternal function, a combined internal parental couple. This links with Bion's (1962a, 1962b) concept of container/contained. Bion's concept of a "container" incorporates both the maternal receptive and the paternal "structuring, penetrative" role—a new thought, a transformation of what is received. Thus it is essential for the development of a capacity to think symbolically that a child internalizes a parental object with both paternal and maternal functions.

The "paternal function" is characterized by benign but firm boundary- and limit-setting, a capacity for "penetrative" insight (new ideas and initiatives); the "maternal function" is characterized by tender receptivity to a child's communications of both pleasure and distress. The combination of these qualities of both firmness and receptivity provides a containing framework within which children in both single- and two-parent families are able to flourish.

These functions can often become polarized in poorly functioning parent couples where one parent of either gender may embody an extreme (parodied) version of a "paternal function"—that is, be excessively punitive and harsh, restrictive rather than limit-setting—or of a "maternal function"—that is, be excessively indulgent and permissive, lacking any limit-setting capacity. In some single-parent families, the single parent may veer from one extreme to the other, embodying either a "paternal" or a "maternal" function, but finding it difficult to integrate and combine the two.

This chapter focuses on situations where the absent father can be powerfully "present" in the mind of the single parent and child, like a "phantom partner", in either a benign or an unhelpful way. Excessive preoccupation with an absent parent can be an obstacle to thinking and can interfere with the remaining parent's capacity to be in touch with her child's emotional communications. The therapist (or therapist couple) can be perceived by the single parent in the transference relationship as a longed-for partner, a containing parental figure, or a critical, persecutory presence.

In the two vignettes below, where the parents had separated, both fathers were an unreliable and unpredictable presence in the family, sometimes disappearing off the scene for months. Anxiety about the effect of the fathers' unavailability or inconsistency on the child, and preoccupations with the past relationship, intruded, filling up the mothers' minds, interfering with their capacity to be thoughtful about their daughters' emotional needs, and thus reducing their availability as well. The children's experience was of an emotionally absent mother as well as father.

In the first example, my colleague and I focused on the anxiety and uncertainty conveyed in the child's play about her father's dependability. Drawing mother's attention to this enabled us to show her how her own unhelpful reliance on father and the worry this caused her were preventing her from attending to her daughter's needs. Paradoxically, my colleague and I needed to help mother face the fact of her single parenthood (to realize the truth of her situation—Bion, 1962a, 1962b), and take steps towards emotional and practical independence, before she could begin to internalize both paternal and maternal functions, which would enable her to parent her daughter in a more integrated way.

*Tanya*

Tanya, aged 4 years, was referred to the Under Fives Service by her health visitor because of her aggressive and disruptive behaviour, and the family was seen jointly by my colleague and me. At our first appointment mother told me that although father had agreed to come, "typically" they did not know where he was. Her style was pleasant but lacked emotional depth, as if she were making an effort to keep herself on an even keel. Tanya appeared to be concerned, looking out for father at the window and calling him on the toy phone. It was difficult for us to talk, as Tanya interrupted constantly, pulling at our clothing. We were quickly divided into two pairings, with my colleague and I exclusively "owned" by mother and Tanya respectively, as it seemed intolerable for either of them to bear feeling excluded. Father arrived five minutes before the end of the session, and Tanya responded excitedly to his lively manner.

The following session father arrived half an hour late. Mother did not appear to be anxious, but it was clear that she was listening out for his car and knew long before we did when he had arrived. As Tanya began cutting and gluing paper, we heard about mother's unplanned pregnancy; how the couple had separated amicably when Tanya was 2 years old; and mother's full-time work and complicated childcare arrangements. We also heard complaints about father's broken promises to Tanya and his unreliability, although these were not mentioned in father's presence. Father felt that he had no problems with Tanya, that she was a happy child, and the nursery had recently written a glowing report on her. We were unsure whether they wanted further help, but, as we were ending, mother mentioned Tanya's difficulty getting on with her peers in group situations, and we offered another meeting for the three of them.

In the third session father did not attend. Mother was anxious about father letting them down, as she did not drive, and she was relying on him to deliver Tanya back to school. Tanya seemed to be less determined to prevent adult conversation, asking my colleague's name, then saying: "You don't remember my name . . . you don't remember my Daddy." We talked about both the mother's and daughter's expectations that people will not hold others in mind when they are apart. Tanya was bothered that father wasn't there, calling him on the toy phone, talking too fast to be intelligible, but she seemed to be telling him to hurry up. We suggested that Tanya might need to keep her father in an idealized position, and she felt unable to let him know how cross she felt with him, for fear that he would disappear altogether.

We heard from mother about Tanya's difficulties in group situations, how she became possessive and clingy towards one favoured child and, when rejected, became aggressive or collapsed. We linked this with Tanya's use of glue in the session and talked about how Tanya might feel she needed to "stick" herself to people to keep them with her. This can feel overpowering to some children, resulting in painful rejection. Mother became interested in how Tanya's play conveyed her feelings. Tanya produced a heart-shaped rubber stamp with the word "love" inside, which lit up when pressed hard onto paper. As she stamped it onto a glue-covered piece of paper, the middle of the stamp fell out and she became upset and angry. We spoke about her attempts to stamp her "love-heart" securely to the paper, and how worried she became when she couldn't make it stay put, couldn't make people she loved stay attached to her, or light up with love for her, like the glowing toy.

As we spoke about her father's absence she wrapped Sellotape around our watches. She agreed that she was trying to stop the time so that Daddy could get there, and she tried to drown out our voices as we spoke. She then tried to tape my colleague into her chair, using copious amounts of tape in an attempt to stick her firmly into her place. We suggested that Tanya was trying to ensure that we couldn't go anywhere, and wouldn't forget her, and how much she longed to take charge and make Daddy stay in one place, close to her. She talked angrily on the phone, then needed the toilet.

The following meeting mother conveyed to us that what she had seen of Tanya's behaviour and play had had a profound impact on her. She said that she had begun to think more about how Tanya might feel constantly left in uncertainty and let down when her father doesn't turn up as he has promised. She felt that Tanya was greatly relieved to have someone who understood how she was feeling, and she told us that she had described Tanya's play and our observations on it to father. She had explained to him that by taping my colleague to her chair, Tanya was expressing her wish to immobilize her father, to ensure that he could not leave her, especially when she felt so helpless to control his comings and goings. We were impressed by mother's genuine sense of having gained "insight" into a new and different meaning to her child's behaviour.

Mother described Tanya becoming furious with her in the car, complaining that her mother had "interrupted her song" by talking to her. Tanya had shouted that she felt like "taking the axe that the huntsman used in *Snow White and the Seven Dwarves* and killing Mummy and Daddy." I linked this to the way in which the flow of our sessions had been disrupted by Tanya's constant anxiety and checking for her father, how it had interrupted her play and the connection between us during the session. Perhaps Tanya's train of thought got interrupted even when there was not an actual external precipitating factor, so that she could become suddenly anxious during group activities, especially when she was waiting for her turn. The waiting could then become unbearable, leading her to interrupt others in order to give them the same experience that she has had and to discharge her overwhelming feelings.

We addressed how difficult it was for mother to face up to the fact that Tanya's father was the way he was and that he wouldn't necessarily change. This meant that she was left having to face the full responsibility of being the only one who could provide a parental function for Tanya.

In discussing the next appointment, mother wondered how to manage, and she was tempted to ask father to help with transport, collecting and returning Tanya to school. We indicated that we did not think it would be helpful to invite father to attend the next session, as we had learnt from experience how disruptive it could be, and we felt that it was cruel to set up a situation at the clinic which mirrored the situation at home. We were having to accept our experience of father as he was without unrealistic hopes of change, and we hoped to demonstrate to mother how facing this kind of fact involved thinking about separateness, independence, and change.

We helped her to begin to think about attending the clinic independently, making other arrangements, without relying on Tanya's father. She was very anxious, asking directions and considering whether she might have the courage to drive to the clinic herself. We also reminded her that we were drawing to the end of our contact, the following being the fifth session.

We explored mother's placatory response to father ("I get annoyed, but I detach myself"), conveying a feeling that she needed to hold back and control her emotional response. We raised the possibility that Tanya's rage may have been in part expressing mother's anger. We suggested that with our support, as functioning parent figures (she had described being rather isolated from her family), it might be possible to be more open and direct with both father and Tanya about her feelings.

The following session they were late and were brought by mother's sister. Mother, in her anxious state, talked about giving up her day job and working nights. I felt shocked that she was contemplating such drastic action, and I considered that we were meant to experience in the countertransference the shock that mother may have felt in our last meeting, when we suggested a major change in her way of relating to Tanya's father. Mother continued: "Tanya won't know if I'm not there, she'll be sleeping." At this point Tanya began to play a hide-and-seek game in which mother had to disappear and appear, and we suggested that she was listening to and understanding the implications of mother's words.

We offered three more sessions to complete the work, in which mother gradually became more competent at driving them to the clinic and managed to arrange better childcare. We focused on helping her find a way of encompassing within herself both a firm paternal role and a receptive maternal role. Mother talked about how bewildered and upset she had felt when Tanya had drawn a beautiful picture, which mother had admired, then thrown it in the bin. We thought Tanya was giving her an experience of how it felt when something beautiful, like the picture of a perfect family in her mind, got spoilt and how Tanya needed her mother to receive and contain these feelings for her. Tanya's distress when things weren't perfect, like the picture she'd discarded, was difficult to bear and could result in mother feeling "rubbish" and inadequate, further damaging her fragile sense of self-esteem and making it more difficult to maintain firm parental boundaries.

We heard about the rushed pace in the evening because of a set early bedtime. Mother seemed to cope by making inflexible rules, as if she could not allow herself to be more relaxed about things. We spoke about the unhelpful polarization of the parent figures that Tanya had in her mind—on the one hand an unreliable but idealized father, on the other a rigid rule-maker. We wondered if there was a way in which the evening period together could encapsulate a tender time of togetherness, as well as firm limits about bedtime, to facilitate Tanya in internalizing a model of harmonious parental functioning which could calm her down. As we spoke about the dilemma of setting firm yet flexible boundaries Tanya became increasingly imperious and contemptuous towards her mother, blaming her for some misdemeanours in a very belittling way. She marched around the room shouting into the telephone, "Stop talking all this rubbish!" We thought that she was protesting against these changes. Perhaps unconsciously she was recognizing that the help mother was receiving was empowering her to separate in a real way from father, leaving space for somebody else to form an adult couple with her. Tanya's oedipal anxieties were also revealed as she became increasingly controlling, recognizing unconsciously the need to "relinquish the idea of sole and permanent possession of mother (which) leads to a profound sense of loss, which, if not tolerated, may become a sense of persecution" (Britton, 1989, p. 84).

In addition, mother's move away from a more "infantile" dependence on father would hopefully prevent her from reverting to the role of a pleading child in relation to him. This had seemed to evoke a cruel contempt in Tanya, masking her anxiety about the powerful position it put her in. As we talked about her need to take charge, she approached us with some Plasticine she had smoothed out, wanting us to feel its smooth surfaces. She seemed to convey her wish to smooth away ideas we were introducing about separateness, boundaries, and difference, to keep things seamless and all the same. Tanya continued, "I don't want to hear all this rubbish", as mother talked about putting her to bed on time. We spoke of Tanya conveying her feeling that she could not just be "put away" at the end of the day without a "smooth" time together, which consisted of her feeling "contained" by a united parental couple, embodied by her mother, in father's absence.

Mother reported improvements in many areas. Tanya was coping better but still had outbursts at school. However, she felt that Tanya was fine now at home and at pre-school. Father had become "more reliable", offering financial help. We heard that her employer was more supportive. We thought that the change in attitude in those adults mother needed for her support reflected similar improvements in Tanya's peer relationships. Perhaps mother, like Tanya, no longer needed to "glue" herself to her friends and colleagues in an over-dependent way. They might, therefore, feel less inclined to push her away, offering help instead.

In the last session Tanya came in pushing a doll in a buggy and asking to do her homework, showing us a grown-up, coping girl. She "tutted" a lot, telling us we were naughty, then glued a picture on the therapy-room wall, agreeing that she hoped we'd continue to think about her after she'd gone. She brought two baby dolls into the middle of the room, as if assured now that we would all attend to her play, and called the doctor on the toy phone, as if to remind us that there were still some difficulties to be dealt with. She played at being a Mummy who was comforting the "stinky babies" who had "done poos which Mummies have to clean up". She suddenly smacked one of the babies crossly, saying it was "naughty".

We felt that mother was more able to "clean up" Tanya's emotional mess and to keep her in mind. I think Tanya also recognized unconsciously that her mother's increased sense of self-confidence could lead to another coupling and more "naughty babies"—since mother was a young and attractive woman. We felt that mother had begun to take into herself a well-functioning parental couple, integrating both "paternal" and "maternal" functions, enabling her to believe that she would be kept in mind and to provide this containment for her daughter.

## Mirja

In this second example, father's absence was also a predominant feature. In contrast to the case above, where uncertainty permeated the family, here mother's unwavering conviction that father's unreliability was the cause of her child's emotional problems seemed to interfere with her ability to be in touch with her child's emotional states. My colleague and I were able to help mother recognize how this overdetermined agenda relating to father was creating an obstacle to her communication with her child, thereby possibly compounding her difficulties.

Mother and daughter, Mirja, aged 4, were referred to the clinic because of Mirja's difficulty sleeping. Mirja had a Serbian mother and a Kosovan father. A colleague saw mother for several weeks on her own, and the content of the sessions focused mainly on mother's grievances about her ex-husband, and her preoccupation with his unreliability in relation to maintaining contact with Mirja. My colleague felt that it was possible Mirja would need individual child psychotherapy input, and it was therefore agreed that I would join her in a meeting with mother and Mirja as a start to the assessment process.

In our first joint meeting we were both struck by the quick way in which Mirja became engaged with the toys (in contrast to Tanya, who had been so restless). Mirja sat at the table with her back to her mother, chattering to herself as she explored the box of toys. Mother commented that the toys were "too interesting", and she seemed to feel excluded. She mentioned several times that Mirja felt sad about not seeing her Daddy, relating most of Mirja's difficulties to incidents connected with her father. The atmosphere was tense, and I felt very aware of intruding into the cosy couple of my colleague and mother, who up until this point had met together as an "exclusive" couple. My sense of intrusion related not only to my physical presence, but to my growing awareness that as an outsider with the potential to perceive the family situation from a different perspective and question fixed ideas, I might be regarded with some suspicion. I wondered whether father may have experienced a similar feeling of exclusion, which may have made it difficult for him to maintain regular contact, thereby reinforcing a cycle of hostility and unreliability between the parents.

Mirja drew our attention to a picture in a story book she had brought along, of a beautiful blonde princess who was standing between two figures (coloured from head to foot in black) whom she described as "baddies". I said that Mirja might have all sorts of worries about how she felt inside, and how she imagined other people, including her Daddy, might see her. Did they think she was a beautiful princess or a "baddy"? She nodded, seeming pleased that we were attending in such detail to the picture.

In the second joint session with them both, as Mirja settled down to draw, mother told us that her daughter had been angry about being brought to the clinic. At this, Mirja turned around and opened her mouth wide, showing me a piece of chewing gum stuck on the tip of her tongue. I said that it sounded as if she was feeling cross today, yet rather than being really "rude" and sticking her tongue out at me properly, she had made this small gesture instead. Mirja seemed excited by this idea and poked her tongue out at me provocatively. I suggested she was testing to see just how rude she could be with us, that she was hoping we would notice the "baddy" parts of her, like in the picture (the two figures on either side of the princess) and wondered what we would think about this.

Mirja mentioned that she banged her head at home so that she could have a "hurt place" and her mother would then cuddle her and make it better. Mother described Mirja getting upset after she had talked to her daddy on the phone. At this, Mirja went over to her mother and tried to cover her mouth to stop her speaking, then slapped the side of her face. Mother was shocked, as were we, and she seemed unsure how to respond. She explained quietly to Mirja in an adult way that it was better to talk about things than to hit people. Mirja lay across her mother's body and tried to kiss her on the mouth as if seeking comfort in an over-sexualized way. She came and lay on the floor, tickling my legs, and I stopped her.

Mother reiterated that she was convinced this behaviour was connected with Mirja's phone contact with her father, as mother felt that Mirja was filled up with unmanageable feelings by these conversations. We acknowledged that this might well be true; however, I began to wonder whether mother's insistence that Mirja's distress was always somehow linked to father might be interfering with her capacity to notice the range of Mirja's feelings, which may not have been exclusively connected to father. Through observing her behaviour, which became over-sexualized at times, I thought Mirja was feeling confused about how one develops and sustains intimate relationships. I also thought that Mirja's concern with the contrasting good and bad figures in the picture she had brought may relate to fear of rejection if she revealed her hostile feelings, showing the "baddy", aggressive sides of herself.

At this point Mirja stuck out her bottom at her mother, touching it and saying "poo" in a rubbishing gesture, as if she were deliberately exhibiting some less savoury aspects of herself (like the poking out of the chewing-gum tongue). It seemed as if she were increasingly demanding to have the messy, distressed part of her, which made her feel like a "poo" baby, deserving of rejection (as she may have felt when father did not arrive for contact), recognized and contained. The strain of behaving like a sophisticated, beautiful princess and keeping these unwanted sides of her at bay was proving to be too much for her. My colleague and I thought Mirja might feel, in phantasy, that expressing these rather unacceptable sides of herself might result in abandonment, and she needed to test this out constantly. Her rude and at times bossy behaviour towards her mother and towards us in the room led me to wonder whether, on some level, Mirja felt that she was "the baddy", responsible for her parents' separation, which might have led to an increase in her feelings of omnipotent control. The more anxious she became about her destructive powers, the more controlling she would need to be, as a way of evading her persecutory fear of retaliation.

In contrast to the previous occasion, when Mirja's back had been turned to mother as she sat at the table, for this session we had rearranged the chair so that Mirja faced her mother directly. Now, as the two of them faced each other full-on, the contact between them felt invasive and over-close. Instead of a father figure mediating between mother and child, imposing some distance between them, helping with separation difficulties, and regulating the intensity of the contact, the absent father seemed to predominate in mother's thoughts in a similarly intrusive way. Her preoccupation with an absent father made it difficult for her to perceive the range of her daughter's concerns and interfered with her capacity to provide understanding and containment for her, thereby creating an obstacle to intimate contact between the two of them.

At a review meeting with mother, a warmer, more trusting relationship was apparent between us all. As mother complained about her partner, and how his behaviour had impacted on Mirja, my colleague and I spoke about how these grievances might serve a function of keeping both mother and daughter both enraged and agitated, thereby preventing feelings of depression about separation and loss from overtaking them. When we suggested that mother's fixed agenda might be preventing her from seeing Mirja's needs as varied and wide-ranging, mother seemed to be relieved.

We talked about our sense of a messy little girl Mirja who was struggling to get through to her mother but who met with a barrier. Mother acknowledged this but went on to describe how at bedtime Mirja clung to her, saying she felt "sad because of Daddy." I suggested that this clinging might be Mirja's way of keeping Mummy with her, especially when Mirja knew that her mother was about to have some private evening space without her. She gave her mother a little reminder that Daddies are "bad", just in case mother had anything of the sort (perhaps a date with a man) in mind for the evening! Mother added that this seemed to happen when she and Mirja had had a particularly nice time together. I recalled aloud how we could all remember a time at the beginning of our work when mother had felt quite wary of me as an intruder into the cosy couple with my colleague, and I suggested that recalling that feeling might help mother understand how Mirja might feel about anyone else coming into her Mummy's life to disturb the cosy couple: if she lets Mummy go, another Daddy figure might intrude, to form a sexual couple, have more babies, to the exclusion of herself. Mother acknowledged that this could be true, citing Mirja's preoccupation with couples while they were on holiday.

We clarified with mother that we felt she was Mirja's main attachment figure, and how important it would be for her to be able to maintain both a maternal and a paternal role in relation to Mirja. We agreed to continue working together, alternating family meetings with individual meetings with mother, to help her consider her parental role in the light of material brought by her daughter to the sessions.

Discussion

In the cases described above, it is striking how the relationship between the parental couple, as perceived by the mother and child, is central to the work. The particular dynamics and circumstances of some single-parent families, or those with unstable parental partnerships, may make the ordinary working through of the Oedipus complex more difficult to negotiate, for a number of reasons. Father's absence or unreliability may confirm a small child's omnipotent phantasy that he has "ousted" father and now has mother all to himself. The ordinary "reality testing" that takes place in a well-functioning two-parent family (accompanied by inevitable feelings of loss and exclusion, as well as relief), when young children are confronted with daily evidence that they have not succeeded in their oedipal wishes, is not readily available. In fact, if a single parent embarks on a series of short-term relationships, the child may experience a repeat confirmation of his destructive omnipotence, accompanied by increased anxiety. A single mother's need to mourn a lost relationship, a previous way of life, or the baby she had hoped to have may make it difficult for her to keep in mind the idea of a creative and benign couple, sometimes concretely filling the absent space in the bed by allowing a child to sleep in the father's place.

In situations where the "triangular space" (Britton, 1989) is intruded into by the "presence" of an "absent" father in the mother's mind, as with Tanya and Mirja, it is difficult for the young child to negotiate the normal oedipal conflicts and to maintain an awareness of the link that exists between the parents, which by definition must exclude the child. Father "there and not there" creates a more ambiguous external situation and may heighten the child's confusion about his own phantasied destructive powers to "split" the parents, and his own phantasied powers to protect and enliven the remaining parent.

Britton writes:

> The primary family triangle provides the child with two links connecting him separately with each parent and confronts him with the link between them which excludes him. . . . If the link between the parents perceived in love and hate can be tolerated in the child's mind, it provides him with a prototype for an object relationship of a third kind in which he is a witness and not a participant. A third position then comes into existence from which object relationships can be observed. Given this, we can also envisage *being* observed. This provides us with a capacity for seeing ourselves in interaction with others and for entertaining another point of view whilst retaining our own, for reflecting on ourselves whilst being ourselves. [Britton, 1989, p. 87]

I hope the examples given in this chapter illustrate how work was often directed towards helping parents (single or a couple) to observe themselves and their children from a different perspective. This often enabled them to begin to internalize the functions of a benign parental couple, in order to facilitate their child's development. The experience of working jointly with a colleague, or finding a way of uniting with a parent to function as a "parental couple" within the therapy room, can be helpful in this kind of work, enabling issues around limit-setting, separation, and individuation to be explored.

Close observation of the developing relationships in the therapy room, and monitoring of the countertransference, are essential tools for this work.

## Note

This chapter is a modified version of an earlier publication: L. Emanuel, "Parents United: Addressing Parental Issues in Working with Infants and Young Children", *International Journal of Infant Observation*, Vol. 5, No. 2 (2002): 103–117.

*CHAPTER 12*

# Oedipal issues in under-fives families: creating a space for thinking

*Michi Gurion*

This chapter addresses the feelings of exclusion and separateness commonly experienced by the young child as he moves away from the exclusive relationship with his primary carer, usually mother, and towards a triangular relationship, most notably with father, but also with siblings, and often a new baby. I shall describe therapeutic work with a family struggling with conflicts, anxieties, and defences associated with the triangular constellation of mother, father, and child—the oedipal situation. Attempts by the child and/or parents to avoid the natural feelings of anxiety and pain associated with this process can have a paralysing effect on the whole family. I hope to elaborate on the nature of these defences and show that one way of alleviating such paralysis is through the creation of a "triangular space" for observation and reflection by the therapist who can provide a "third position" (Britton, 1989) on the various points of view within the family. This is a space bounded by the three people within the oedipal situation and their potential relationships. It includes, therefore, "the possibility of being a participant in a relationship and observed by a third person as well as being an observer of a relationship between two people" (Britton, 1989, p. 86). This "space for thinking" allows the possibility of new ideas to be created within the therapeutic setting.

The first year of life is dominated by the relationship between infant and caregiver, usually the mother. The infant begins life entirely dependent upon this relationship for his very existence. If all goes well and the baby's fundamental needs, both physical and emotional, have been met, he will have internalized figures who are a source of strength and containment for him. The experience of weaning, so central during the second half of the first year, confronts the baby with the reality that he does not have exclusive possession of the breast. Relinquishing the intimacy and exclusiveness of the feeding situation may be painful for both mother and baby, and the gradual shift towards acceptance of the parents' relationship with each other is filled with conflicts and anxiety.

Not only does the child begin to perceive his parents as a couple from whose relationship he can be excluded, he also recognizes, in the words of Hanna Segal, that "the nature of the link between the parents is different in kind from the relation of the child to the parents and at the moment unavailable to him. . . . It is not only that they exchange genital gratifications, but also the fact that the parental intercourse leads to the creation of a new baby" (Segal, 1989, p. 8). This realization of parental sexuality and partnership, as well as his growing awareness of difference between adults and children, will inevitably generate very strong feelings of loss, envy, and jealousy. Rivalry with one parent for the attention of the other is a common consequence of such recognition. However, it may also encourage him to find comfort in other relationships and activities, most significantly with his father.

Working through these ordinary but painful anxieties and conflicts is facilitated by the presence of a securely based internal parental couple in the child's mind. The absence of a "united" parental couple can make it more complicated for the child to establish an oedipal triangle. Parents' own unresolved oedipal conflicts could lead them to over-identify with their child, thus discouraging separation and growth. The birth of a new baby can stir up a sense of displacement in the child, and this in turn might make parents feel guilty and reluctant to set ordinary boundaries. There is always the child's own personality and unique way of perceiving and interpreting parental and sibling behaviour to be taken into account, too.

The resolution of the oedipal situation through relinquishing the sole possession of mother and the acceptance of the parents' relationship with each other creates what Ronald Britton calls "a triangular space".

In my description of the work with this family, I provide a detailed account of the thoughts and feelings evoked in me during the meetings to indicate how the use of transference and countertransference can be helpful in identifying areas of difficulty within the family.

## *Oedipal rivalry*

This case illustrates a common family problem: a 2-year-old who feels pushed out of place after the birth of a sibling. In this case the little girl turned to her father for comfort, as little girls often do; but in her mind this took on unusual proportions, as in her imagination she had rearranged the family into a new set of couples: herself and father on one side, and mother and baby brother on the other. This was her way of denying the fact of her parents' intimate couple relationship.

Mrs A contacted the local child-guidance service asking for help with her 2½-year-old daughter, Maria, due to her waking up frequently at night and demanding mother's sole attention during the day, unable to play on her own. The family was under strain at the time of referral, with maternal grandmother suffering from cancer. In addition the family's home was undergoing some renovation and was in chaos.

Although the whole family was invited for the first meeting, mother chose to come on her own, as she had her doubts about "this kind of service" and wanted to check what was on offer. She did so, in the first instance, by bombarding me with many direct questions about the work in the clinic, and she demanded to know what exactly it was that I was doing, as if I had some hidden menacing agenda.

(I thought that she may have been frightened of what *I* might ask *her*, and putting me on the spot by reversing the situation was a way of protecting herself from the unknown). I tried to answer some of her questions, although I soon realized that my answers in themselves were not what really mattered. What was more important was how I absorbed the questions and bore the accompanying feelings. (Being put on the spot in this manner gave me some first-hand experience of her own state of anxiety and feeling of being overwhelmed. It also indicated how her daughter might be experiencing her mother, perhaps being on the receiving end of a great deal of anxiety.)

Mrs A became very tearful as she spoke about the burden she was carrying: the care of her two children, Maria and Daniel (11 months old), as well as her own parents, particularly now that her mother was very ill. She said that both she and her husband were bewildered by the change in Maria. She used to be a wonderful baby before her brother was born but in the last few months had become so demanding and clingy, day and night, that both parents were on verge of collapse. The baby, however, appeared very calm and contented and slept through the night.

Mrs A herself was calmer by the end of the meeting and was able to link Maria's difficulties to the strained situation at home, while she was already having to struggle with the arrival of her new baby brother. We spoke about Mrs A's fear of losing her own mother and the way both mother and daughter shared the same fears of abandonment.

Mrs A thought that her husband would not want to come to these meetings, as "he did not believe in such things". (I thought that Mrs A herself arrived at this meeting with no hope of being helped, perhaps expecting to be blamed or to be told that something was wrong or abnormal in her responses. At the end of the meeting she felt calmer and more gathered, and I thought that perhaps she had wished that her husband had come with her to this meeting. Perhaps she now attributed her own suspicions to her husband.)

I was left with many doubts and questions in my mind (not unlike Mrs A): Why was Mrs A so suspicious of this service? Had I managed to reassure her? Why had I been so eager to reassure her? Would she be able to persuade her husband to join us for the next meeting? Under their scrutinizing eyes, would I be able to come up with the goods?

(This state of mind of feeling unsure about one's ability to help is not unusual, particularly with under-fives families. These parents can often feel helpless and inadequate themselves, and the need to ask for help is often humiliating and shaming, in some cultures more than others. Projecting these difficult feelings into the therapist can, in fact, enable parents to feel liberated and take up a more confident stand as parents.)

## The princess

A more convenient, after-work time and mother's sense of relief after the first meeting seemed to enable the whole family to attend the second session. Mother's initial description of her daughter as anxious and sensitive did not prepare me for the picture I was presented with. Maria appeared as a very self-assured, domineering "princess", whose long hair fell elegantly over her face like a veil, also keeping her eyes quite hidden. Her presence in the room as a central figure was unquestionable, while her younger brother, Daniel, seemed to be rather inconspicuous. Mr A was quiet to begin with but did not come across as suspicious of this kind of work in the way that his wife had anticipated.

Maria went straight to the table where a few drawing materials were laid out, and she stayed standing by the table, presumably to keep her height (or highness!) at all times. There was also a sense of her not really needing anything that was on offer here, as if she were just passing by or on her way to somewhere more interesting. She started drawing many circles on one sheet of paper followed by another and another. She then distributed them to all people present in a dramatic, teacher-like manner. Mother explained that Maria was presently learning about triangles, squares, and circles, "but circles are her favourite". (I thought of her need to be in the centre, within a circle, rather than within a triangle or square, shapes that are associated with more than two. A triangle, with its apex and sharp corners, could be associated with feelings of exclusion and loneliness highlighted by the sharpness of the edges, in contrast to the soft never-ending shape of a circle). On completing this activity she found herself having nothing to do (as if having to face being a child in the corner), and the tension in the room started rising as she began to grab things from her brother, who faintly protested. Her parents seemed somewhat helpless and did not intervene.

Soon the atmosphere became heated as Maria continued to intrude into Daniel's territory (projecting her disturbance and discomfort onto him). The latter became increasingly agitated and eventually cried. When parents made a comment about it, albeit mildly, Maria immediately veered towards mother's bag full of "bribes", which mother said she takes "just in case". (I thought that mother needed to be always ready to appease Maria, to sweeten her own bitter feelings of guilt or anger.) Mother seemed to expect Maria to be what she called "mean to her brother", and she was ready to appease her by giving her a sweet (as if mother could not be experienced as mean in the eyes of her daughter. I was here reminded of Mrs A's anxiety in the previous meeting and was puzzled by the contrast between her description of Maria as a very sensitive helpless girl and the way Maria presented here—in full control and possession of her parents.)

I made a comment about Maria needing to feel all right at all times and her parents' wish to please her. Father responded to this by making a connection to his own childhood and said he had always been a very anxious child. He remembered, for instance, how all the other children in his neighbourhood used to climb up the trees while he would stay at the bottom collecting the apples. Maria, who must have felt out of focus at this moment, moved swiftly to sit on her father's lap, spreading herself all over him, and proceeding to command him to get her this or that (as if Maria were the assertive climber in father's eyes). Father did not challenge her, yet I could not help but notice how determined she was in avoiding eye contact with me, as I was beginning to get a clearer picture of her state of mind. (I thought that she probably perceived me as a threat to the status quo and that I represented a need and a vehicle for change, in her eyes the unwanted intruder who needed to be defeated through exclusion.)

I heard from Mrs A that in the night Maria wakes up and comes to her parents' bedroom. Mother does not like her getting into their bed, so father usually takes her back to her own bed and stays with her until she falls asleep. (I thought that although the parents were clear in keeping their bed out of bounds, Maria did manage to get her father out of the matrimonial bed and have him all to herself. Her waking up several times at night could be triggered by her fear that he would slip back to mother.) During the day, however, she follows mother everywhere and demands her exclusive attention. (Out of guilt for taking her husband away from her? Or a way of being mother's shadow, as if by sticking close to mother she can instantly "become" mother and avoid having to know about being a little girl?)

I asked the parents whether they thought Maria might be checking on them at night, as she seemed to have a very strong need to be right in the middle so as not to feel excluded. Both parents were amused by this, and mother became more animated and said simply: "Oh yes, Maria is married to her father." I said that she seemed therefore to be in competition with mother, who is already married to her husband. Here Maria became very upset and strongly protested: "*My* Daddy! Mummy is Daniel's Mummy and Daddy is *mine*." Mother said that sometimes she teases Maria by saying, "He is *my* husband" and Maria protests back: "No, he is *my* Daddy."

As we continued to talk about this Maria asked mother for her ring (her wedding ring was the only one on her finger), and mother let her have it. In gratitude Maria kindly offered her her own cheap plastic one. I was reminded of the circles and Maria's dislike of triangles and squares, while circles may be evocative of a couple enclosed with no corners to bump against (the wedding-ring circle as a symbol of the relationship between mother and father).

This prompted a lively conversation as the parents began to show more interest in understanding aspects of their daughter's behaviour. They were able to recognize that Maria's night-time waking and day-time clinging to mother during father's absence at work illustrated her need to keep an eye on her parents, partly to make sure that they do not produce any more babies, as it were, but also to protect herself against feeling abandoned (it is likely that her increased hostility and intrusiveness would have brought greater fear of retaliation and abandonment). There was also a fear of being left with nothing, particularly as Maria would perceive her baby brother as snatching her own place with mother. They could also see her following mother's footsteps as not only literally clinging or gluing herself to her but as also wishing to *be* her, in order not to be faced with the painful reality of the difference between her and her mother, who after all produced lovely babies. The parents were both relieved and keen to proceed with the work.

(Although I could see that the current situation at home may have exacerbated Maria's need to keep a vigilant eye on her parents I was not yet clear what made it difficult for these parents to manage her demands and bear her feelings. I wondered whether some of these difficulties were already experienced prior to the arrival of the new baby but were intensified by his birth. Perhaps Maria was a particularly demanding, envious baby who had found it especially difficult to bear the position of needing mother and perceiving her as the holder of all good things. Certainly both parents seemed to find it very difficult to challenge her in an ordinary way: they were almost too empathetic towards Maria, understanding her discomfort and frustration and wishing only to take those feelings away. It seemed as if they were both very identified with her vulnerable feelings and were therefore less able to take a parental stance of setting boundaries in a clear, albeit friendly, manner, perhaps for fear of hurting her and possibly becoming unpopular in Maria's eyes. This in turn fed into her omnipotence and her phantasy of being at one with her parents. Their helplessness therefore made her feel all too powerful, thus controlling her own vulnerable part in a rather grotesque way.)

*Recovery*

At the third meeting the parents reported improvements in Maria's sleep and behaviour during the day, although they were not readily attributing it to the work at the clinic. However, I was particularly struck and encouraged by the change in them as they were less distant from each other and spoke together as parents, sensitively describing Maria's behaviour. For instance, they seemed more aware of her tendency to overdramatize and spoke about her "crocodile tears". They thought that she recently felt "her nose had been put out of joint", firstly by her brother's arrival and more recently by parents' preoccupation with the building work and grandmother's illness. They thought that Maria had become more miserable. Indeed, in the room she seemed more ordinary and less conspicuous. In this meeting the parents were relaxed and open about their own childhood experiences and connected these to their feelings and attitude towards Maria. Mr A described his own father as a very volatile man who always needed to be appeased by his son. Mr A's response to his daughter's capriciousness and intimidation was not, in his mind, dissimilar to his response to his father. (One could also see that he needed to be a different father to his daughter by being soft and giving, rather then distant and strict.)

Mrs A was the older of two girls and viewed her younger sister as her father's favourite. She described being made to feel unbearably excluded. She thought that Maria's birth had stirred up a lot of feelings in her, probably reminding her of the birth of her younger sister. (This would link both to her reluctance to upset Maria and also to her competitiveness with her over father/husband. At the same time mother may have relished seeing Maria's assertiveness and demand for attention, which she herself may have lacked when she was a child. Interestingly in both parents' accounts, their own mothers were not even mentioned.) Mrs A made reference to issues around separation by becoming aware of her habitual anticipation that Maria will not manage without her whenever she leaves the home. (This may also reflect Mrs A's own fear of not being as needed and feeling disposable.) We thought together that this anticipation was like an invitation for her daughter to feel abandoned and excluded, in the way she had felt as a child when her father and younger sister left her at home and went of to the park together. (I thought of both Mr and Mrs A as having suffered a degree of deprivation and rejection in their childhood. Their need to be loved and wanted had been activated by their first child. Perhaps both unconsciously encouraged Maria's dependence and need for them, to counteract feelings of rejection and exclusion by their own parents.)

The change in atmosphere during this meeting was striking, as scepticism and wariness gave way to thoughtfulness and sadness. Mrs A was particularly touched by these discoveries. She was pleased to be able to recognize something about herself and to differentiate between her own infantile feelings from those of her daughter.

## Exclusion of the therapist

After the previous productive meeting, the parents cancelled the next three appointments (corresponding to the three meetings we had had). (I wondered whether the contact that was made with me, although helpful at the time, had also increased their anxiety as it brought them into contact with painful feelings in relation to their own childhoods. Perhaps the parents were then able to unite through having a "common enemy". In the second session they had described their daughter with some hostility as having "crocodile tears". This may have evoked guilt in them, and so perceiving the therapist as "the enemy" would appear less dangerous.). By the time we eventually met, the impressions of the previous meetings had faded away. Although the parents again reported significant changes in Maria's sleeping patterns, as she now slept more or less through the night, they seemed more distant and less interested in continuing the work from where we had left off.

I suggested that the subdued mood and the cancellations may be connected to the previous meeting when perhaps they felt they had spoken too openly about their painful feelings and childhood experiences. Perhaps they wanted to put it all to one side. I also wondered whether in their minds they might have anticipated this to be the last meeting, as we had not booked another one. The parents did not take this up, but the focus of the meeting seemed to be shifting elsewhere. Their minds were now full of the very ill grandmother, and mother's own anxiety seemed to be on the increase. Maria seemed more genuinely mindful of her mother's upset feelings, and, interestingly, mother's concerns were focused on Daniel, whom she described as aggressive towards his sister when he could not get his own way. I wondered whether mother's hostile feelings towards her own sister and father were very much stirred up and lodged now with Daniel. Mother said she was afraid he would grow up to be a thug.

They turned down the offer to come for another meeting as they felt there was no need for any more help. Perhaps they, too, like their daughter, found it difficult to acknowledge their need for help.

## Discussion

Although these parents were not naturally inclined to engage in this kind of work, they were nevertheless able to respond to the ideas suggested by the therapist and felt understood. This in turn enabled them to resume their parental position in understanding and containing their daughter. Although they could see the benefit of such a process, it is possible that they were reluctant to continue with this work for fear of being drawn back to the pain associated with infantile feelings and becoming too needy and dependent on the therapist. Nevertheless, being helped to think about their daughter's behaviour and perceptions, rather than acting on their own feelings associated with their own childhoods, did help to bring about a shift in their perception of their daughter, so that they no longer saw her as father's "demanding father" or mother's "favoured sister", but as a little girl full of her own pain and conflicts. Just as they were able to own up, albeit temporarily, to their own pain, so their daughter was able to resume a more ordinary position within the family.

Perhaps the most important change was in mother's position. Filling me with doubts at the start and cancelling appointments at the end can be seen as an enactment of the drama that took place with her daughter. In the same way that I was to feel inadequate in my role as a therapist, so she was displaced by her rivalrous daughter and was made to feel redundant in her role as mother and wife. It is likely that this constellation reminded mother of herself as a child being displaced by her own younger sister. If she saw her daughter in this light, being very powerful and precious, then it would no doubt paralyse her in her attempts to contain and bring her daughter gently down to earth. Projecting these feelings onto me not only enabled me to have a direct experience of her situation but to offer containment through this understanding, rather than act on these feelings. This in turn freed mother to resume her parental position.

The emotional demands on her at the time of the referral must have tipped the balance for her. It is also possible that Mrs A, whose mother seemed absent from her own childhood stories, had projected her own oedipal wishes *vis-à-vis* her own parents onto her daughter, which would explain her increased guilt over her very ill mother.

## Conclusion

These parents became more aware of their daughter's feelings and needs as well as their own feelings evoked by her. This increased awareness and readiness to observe their daughter led to a shift in their view of her, which helped them to regain to some extent their parental capacities and resume a more containing function towards their daughter.

The therapist in her observational, receptive, and non-judgemental stance could be thought of as offering to the family a similar kind of parental function, where projections could be received and feelings thought about. It is through the careful monitoring of such feelings and thoughts lodged in the therapist (countertransference) that a clear picture of the nature and extent of the difficulties could emerge in a relatively short time.

# Separation and loss; weaning and growth

This section touches on a central aspect of an infant's development—the struggle to cope with separation and loss in a life-enhancing way—which is often at the heart of the behavioural and emotional difficulties for which families are referred to an under-fives service. Also described is the clinical work undertaken in community outreach settings where the Under Fives model has been adapted to the particular context. The chapters explore the theme of separation and loss across the under-fives age range, with Dilys Daws (chapter 14) focusing on babies' sleeping and feeding difficulties and later chapters describing work with toddlers and "rising fives".

Holding the balance between states of hope and despair, life and death, loss and gain, and helping families in this task, is the theme running through this section. This is most starkly conveyed by Elizabeth Bradley (chapter 15), who describes the unbearable conflict for parents of coping with a dying child while attempting to welcome a new baby into the world. This highlights the complexity of working with parents dealing with traumatic loss who may have pre-existing mental health difficulties. In this case, mother's childhood terror of catastrophic loss, combined with her persecutory guilt at conceiving a new baby as her daughter is dying, posed a challenge to the therapist to hold a balanced view in the face of such distress. The impact of previous losses—stillbirths, miscarriages, or terminations—on parents and subsequent children emerges as a common theme in work with under fives and can be one cause of ante- and post-natal depression.

Hopefulness and lack of hope are used as a measure of potential for change by Meira Likierman (chapter 13). In her chapter she suggests that what differentiates the three clinical cases she describes, all of whom were referred for "separation anxiety", is the degree of "hope for change" held by each child. The ability to feel hopeful in these children is, she suggests, dependent on the reliability and capacity of the parental couple to think together about their children's difficulties. This emphasis on the positive effect of a well-functioning parental couple on young children's mental health, and the consequent focus on parent as well as family interventions, is a major factor in this model of work with under fives. Anxiety about difference, which, Daws reminds us, is implicit in developing a sense of separateness, becomes difficult to tolerate unless a child feels contained by his inner sense of a safe parental couple. This includes the capacity to cope with feelings of aggression including murderous oedipal feelings towards parents and potential new siblings.

Likierman illustrates, through detailed description of her clinical interventions with families, the difference in quality of parental functioning. On the one hand, a previously harmonious couple, whose son Rajeev developed serious "stranger anxiety" when his mother had been suddenly hospitalized, were helped to understand the cause of their sudden marital disharmony and the effect it was having on their son. His early good start in life and the "hopeful" environment provided for Rajeev indicated that a brief intervention, allowing for the "repair" of misattunements resulting from the traumatic separation, would suffice.

The furious parental rows described in the case of 3-year-old Mina augur less well. However, the way in which Mina used the wild animals in the sessions to dramatically enact the fights between her parents enabled them to recognize the harm they were doing to her and to effect some changes in the family.

The more severe example of George points to one of the dilemmas in this work: that it is extremely difficult to judge from a short referral the severity and complexity of the problem until one has undertaken some form of assessment as part of the service. The referred symptom may be the same, but the manner in which George has responded to what appears to be a "less hopeful" environment is cause for concern.

In this case a parental couple who are estranged and polarized in their approach to their son, and for whom the death of their first child is clearly still unresolved, appear unable to contain his communications of anxiety and distress. His way of coping has been to become excessively identified with his mother, literally attempting to get "into her shoes" by his wish to become a "girl-boy". This extreme form of identification as a way of maintaining "possession" of his mother seriously impedes the development of the process of separation and individuation described so clearly by Daws. In addition, the "relish" with which George destroys the drawing he makes in the session betrays the "self-destructive tendencies" and potentially perverse nature of his defence against vulnerability, which is a worrying feature of a number of children seen in our service. Unlike many families where brief work is indicated, this case is likely to require ongoing involvement—

marital, family, or individual child psychotherapy for George—in order for real change to take place.

It seems important to keep in mind the developmental value of separation and weaning, the fact that this process is not only about loss, but about "letting go", mourning the loss and moving on towards a new gain. As Daws vividly reminds us through her vignette describing baby Penny's weaning from the breast and her sudden spurt in language development, loss and frustration—if not too overwhelming—can spur us on to the next stage of growth and creativity.

CHAPTER 13

# Spanning presence and absence: separation anxiety in the early years

*Meira Likierman*

The realities of separation are part of all social relationships, including the earliest mother–infant bond. The newborn depends on the mother's nurturing presence, but, being out of the womb and in the world, he is bound also to experience normal gaps in her care. The first separations in life might take the form of the baby coming to the end of a breastfeed, being put in his cot to sleep, or being handed over to another adult. O'Shaughnessy notes that: "The feeding infant does not have an association with the breast, like a strictly business association. He has a relationship to it, which spans absence and presence, which goes beyond the physical presence of the breast to the breast in its absence" (O'Shaughnessy, 1964, p. 34).

As the baby develops into a toddler, he becomes much more aware of the many small gaps in his care routine. The mother attends not only to him, but to his father and siblings. In an ordinary day, his parents concern themselves with their other children, with each other, with members of their extended family, and, more generally, with their lives.

When the small child is feeling resilient, he can negotiate gaps in care and attention, awaiting his turn with a sense of hope that, sooner or later, his needs will be met. However, at times when the child feels more fragile, he tends to regard small inattentions with anxiety or anger, experiencing them as insults to his person or even as fundamental threats to his existence. Is he being deliberately humiliated when parents turn their attention away? Or, worse, will he cease to exist when he is not held in the parental gaze, when the mother leaves the room or the father goes out?

Such anxieties surface periodically in all small children. In the long term, they may underpin their response to more obvious physical separations, such as going to nursery school or childcare. When a child shows intense anxiety on parting from parents the clinician may be tempted to jump to conclusions and cast the behaviour as pathological. However, some anxious clinging is both normal and universally expressed. Its full significance can therefore only be evaluated in relation to contextual factors. Of crucial importance is the child's ability to be hopeful that his needs will be met after periods of inevitable waiting and frustration. Such hope depends partly on a parental emotional provision that is reliable, rather than continuously and flawlessly available.

This chapter addresses the manifestation of separation anxieties in three small children from different families, all referred to the Tavistock Under Fives Service. As described elsewhere in this book, this service offers brief interventions to families. The model is informed by psychoanalytic theory and by the use of here-and-now countertransference in the sessions. The clinician draws on her own experience to make emotional contact with the family, contain its distress, and, through offering insight, facilitate shifts in the family dynamics.

The anxiety that prompted these three families to refer themselves to the Under Fives Service was their child's fear of being alone, especially, but not exclusively, before going to sleep at night. In one family, anxious clinging was used as a piece of communication, with the child trying to let her parents know about a temporary distress in her life. In another family the child's separation distress represented more serious developmental difficulties. Instead of being used as a temporary means of working over normal childhood issues, it was becoming established as part of a malfunctioning system and contributing to this system.

The three sets of parents who referred themselves to the service all had single children. Exploration revealed that precisely the same symptom was expressed in differing family contexts. What also differed drastically in the cases was the degree of hope for change held by each child. Where there was very little hope in the child, and little corresponding environmental reliability, the symptom began to act as a powerful independent force, drawing the family into a vortex of complications. I conclude that in a child under the age of 5 years, separation anxiety needs to be evaluated in relation to the family context and the degree of hopefulness that this enables the child to develop. At an optimal level, the child needs to feel that his family is sufficiently intact to contain his separation anxieties while he struggles to work through them.

Where a two-parent family is involved, the child's hope is that between them, the parents will offer a supportive framework for her emotional life. Obviously this unconscious hope is also part of a conflicted oedipal system that challenges the parents' strength as a couple. Childhood symptoms can indicate that the parental structure is under strain and that the child has become anxious about his basic security.

## *Mina*

Mina, an only child, was 3 years and 2 months old at the time of referral. Her parents, Mr and Mrs T, were concerned because Mina was afraid to go into her room alone, and refused to be left there at night to go to sleep, claiming that there was a roaring lion in her bedroom. Careful questioning by the parents failed to reveal where this notion had come from.

All this was reported to me in the first meeting, to which the whole family was invited. Yet Mr and Mrs T had chosen to come without Mina and were sitting opposite me, father in the armchair and mother on the couch, their demeanour and body language conveying a strong sense of estrangement from each other. They told me at once, and with guilty anxiety, that Mina's fears may be their fault. Their marriage was not a good one, and Mina was witnessing loud arguments between them. In fact, they were actively thinking of a divorce, and lawyers had been contacted. They explained that the trouble between them started only after Mina was born. Mr T was so besotted with her that he gave in to her every wish. Mrs T resented it, as she was left with Mina all day and so had to cope with the consequences. This argument between them escalated and soon brought to the surface other fundamental difficulties, revealing how much they felt like strangers to each other. At this point Mrs T looked at me and explained to me that they had come from very different cultures.

Mr T explained that he was Turkish and had come to England in his childhood. His background was poor and struggling, and he remembered having to help in his father's failing small business after school. He was the eldest of four, and was expected to do the most. When he was 13 his mother became ill with multiple sclerosis. The relationship between his mother and father deteriorated, and his father left home. Mr T became a young carer, the only one to live with his mother. From time to time he also helped in his father's still struggling business.

When he was 19 his father died suddenly, as did his mother, two months later. He had thought before of going into higher education, but now he was left very anxious. He decided to continue to run his father's small business and did so with the help of his third brother. They managed to turn the business round by doing much of what the father had been disinclined to do when he was running it. The business grew and expanded and they bought more outlets, finally selling all of them for a substantial profit. Mr T was now economically comfortable and had branched out into new business ventures. It was at this time that he met his wife. She was French and had come to England to learn English. She explained how her background differed from his. She was the first child of a comfortable Parisian couple and had one sister. They were brought up in luxury, but also with a lot of coldness. Her mother in particular was very critical and remote, and both of her parents had been fixated on social status.

I wondered about Mina's parents as a couple. I said it seemed to me that in spite of their differences, they had something common, in that they both brought needy aspects of themselves into their relationship. Mrs T agreed at once, and with tears in her eyes she told me that she fell in love with Mr T because he was so passionate and so capable of intimacy. She said she still wanted the marriage to work. She looked at me with a pleading expression. Mr T did not respond to this, and finally I remarked on his silence. He said coldly that there was no point to this. He no longer loved his wife. She was much too harsh with his daughter and spoiled the atmosphere at home. Why was it always he who had to carry the burden of everything?

Time was running out. I pointed this out and also suggested that if indeed they were contemplating a separation, we should give careful consideration to the aim of our sessions. I linked this suggestion to the "roaring" that they did in front of Mina when they rowed loudly in her presence. They agreed that it was understandable that she reacted with anxiety. They asked to bring her to the next session.

First session with Mina

When I picked them up, I found Mina on her mother's lap in the waiting room. I was struck by her good looks, with dark eyes and curly hair and very obviously resembling her father. Mrs T urged her to get off her lap in order to go to the room, and Mina grumbled incoherently and weepily. I said to her, "You must be Mina", and introduced myself.

In the room Mina immediately demanded to sit on mother's lap and put her thumb in her mouth, staring at me with a hostile expression. The parents began to talk. Father said that they had thought over what I had said and decided to make an effort to sort things out in relation to Mina. They also thought they might give the marriage another try. He seemed genuinely emotional, and I felt some surprise but did not say anything. Mother nodded agreement. Mina began to wriggle on mother's lap, and after a while mother put her on the floor. She stood uncertainly in the middle of the room. I pointed to the box and said that these were things for her to play with when she came here with her Mummy and Daddy. She turned her back to me with obvious hostility and seemed to want to get back onto mother's lap.

I said that Mina was not happy to be here in this room which she doesn't know with a lady whom she doesn't know. She half turned her face to me, and this time, she had a flirtatious smile. I smiled back, and she walked to the box and picked it up. With some difficulty she carried it to the couch where her father was sitting. As soon as she was close to him she tipped the box upside down and all the toys scattered noisily on the floor. Mother protested, "No, don't do that Mina, it is not nice, you will break the lady's toys." Mina looked defiantly at mother, then at father. Father said that there was no reason for mother to make such a fuss. Mother burst out angrily, "It is all very well for you. I am the one who is left alone with her all day and have to cope with the consequences of your spoiling." An argument ensued, in which mother accused father of taking too soft a line. Each parent maintained that their position was completely right. They were loud and uncompromising.

Mina began to cry. Mother said to father: "See what you have done?" Father said, "I didn't do this, you did, you started it." I began to talk but was immediately interrupted by the continuing row. I felt as though my words had been swept aside quite violently. A feeling of helplessness descended on me. Mother picked up the crying Mina and tried to settle her on her lap while still arguing.

I intervened with more deliberation, saying that perhaps they were showing me what it was like at home when they argued. And now I could witness how bitter their rows can be. Both parents calmed down for a bit and listened. Then father agreed with me. I added that something had sparked the fight in here. It seemed that when Mina tipped the box it made them nervous and they were not sure how to react, whether to scold her or not. There was a silence. Mina stopped crying and began to suck her thumb. She was looking at me. Father began to say that I was right, that he was confused about discipline. He did not trust himself and so often wanted to be guided by his wife, but he tended to feel that she was completely wrong, and she felt the same about him. She seemed to require so much harshness from him. And he looked at Mina and said, "She is so small and so vulnerable."

I wondered what it meant to the parents that Mina had tipped over a box of toys. Perhaps it was like spilling out all the family problems in my room. They were both listening, and mother nodded. I then said that this appeared to not only generate anxiety about what might be spilled out and how I would cope, it also raised discipline issues. I added that parents often learn ideas about discipline from their own parents. They had told me about their respective backgrounds. It seemed that there was a connection. When Mina had tipped the box, perhaps mother had in her mind her own background and how such an action would have been viewed within her family. Father was very preoccupied with the thought of Mina's vulnerability, and vulnerability had played a big part in his own life. He had himself been a vulnerable child, a young carer who had also witnessed vulnerability in his mother when she had become ill. They were thoughtful.

Then father said that he did not agree and did not see what his past had to do with anything. Mother felt differently. She felt I was right, and acknowledged that she felt she had a harsh voice inside telling her that her daughter needed to behave well the entire time. I pointed out that they had both drawn my attention to how the past only mattered if it was still present, inside their minds, like the critical voice that mother was describing and the great pity for Mina that father was describing.

Mina picked up the large baby-doll and asked me: "Where is the bed?" I noted that there was no toy bed for the doll. I also said that Mummy and Daddy had been telling me that Mina did not like to go to her bed at night. Perhaps she wanted to play a bed game and could show me things about bedtime? Mina looked dissatisfied, dropped the baby-doll, and went back to sit on her mother's lap. She was sucking her thumb again. Father then explained that each time they put her to bed at night she cried and mother had to stay with her in her room. She often did not fall asleep until eleven or twelve at night. This meant that she was exhausted in the daytime and weepy. I pointed out that it also did not leave them much of an evening together. They both nodded vigorously, and mother said that ideally Mina should go to sleep at seven and leave them a bit of an evening. She was speaking in lowered tones and was very watchful of Mina.

I said that they both seemed to agree on this but also seemed to feel guilty for wanting time together. Father said: "It is all our fault—if we didn't row so much, she would not be so disturbed." I questioned whether not wanting to go to sleep on time was a sign of being disturbed. Mother said lots of children probably did not want to go to bed when told. She felt mystified about how to persuade Mina. She felt her husband should be firm, and she claimed that, without this, *she* could not be firm. I pointed out that this did not appear to leave much space for both of them to discuss the problem together and then cooperate over a solution. They looked thoughtful.

I then pointed out that they seemed to be feeling very guilty about Mina, especially because they rowed in front of her. They seemed to be worried that they had already damaged her. Might this be a reason for their inability to put her to sleep at a reasonable time, and their inclination to give in to her every whim in the evenings? Both parents nodded and said that they would try to work out something before next time.

*Discussion*

The most worrying aspect of this session was the almost complete inability of the parents to hear one another, or anyone else, when arguing. The content of the arguments might be described as unremarkable. However, the parents obliterated each other when making their point, and I, too, felt obliterated when trying to enter the discussion. While arguing, Mrs T was trying to settle Mina on her lap in a way that was highly disturbing for the child. Mina's response to me was initially grumpy and hostile. I felt that she was rather moody and depressed, with a very avoidant attitude to a new object, as if reaching out to others was pointless. I would describe Mina as feeling relatively hopeless about the family situation and describe the parents as conveying a sense of hopelessness about their own relationship, in spite of their desire to try again.

This led me to wonder what Mina was using her anxious clinging to express. In the session she cried when the parental quarrel began, as if trying to stop the quarrel with her crying. Was she also using her separation anxiety at night to check the intact presence of both parents?

And yet there was a complex oedipal dimension to the situation, because Mina also used her symptom to separate the parents. Their own personalities complicated the situation. Father seemed angry about his background, in which his parents were experienced as needing support prematurely. He had been a "parentified" child who had taken the partner role with his mother when she became ill. I felt that resentment had simmered in him ever since, and while he was made to work too hard and grow too fast, he seemed to want his daughter to have the opposite, an ideal, protected childhood. He paired himself with his vulnerable-seeming daughter, projected a tough, demanding parent figure onto his wife, and hated her as such. Mina was exploiting this situation to gain his attention and so reinforce the split between the parents. But in parallel, she was also trying to influence the parents to stop quarrelling.

Subsequent sessions

*Looking for the bed: the work develops.* In our second meeting Mina seemed a lot more pleased to see me. She ran ahead of us to the room and began to inspect the toy box. She had abandoned her position on mother's knees and was playing actively. She played a game in which she undressed the baby-doll, sat her on the potty, and gave her a bath and a drink in preparation for bed-time. However, when it came to actually putting the doll to bed she seemed lost, asking again, "Where is the bed?" I noted again the absence of a toy bed.

The parents, meanwhile, reported that they had put her to bed early and that they had been firm; to their surprise, she had settled and was now going to sleep at seven, giving them more of an evening. They seemed happier together and were now sitting side by side on the couch. They were able to tell me much more about their backgrounds. Both parental grandparent couples had had very poor relationships, and mother and father had both witnessed a lot of arguing.

In the third session I provided Mina with a large toy cot, borrowed from a colleague. Mina reacted to this by trying to get into the cot herself and then realized that she was too big and abandoned the effort. I said to her that perhaps she was not sure at that moment who the toy bed was for, the dolly or Mina. However, she did not use the cot symbolically in her play. Again she undressed the doll, bathed her, put her on the potty, and then stood looking lost. She soon moved to play with other toys.

Two sessions after this I found to my dismay that my colleague's room was locked, and I could not get hold of the toy cot. I started the session with some trepidation, but, to my utter surprise, Mina emptied the toy box just as she had done in the first session, declared it to be a bed, and then climbed into it, sitting down and grinning. Moments later she got out, played at preparing the doll for bed, and put the doll to sleep in the box. After this she took the lion and crocodile and raced around the "bed" with them, making them roar. I suggested that the doll in the bed was like Mina in her room at night, and maybe she was having bad dreams about fighting and cross feelings.

At this point Mrs T reported how, the day before, when she had argued with Mr T in front of Mina, Mina turned around and said to her, "Mummy, don't fight." I took up how the lion and crocodile were like a Mummy and a Daddy fighting and making Mina very frightened and cross. I then wondered what the fight had been about. As usual, they had quarrelled about how to handle Mina. Father came home from work and asked Mina for a hug. She was absorbed in a game and did not respond. He was very offended and began to nag Mina in what mother perceived as quite an aggressive manner, telling Mina off about not being nice to him. Mother intervened and said "don't bully her" and a row ensued. I commented on how the roles were a bit reversed—this time it was father who was angry with Mina, and mother who was protecting her. Both of them expressed their confusion about how to communicate effectively with each other about their parenting of Mina. I pointed out that neither had a model in their minds of a couple communicating. This time, both agreed with me.

In the remaining sessions Mr and Mrs T reported greatly improved communication over Mina. Each listened to the other more, and they were able to weigh up pros and cons of behaviour. However, their overall relationship still felt shaky, and they were resolved to seek marital therapy. They also reported that Mina's symptom had subsided. She was now fine in her room alone and was able to go the sleep at a reasonable time.

*Discussion*

Hope and hopelessness were almost equally balanced in this family. The child was able to use a symptom to communicate distress over the parental situation, yet when she sensed the improvements of which her parents were capable, she was then able to relinquish her symptom. The parental rift had initially led Mina to try to break the parents' evening together, and she had succeeded. This in turn had heightened her anxiety about separating the parents and breaking the security of the home. She was left with aggression and fears of retaliation for her hostility and damaging behaviour. I assumed that this unresolved aggression invaded her dreams at night and made her fear being in her room alone. When this happened, she did not have a safe parental couple in her mind to which she could turn for help. Yet when the parents actually acted jointly to create a space for themselves, she responded. Some degree of hope had to be experienced before the terrified clinging could be relinquished.

Although it did not seem so at first, there was even more hope in the next case that I describe.

*Rajeev*

Rajeev was the 16-month-old only son of an Asian couple. He was still in nappies and had not begun to talk as yet, although he had recently started using single words and a range of sounds to make himself understood. Rajeev was referred because he screamed if put in his bedroom on his own. The health visitor thought that the mother, Mrs A, would benefit from counselling. Mrs A's other worry was that Rajeev had a phobia of people other than his parents touching him. He went rigid and screamed if anyone so much as approached him. Mother mentioned an incident when she was talking to a friend in the street and the friend addressed Rajeev with a friendly smile and leant over the buggy to greet him. Rajeev burst into screams and could not be consoled for hours. Rajeev was described as following Mum around the house and even to the toilet. Mrs A felt exhausted. I also gathered that father worked very long hours as a solicitor and was often not at home to support mother.

I learnt all this in the first meeting with the family. Mr and Mrs A were sitting on the couch opposite me, with Rajeev seated between them, looking apprehensively at me. I asked the parents when they first noticed his behaviour. They said that they could remember the moment well. Rajeev had initially been a very contented baby, a real delight. He fed and slept well and seemed to respond to others happily. He had been a planned baby and was conceived in the context of a good marital relationship. The marriage was an arranged one, but they fell in love almost as soon as they were introduced. All the grandparents were alive, and there was a positive relationship with all of them. However, Mrs A's parents were in her country of origin, and although she visited them, she missed them when in London. Mr A's father was described as a warm man but too old to help with Rajeev. Mr A's mother was much younger than his father. She was struggling to be helpful to the young couple but had never been very practical with children. Mr A and his two brothers had been brought up with the help of a nanny, and although his mother was not a remote type of person, the nanny had dealt with the practicalities.

A year earlier, when Rajeev was only 6 months old, Mrs A suddenly contracted a severe viral illness and needed to be hospitalized urgently. From one moment to the next she was taken to hospital, and Mr A urgently called his own mother to come and look after Rajeev. Grandmother agreed to come over at once. Yet when Mr A returned home from hospital that evening, he found Rajeev crying inconsolably and his grandmother looking quite lost. It turned out that when she tried to feed him from a bottle, she prepared it in the wrong way, not realizing that the teat was blocked and that Rajeev was sucking forcefully but getting no milk. Rajeev's fears seemed to start from that time. From being a contented baby he became fearful and cried each time he lost sight of his father. He transferred this behaviour to his mother when she returned from hospital two weeks later, and this developed into the kind of clinging that they now described to me.

As they were talking Rajeev looked at me intently. There were some toys on a small coffee table in front of the couch, and I pointed to them and said that he could play with them. He reached towards the little table and tried to lean forward to get hold of one. However, he was clearly too scared to do so, since it meant moving fractionally closer to me. I told the parents that I could see what they meant about his stranger anxiety. Rajeev continued to stretch out his arm towards the toys and began to grunt. Mr A picked up a handful of little wooden bricks from the table, which he put down on the couch beside Rajeev, who looked delighted. He took the bricks one by one and threw each on the floor, saying "*dow*" emphatically. I noticed that he swung his arm upwards before throwing each brick, as if about to hurl it forcibly. In fact, he then dropped his arm limply and let the brick drop onto the floor, saying "*dow*" in an incongruously enthusiastic way.

I said to Rajeev, "I think you are saying *down*, and showing me that the bricks are falling *down*." Rajeev looked at me mischievously and, half smiling, picked up another little brick and swung his arm dramatically upwards. This time when he lowered his arm and let go of the brick, I said *"down"* together with him. He was clearly enjoying this, and we repeated the game until all the bricks had been dropped. At one point I shifted in my chair and moved slightly forwards. Rajeev stopped his game at once and froze. I said Rajeev did not like me to come too near him. He did not appear to grasp what I said. I realized that while he was able to grasp single words (such as "down"), and probably also short phrases, fluent speech was still somewhat beyond him. Rajeev turned to his mother and said "Mamama" tearfully, and mother took him onto her lap. He looked at me anxiously. I said emphatically "Look, I am moving *back*," and I sat right back in my chair. He relaxed a little. I again said to the parents that I could now see what they meant about his fears. They seemed relieved. It was time to finish and we made another appointment.

*Discussion*

There was much that seemed optimal in the circumstances of this family, good relationships all round, a good marital bond, comfortable circumstances and a wanted baby who was initially contented. I did wonder at how uncomplaining the parents seemed. There was a faint echo of a complaint against a kind but remote and useless internal object, hinted at by the mention of the unpractical grandmother, the too-old grandfather, and the faraway maternal grandparents. Rajeev also betrayed anxiety about aggression when throwing the bricks. His intention, signalled by a dramatic swing of the arm upwards, was to hurl the brick with great aggression and signal real threat to me. However, the execution of each throw was very timid. I nevertheless felt that I was in the presence of a "good-enough" setting. The parents communicated with Rajeev in a warm and kind manner and were obviously fond of each other. I felt that they would have never consulted our service had their lives not been disrupted by a trauma that had upset the family equilibrium and brought to the surface great anxieties.

Talking about things that are "Gone"

In our next session only mother and Rajeev were able to attend. They sat together on the couch opposite me, and Rajeev immediately reached out for the bricks. Yet again he threw them and we said *"down"* together. I noticed that he became slightly more animated in his throwing. He stopped making large swinging gestures but threw the bricks more forcefully, shouting *"down"* excitedly in time with me. He grew increasingly boisterous in his throwing. I noted that Daddy was not with us today. Mother was telling me that Rajeev had been slightly better. Although he had been following her around the house as usual, when he lost sight of her he did not burst into tears quite so quickly, nor cry in such a broken-hearted way.

While we were talking, Rajeev had finished discarding the bricks and was now sitting looking perplexed. Suddenly he heard sounds coming from the direction of the window and looked intently at it. We all listened quietly. It was the sound of a car coming into the car park. I said, "Shall we go and see the car from the window?" Rajeev immediately began to get off the couch but then realized that he was closer to me and froze. He turned to mother tearfully. I suggested to Mrs A that she should take him to the window, and I told Rajeev that I would come too but would keep a long way away from him. Once again he did not seem to grasp my sentence fully until I showed him how I was keeping myself at a distance. Mrs A held Rajeev up at the window, and I stood further along the window ledge. At first Rajeev looked at me with trepidation, but then he gradually seemed more reassured and turned his attention to the car park outside.

Rajeev inspected the cars that were coming into the car park and looked at length at cars that were leaving, sometimes looking in their direction for a while after they had gone. I began to say *"Gone"* each time a car left the car park. After a while Rajeev joined me, and we said *"Gone"* together as we looked after departing cars. I then began to point to cars when they came into the car park, saying: *"Here it comes,"* and later when they left we said *"Gone"* together. The session drew to a close, and we made a further appointment.

On the third session father, mother, and Rajeev attended, the parents reporting more improvements. Rajeev now let mother leave the room without crying, although only for short periods. We went to the window again, and this time I suggested that Mr A might take Rajeev, as he had missed out on doing so in the previous session. Rajeev looked after disappearing cars and said *"Gone"* emphatically and with glee. Mr A looked mildly amused at first, but then he joined in with Rajeev saying *"Gone"* when cars left the car park. After a while Rajeev fidgeted to indicate that he wanted to be put down. Mr A lowered him to the floor, and Rajeev immediately clung forcibly to his father's knees. Father picked him up, and they sat down on the couch next to mother. Rajeev indicated that he wanted the bricks, which his father got for him again, and Rajeev threw them one by one on the floor as before, yet again saying *"Down"* excitedly. I noticed that his throwing was much more forceful. Mother related to me how he had been better, except for one occasion. On Tuesday mother had had a hospital appointment for herself. She got into the car, and father came out with Rajeev to wave goodbye. When mother waved, Rajeev again got into a panic and cried inconsolably.

Rajeev was looking at me with an alert expression. I said Mummy was telling me how he cried when she went away in her car. Rajeev continued to look at me slightly blankly. At this point I made a decision to accompany my verbal interpretation with a demonstration with the small toys. I took a toy car from the table and sat the mother-doll in it. I made the doll wave to Rajeev and said: *"Bye bye."* I then made the car "travel" and disappear behind my back, saying: *"Gone."* I said Mummy was telling me that when she was *gone* with her car, Rajeev cried. Rajeev looked at my demonstration in alarm, pushed his two middle fingers into his mouth, sucked anxiously, burst into tears, and demanded to go on mother's lap. I brought the mother-doll and the car back into view and said: *"Here she comes."* Rajeev settled for a bit, sighing tearfully. He looked very anxious. I held up a boy-doll, saying: "This is like Rajeev, and Rajeev is worried. He thinks that when Mummy was gone, something bad happened to her. Maybe she fell *down* like the little bricks and so would not come back any more." Rajeev sucked his fingers anxiously and continued to watch. We were getting towards the end of the session. Mrs A began to put Rajeev's coat on. To our surprise, he turned around and hit her. I said Rajeev was cross with Mummy, because she left him to go to hospital and he was so frightened when she was *gone*. We made a further appointment. When Rajeev left with his parents, he looked more relaxed than I had expected.

In our next session Rajeev picked up the toy car and mother doll from the little table. He gave them to his father and grunted urgently. His father looked puzzled, asking: "What is it Rajeev, what do you want?" I suggested that maybe Rajeev wanted me to go back to what we were doing last time. I repeated the mother-doll-in-the-car sequence, saying *"Gone"* when the car was behind my back. This time, Rajeev did not climb on mother's lap. Instead, while pushing his two middle fingers into his mouth, he reached out and grabbed his mother's breast and held it anxiously. Mrs A giggled gently, and Mr A laughed a little. I pointed out that they both recognized how the breast meant comfort to him, and they both nodded smiling. I made the toy car come back several times saying: *"Here it comes"* and *"Hello"*. Soon Rajeev joined me with a *"Gone"* each time the car disappeared behind my back.

I pointed out to the parents how scared Rajeev was of losing mother, as they could plainly see. Mr A responded by telling me much more about his own feelings during the time his wife had been in hospital. He had been in such disarray and had really feared that he would lose his wife. At this point there were tears in father's eyes, and Mrs A held his hand. She joined in and spoke about how helpless she had felt when in hospital, and how weak she had been when she came home. Mr A said that he worried and really struggled to help Rajeev. He was also sometimes angry about fate. I commented that maybe he was even angry at how helpless the women seemed, his wife who was ill and his mother who was not practical. After some hesitation, he agreed with me. I suggested that the mother's sudden illness had been a trauma for the whole family and had scared Rajeev. It had also, understandably, aroused some anger in all of them.

Mrs A admitted that she had been angry with everyone, especially when she came back from hospital and felt very weak. She kept wishing that people around her—her husband and mother-in-law—would respond to Rajeev in a less clumsy and more observant way. It was typical, for example, that her husband would keep Rajeev waiting for his bottle longer than she thought appropriate, and would talk to him while preparing it in a rather slow, clumsy way. Mother thought the talking was useless when a baby was hungry. We discussed the unique tie of mother and baby, and Mrs A said she wondered if it was possible for anyone to be as much in tune with Rajeev as she was. Mr A responded, defensively, that he did the best that he could. Mrs A continued that her husband's different way of responding to Rajeev when she was convalescing made her worry that he was damaging Rajeev through inappropriate interventions. It was frightening to see father not in tune with Rajeev when she was so weak and could do little herself.

Mother and father looked at each other in some surprise, and father said, in a hurt voice, "But I had no idea that you felt this way." I pointed out that maybe Mr A felt a little attacked right now. I wondered if Mrs A needed to blame him, but that somewhere in herself she was really blaming herself because she felt that it was as a result of her hospitalization that the problem had started. Mrs A was now tearful, but she nodded assent. She said she felt that deep down she had betrayed her child by becoming ill. Mr A held her hand.

In our fifth, and last, session all the family attended. Rajeev signalled a desire to go to the window. I asked "Will Rajeev come with me?" and to my surprise he agreed and allowed me to hold his hand. Later in the session, both parents told me that the problem had now subsided considerably. The clinging had decreased, but, most spectacularly, there no longer seemed to be a stranger phobia. Rajeev was happily approaching and touching other people and allowing them to approach him. We decided together that the counselling could be concluded.

*Discussion*

While this family had some difficulties, on the whole they presented a very hopeful environment for Rajeev. His good start in life also meant that he had some internal resources, a good early object relationship on which to draw. The trauma of the mother's hospitalization when he was only 6 months old led to the distress that created a set of alarming-seeming symptoms. However, the alarming appearance of his stranger anxiety was not an indication of severe, long-term pathology. In the course of our work, it became apparent how much it was used to communicate Rajeev's own alarm, and how the degree of fear that was communicated was in direct proportion to what the environment was willing to bear.

Rajeev's phantasies were readily expressed in the first session. He not only felt traumatically abandoned, but very angry. His game with the bricks indicated his phantasy desire to reverse what had happened to him. Instead of feeling dropped by the mother, he played at an aggressive throwing away of a maternal object. However, the degree of anger experienced by him led to anxiety about the omnipotent power of his throwing. He struggled to curb his anger, hence the limp kind of "throwing" that I witnessed at first. As Rajeev became more able to express aggression, he became better able to separate.

The parents had the capacity to provide a good environment, but this environment was shattered when the mother became ill. Her illness traumatized both parents, stirred their anger, and led each to want to blame the other. There was thus mutual anger and accusation—an unconscious parental row that deprived Rajeev of the safe environment that he had known in the first six months of his life.

## George

The situation of George was much more complicated and less hopeful. George was nearly 4 years old at the time of referral. He was afraid to be alone in his room altogether, claiming that he worried about "burglars". The symptom had started when he was 2, but the parents did not seek advice, hoping that it would pass. Over time George learnt to make less of a fuss at bedtime, but he found all sorts of manoeuvres and excuses to take him out of the bedroom and into his mother's company. Mother felt that he was hiding the extent of his panic at being alone. He usually fell asleep in the sitting room late each night when he had become totally exhausted, and he was then carried to his bedroom. Mrs S mentioned incidentally that there was another aspect of his behaviour that puzzled her. George said he did not want to be a boy but preferred to be what he called a "girl-boy". In the dressing-up corner in his nursery, he preferred to dress as a fairy or nurse, never as a policeman or superman. He spent more time with girls and talked about wanting to be a bride when he grew up and got married. He often sneaked into mother's bedroom in her absence to try on her clothes, and once he stole her skirt. I noticed that while reporting all this to me, mother looked extremely concerned about George's fear of being alone but only vaguely perturbed by George's desire to be a "girl-boy".

George and both his parents had come to the first meeting. The parents were sitting together on the couch while George seated himself in the child's chair next to the little table, busying himself with drawing. The parental couple had a rather contrasting appearance. Father, a man with a formal, reserved demeanour, avoided eye contact to an unusual degree and seemed very lacking in affect. Mother, who explained that it was with great difficulty that she had persuaded him to come, was emotional and rather loud. Both parents kept an almost invisible boundary between them, sitting next to each other in unrelaxed, guarded postures. George looked very like his mother.

In response to my enquiry, Mrs S explained that George was their only child. Before George was born, a daughter had died a cot death soon after birth. When telling me this, Mrs S became emotional and tearful, and Mr S shifted uncomfortably in his seat, looking around the room. I discovered that Mr S was a university academic and that mother was a housewife. She complained that her husband was a remote person who lived in a world of his own. She could not enlist him to help with the care of George. And George needed a firm hand because he was too rough. I asked what mother meant, and she explained that George was noisy around the house, used rude words at times, liked watching cartoons that had violence in them, and often asked for a toy gun. She worked hard to stop these tendencies. She felt that her husband should help, but he was absorbed in his academic work and spent most of his time on it, continuing his research at home. She did not want to allow rough play and toy guns. I referred to her earlier report that George wanted to be a "girl-boy" and wondered what she made of the rough play and desire for toy guns. She said that she did think these were boyish, but not the aspect of maleness that should be encouraged. She felt that everyone could be taught to be peaceful.

I asked George if he was listening to what we were talking about. George looked at me and said, "Yes, she is telling you that I want to be a girl-boy." He looked uncomfortable, turned away from me, and held up his drawing for all of us to see. He had drawn a large aeroplane that took up almost the entire page. He then addressed his father with a somewhat precious lisp: "Look, I've drawn a 747." I noted that George had just heard us talk about his wish to be a "girl-boy", but he had drawn a boy sort of picture, which he wanted his daddy to like. Mr S looked a little rigidly at the picture and commented that certain 747 features were missing from it. George looked crestfallen for an instant, but he quickly sat down, tilted the little chair precariously onto its hind legs, and began to swing back and forth on it.

I pointed out that father was interested in the outside of the aeroplane, but that George had also drawn an inside. The aeroplane was full of people, all looking out of the window, and three of them were smiling and waving. Maybe these three were like George and his parents, and George drew them looking happy to be in this place. Again Mr S shifted uncomfortably and surveyed the room. His eyes rested on some books on a shelf. He seemed to be trying to read the titles. I said it looked as though he wondered where I got such ideas from. He smiled dryly and made very brief eye contact with me.

George smiled at me, stood up, tilted his head shyly to one side, and with a slightly effeminate ballet twirl turned back to his chair and sat down with his picture. I said that it seemed that George was showing some pleasure at being here with his two parents. Mother said that George needed both of them, and there were tears in her eyes again. She looked at Mr S for a moment, as if checking something, and then proceeded to tell me that things were rather difficult between the two of them. She told me that Mr S did not spend all his time at home but went back to stay with his widowed mother outside London a great deal of the time.

Mr S responded formally, saying he meant to spend more time at home with her and George, but it was difficult. He did not elaborate on this and seemed devoid of feelings about it. Mrs S said that the situation had gone on for ten years. I commented that they had only now found themselves seeking help. Perhaps they only now felt that it was possible to think of changing things? Mrs S looked strangely at me and asked with some surprise what I meant by "changing". She seemed to have little notion that she could expect something different. Yet she clearly knew she did not like things as they were. She complained that Mr S spent about half a week with his mother and, furthermore, that his comings and goings were not predictable. When he was with them, he was, in any case, cut off a lot of the time. Mrs S now looked heated and agitated. I commented on how angry this seemed to make her. She denied that she was angry and said she thought I would agree that the situation was bad for George. Her husband responded that he did not see why that should be so. He added a little sardonically that no doubt I would attach importance to what his wife said, but he was not sure about my ideas, and, in any case, psychoanalytic ideas were not proven.

I said he seemed worried that I might attack him with psychoanalytic ideas, but maybe he really wanted me to take on board the realities of their predicament. Something made both of them unable to change a situation that apparently bothered them. I also wondered about the painful aspects of their parenthood—the cot death of their firstborn, and George's current fears. Mr S softened a little for the first time and said quietly, with his gaze lowered, that I "had a point."

Sometime during this exchange George began to scribble on his aeroplane drawing with a pencil, at first lightly, and then with increasing intensity, gnashing his teeth and grasping the pencil tightly with his fist. He proceeded systematically, and with some satisfaction, to scratch out the faces of the people in his picture, making holes on the page and leaving intact only a single face at the centre of the picture. Some pencil marks were transferred to the table, and Mrs S protested in obvious dismay, saying to me, "You see what I mean, he is so rough." Mr S looked at her but made no comment. George ignored her and then said with relish, in an artificial, high-pitched feminine voice, "Look, I've made holes."

I pointed out that the holes had scratched out all the people in the aeroplane except for one person. Perhaps George had been listening to what we were saying and now showed me how the happy family that he had drawn was not safe and happy any more. I also pointed out that one person was left alone in the picture in the middle of a lot of holes. Maybe this was how George felt when he was asked to be alone in his room at night. George again tilted his head shyly to one side. I said to him that he might have been worried by all the things he heard us talking about. Mrs S said impatiently, "Oh, he knows." I established that mother meant that she had often complained to George about his father's stays with his own mother. George stood up with some urgency and, interrupting our conversation, said loudly, "Yes, and he goes to his Mummy." I said that George now felt that he and his Mummy were angry together with Daddy and his Mummy, like a fight in the family. I spoke again about George's fear of being alone in his room. Maybe he sometimes felt full of angry feelings, and was afraid to be alone in his room with such feelings. And if the angry feelings got even worse, they made him want not just to be with his mummy, but also to become like her, a girl-boy with a hole in his body. Mrs S was listening to this, and she again became tearful. Mr S was very still and very attentive. George sighed a little and then announced that he was going to draw a new aeroplane on a new page, which he began to do.

Mrs S began to talk about her own background. Both her parents had died when she was 4 years old, and she was fostered long-term by a couple who had a permanently shifting population of short-term foster children. Mrs S disliked her foster-father in particular and said that he did things to her that should not be mentioned in front of George. She felt very "semi-detached" in her foster home, because her foster-mother was always busy with other children. I wondered if her experience of her foster-father made her worry about aggression and boyishness in George. Once more her eyes filled with tears. She said that she loved George greatly but always worried that he will end up disliking her or being angry with her. If that were to happen, she would feel devastated and completely alone in the world.

It was time to end. The couple agreed readily to come to further appointments, and I explained to George that we needed to meet again, because there was a lot to think about. I told him that I wanted to think not just about him and his worries, but also about his parents, because they too had worries, and I felt that he noticed this.

## Discussion

The situation in this family was too complicated for a brief counselling intervention alone. The parental couple found it very difficult to think, either together or apart, about ways to remedy their situation, and the nature of their contact was particularly complicated. I experienced Mr S as emotionally avoidant to the point of conveying an autistic quality. Mrs S seemed to be colluding with a difficult situation, repeating the abusive and "semi-detached" deprivation of her childhood. There was intense but hidden aggression between the couple, and, in addition, I did not feel that they had dealt sufficiently with the cot death of their first baby. While Mr S was too emotionally remote from George, Mrs S was rather swamping, burdening George with the sadness, anger, and neediness of her otherwise "semi-detached" life. There was a great deal of pressure on George to engage in an ideal, unaggressive relationship with his mother from which his father deliberately excluded himself. Separation and individuation under these conditions seemed an almost impossible task.

Although George was clearly pleased and grateful for the contact offered in our session, I felt that at a deeper level he did not hold out much hope for improvement in the family relationships. The parental inability to unite in caring for George had its roots in highly complicated factors and overwhelmed George's hope of protesting and being heard. His fear of separation was no longer a simple cry for help and betrayed self-destructive tendencies, seen in the relish with which he isolated himself in the midst of holes in his picture. I also wondered how Mrs S's need to stifle George's aggression played a part in his gender-identity issues. In the session I witnessed barely disguised aggression, seen in George's ignoring of his mother's plea to stop scribbling on his picture and his cynical, high-pitched caricaturing of female "holes".

George thus reacted to the stress between his parents with a hopelessness that became embedded in his identity, influencing his entire way of experiencing himself. Failing to reach his remote father or separate from his emotional mother, George aggressively scratched a hole in his being and, in phantasy, turned himself into a "girl-boy". With this gesture he also stole into his mother's identity, much as he stole her actual skirt. His fear of "burglars" in his room made sense as his phantasy fear of retaliation. George's distress was no longer in a communicable state—it took on a perverse quality, as if he had nothing left to do except turn on himself and his good objects and enjoy scratching out any sustaining relationship between them.

With such a situation it was clearly impossible to resolve difficulties in five or even ten sessions (as a second set of five sessions is often agreed upon with some families), and while the family did attend all the sessions that were offered and some relief was felt, further referrals became necessary.

## *Conclusion*

I have shown how, in three cases of separation anxiety, the permutations of the child's symptoms varied greatly and were closely related to the degree of hope experienced by the child. Rajeev showed an acute and painful separation anxiety because he sensed that his parents were able to tolerate it. In spite of their temporary difficulties, they had a strong bond, and Rajeev was thus able to sustain a hope that his expression of distress would be picked up. Unlike him, George stifled his fear of being alone in his room, struggled to hide his anxieties and aggression, and used stealth as a means of seeking proximity with his mother. But this kind of proximity provided no relief and containment for his distress. His mother noticed George's fear of being alone, but she had too many needs of her own to have the space to respond to him. George thus had little hope of his distress being picked up in a direct way by two communicating parents. Mina's situation was in between such two extremes. She had some hope that her parents could stop fighting, to the point that she even asked them to do so, and she partly used her anxious clinging in a provocative way, to obtain a united reaction from them.

A number of factors contribute to the child's capacity to retain a hopeful outlook in childhood. I have tried to show that one crucial factor is the reliability of the parents and the child's experience that his needs will be met in spite of frustrations. The child's trust partly grows from the level of tolerance and containment offered in the family, and this, in its turn, depends on the psychic structure provided by the bonded minds of the two parents. It is within the safety of this structure that the small child can begin to face many small doses of ordinary loss. She can thus build up the confidence to endure more extended separations and, while doing so, retain the hopeful conviction that she has not been abandoned.

CHAPTER 14

# Sleeping and feeding problems: attunement and daring to be different

*Dilys Daws*

*Attunement and autonomy*

In psychotherapy we work with emotions, our patients' and our own; this is most evident when we work with parents and infants. The first duty of parents of very young babies is to attend to their physical needs—to keep their baby alive. This requires knowledge, skill, instinct, and emotionality. As therapists, we may ask, how do new parents feel about this awesome task? How do they feel about their tiny helpless baby? Where do emotions connect with instincts? How do love and hate fit in to this life-and-death reality? Are parents developing the love and secure attachment that can grow from the proximity necessary in feeding a baby and keeping it safe? Or are the cues of infantile needs triggering hostility to their baby from parents who feel unable to meet his needs (Fraiberg, 1980)?

Our ability to work with parents and infants is drawn from our own experience, which, remembered or not, may lead us to empathize with the situations of others. But human experience is somatic as well as emotional. You could say that emotions are bodily reactions, which are at core an appraisal of self and environment. In parent–infant work, bodily realities are everywhere. Babies are fed in front of the clinician; their nappies are changed in the room. These basic bodily functions and the emotions that accompany them are experienced directly between the baby and his parents. The therapist who witnesses their activity may be the recipient of transference communications from the parents, but mainly she is in the privileged position of observing behaviour and emotion; she also observes the parents' perceptions of their baby, influenced by their own past experiences—in other words, their transferences onto their baby.

It is obvious that babies need the physical mediation of another person to satisfy their hunger or to deal with other physical states. As Stern says: "others regulate the infant's experiences of somatic state . . . namely, the gratification of hunger and the shift from wakeful fatigue to sleep. In all such regulations, a dramatic shift in neuropsychological state is involved" (Stern, 1985, p. 103).

Parents use their emotions to attune appropriately to their newborn baby and his need to be looked after. Stern (1985) has described the importance to intersubjective human understanding of "affect attunement". Parents attune to their baby by "the performance of behaviours that express the quality of feeling of a shared affect state without imitating the exact behavioural expression of an inner state" (p. 142). By showing their baby they know how he feels, they add a dimension to the excitement of ordinary interchanges such as bathing, feeding, playing little games with him, and so on. First, they imitate the baby, and then they add a different mode of behaviour—for instance, if a baby is beating time with his hand on a toy, the parent may join in by singing to this beat, or by moving her own body in time to the baby's singing sound.

This feeling, of being in touch with each other's emotional state, plays a major part in allowing the baby to feel safe enough to "let go" into sleep. We as therapists are also using our ability to attune to the families we see. We need to be in touch with their state of mind before we can think about how to change it. By knowing their emotional state and then daring to be different, we help parents to have the courage to recognize that their infant's state of mind may not be the same as theirs.

## *Sleeping and feeding problems*

In thinking about both sleeping and feeding problems we must think developmentally, as well as noticing the emotions that pass between parents and babies. Babies' feeding and sleeping patterns are an aspect of their own temperament and personality, but they develop within the relationship with their parents, and the setting up of a sleep–wake and feeding rhythm is influenced by the interaction between parent and baby. Achieving this rhythm and pattern is the main preoccupation for mothers and babies in the early weeks. It is the process through which they get to know each other and through which the baby gradually achieves autonomy. The negotiating of this, as much as its achievement, influences future relationships.

New-born babies at first sleep much of the time and wake mainly for feeding. Often, they fall asleep at the breast so that neither the end of a feed nor the going into sleep is experienced as a separation from the mother. If this continues after the first few weeks, then the baby actually misses out on what could be thought of as an emotionally maturing piece of experience: of at least sometimes digesting a feed while awake and away from his mother's arms, or of going to sleep without the help of the mother.

As clinicians, we listen out for how these processes have or have not happened—what is noticeable, by its appearance or by its absence. If a baby always goes to sleep while being held by a parent, then if he wakes later on, alone in his cot, he may feel that only the parent can help him back to sleep. Or if going to sleep is associated only with breastfeeding, he may demand a breastfeed to help him deal with each arousal. Weaning can then feel like a desperate problem, involving the loss for a mother and baby of their known way of the baby getting to sleep. The difficulties may also apply when the baby is bottle-fed, though the fact that fathers or others can also give the baby a bottle may disperse some of the problems experienced by the exclusive mother-and-baby couple.

Playing at the breast, during or after a feed, may also connect with good sleeping. This leads us to think about the need for mothers and babies to play with *ideas* about their relationship in order to enjoy and manage feeding, transitions, and separations, including "letting go" into sleep.

One problem for a mother in getting a baby to sleep is the basic act of putting the baby down—that is, of separating herself from her baby and the baby from her. There are two important issues here. First, all babies need closeness and intimacy with their parents to develop both a sense of themselves as individuals and in relation to other people. Second, all babies need at appropriate moments to take steps away from their parents, both literally and metaphorically, in order to begin to grow. However, these stages of development may themselves be the cause of sleep problems. A baby who is learning to crawl or to walk may be so gripped by the excitement of his new achievements that he is unable to "let go" sufficiently to relax into sleep. The separation that his mobility implies may also lead to feelings of insecurity. If he walks away from his mother, will she still be there when he turns to come back? Some parents may themselves feel excluded as the baby starts to discover objects and places in the home, and they may feel bound to stop exploration rather than teach the baby how to safely climb the stairs. Difficulties in weaning may also highlight unresolved problems in the feeding relationship, and success in weaning can correlate with ability to sleep.

These steps of development coincide naturally with many mothers' feelings about being ready, or indeed having, to return to work. A baby's distress at this change may cause wakefulness, or there may simply be a need for the mother and baby to spend waking time together in order to make up for the unaccustomed time apart.

## Working therapeutically with families

For many years I worked in the Under Fives Service at the Tavistock Clinic as well as doing "outreach" work at the baby clinic of the James Wigg GP Practice, which I still continue to do. I found that many of the referrals were for sleep problems and that many of these could be "cured" in the first one or two sessions, though the work might need to be consolidated over a few more weeks. This led me to look at the process within the family and to write about it. My work in the baby clinic also includes consultation with the GPs and health visitors where I try to attune to their dilemmas in dealing with the innumerable problems of young families and their attempts to assess the seriousness of these. I hope to help the professionals in turn to attune to parents and infants so that the emotional essence of problems can be communicated. Doctors and health visitors then often find that when active offering of solutions is replaced by reflective listening, parents are relieved at feeling understood and may find their own solution (Daws, 2005).

Exploring the reasons for a baby's sleep disturbance often leads the therapist to a human drama that is going on in the family, sometimes a re-enactment of patterns going back to the parents' own experience in their childhood. Repeatedly, this involves dealing with and surviving separations (Daws, 1989, p. 56).

I use much the same clinical method when working with sleep problems as I would for any other presenting symptom. That is, I take the nature of the problem itself seriously. The effects of sleepless nights are likely to leave the family exhausted, distressed, and angry.

I start by letting parents talk to me in their own way, so that I get the particular flavour of what they consider to be the problem and its origin and their predominant emotion. I think of the emotion the parents convey in these first few moments—be it anger, anxiety, or responsible concern—as similar to the one the baby is finding directed towards him during his sleepless nights. I then explain that I would like to ask about the baby and the family in general, so that we can discover what links there may be. Once I have started to ask questions I am, perhaps, felt to be looking after them, and the emotional intensity often subsides. One mother said to me appreciatively, "You don't just say 'um' and you don't tell me what to do."

My questions are directed towards three different areas. I start by asking for details of the baby's timetable. I ask what happens during the day and the night, and a vivid picture builds up in my mind of what happens in this family, and also of their assumptions of what should happen. My mental picture involves the physical placing of where the baby sleeps as well as the permutations of who sleeps with whom and where. I am interested in the minutiae of detail of parent/infant lives—standing back to see from the outside and yet fascinated by the practicalities and symbolic importance of bottles, spoons, cots, and beds. These details themselves can begin to clarify a confused situation as the parents both inform me and think about the logical connections of what they are telling me.

Second, I make a free-ranging enquiry into memories of the pregnancy, birth, and early weeks. I tell parents that I need to know the baby's life-story to make sense of what is happening now.

Finally, I ask about the parents' relationship with each other and with their own family of origin, so that we can see the bigger picture of which this particular baby is a part.

The parents I see have usually been offered much advice already and often tell me they have "tried everything". However, because I do not at once offer solutions, they are less likely to react negatively to my enquiries. They are able to free associate: *unconscious threads* draw together and connections emerge as their minds move freely from one related theme to another. They may perceive me as interested, receptive, and capable of holding on to a great deal of information—and, in fact, it is striking how they can convey economically much focused information. It seems as though all ordinary parents have a story to tell about their baby, as dramatic and moving as any work of literature.

The unfolding of this story is a major part of the work, and this first session is the key to it. Jumbled, incoherent thoughts come together as I listen to this story. Palombo (1978) pointed out that one of the functions of dreaming is to assimilate the events of the day into settled long-term memory. The parents of sleepless babies that I see have lost much of their time for dreaming. I often feel that my consultations allow parents to assimilate their jumbled thoughts and make sense of them.

Themes emerge about the nature of their relationships. The meaning of not sleeping may change with the age of the child, but underlying it seems always to be some aspect of the problem of separation and individuation between mother and baby—in other words, the nature of attachments. Feeding and weaning problems are closely related. Bereavements, marital conflict, difficult births, and psychosomatic tendencies can all link with sleep problems. Ambivalent feelings are a crucial factor in all this. Making these links enables parents to separate their experience from that of their infants and frees them to solve the problem themselves.

When a family is able to discuss such issues, allowing me as the outsider to have some new ideas of what might be helpful, it shows they are ready for a change. For instance, I may approach the thought of a "transitional object" (Winnicott, 1971) by asking if the baby has a teddy bear. I may be told that he has several cuddly toys, but when I suggest that *one* significant toy could be important, parents may be able to create a shared idea with the baby that a particular toy has a job to do. Often, of course, blankets, dummies, or the baby's own thumb may become the source of satisfaction that allows separations from the mother, at the same time as providing a link or memory. If the therapist's attunement to the stuckness involved in the original problem can also encompass an idea that change is possible, then the parents' own belief in the possibility of change between them and their baby may be liberated. Thus it is essential that the therapist does not have a rigid agenda of how the family should change but can, rather, share with the family a "transitional space" where thoughts of a new satisfaction of sucked thumbs or cuddled teddies are mutually enjoyed by all in the room.

This highlights why it is necessary for the baby to be in the room. Babies are often in tune with the emotional atmosphere, and there may be a remarkable connection between what parents talk about and small babies' actions and vocalizations. For example, the fact that some babies cry excessively may connect with some inconsolable experience in the parent's own history. When the parent is able to talk about this with the therapist, he or she may then be able to console the baby (Hopkins, 1994). The parent's reaction to a baby crying in the session may in itself be useful material for the work. Some mothers or fathers may want to take the baby out for a walk in the corridor as an attempt to get away from painful issues stirred up in the room. Persuading parents to stay in the room with their crying baby can sometimes enable them to share difficult feelings with each other for the first time. The same may be true of a mother's attempt to try to soothe her baby silently. As one mother said, on having this pointed out to her, "If I did say anything to him, it would be too horrible." The opportunity to put her "horrible" thoughts about the baby into words to the therapist came as a release. Once such thoughts are spoken out loud, they may become more bearable. Equally important is the impact of the mother's ambivalence towards the baby and of unacknowledged feelings.

A therapist who is able to be non-judgemental, attuning to a wide range of emotions, can allow parents to own their hostile feelings towards the baby. In this case, the mother was able to have a different feeling towards her baby and to hold him close to her and put into words what *he* might be experiencing. Having had her own feelings understood, she was no longer preoccupied with the force of them. The baby sensed this difference and was able to be comforted by her.

As with sleep, feeding problems often have a relationship context. They fall into two main categories—"too much" or "too little". When babies are feeding too often, I get a distressed account of how exhausted the mother, and sometimes the father also, feels about unremitting feeding. I then ask the parents about the how feeding—breast or bottle—was established. I ask about their own parenting, particularly what they know about their own early feeding.

As I listen to this reported story, I also think about how it is communicated. I think of the parents' attitude to me as a transference of aspects of the problem. How they expect me to behave towards them may be based on aspects of how their parents actually treated them in their childhood, or misreadings of this. Some mothers and fathers seem to experience me as an ideal mother figure who will understand them, listen to them, and attend to their needs. They may also try to extend the work with me—for example, moving into my room as though to spend an enjoyable hour basking in my attention. They enjoy me pointing out the family dynamics—but they do not intend to change! These are the parents who find weaning difficult. Others are irritated by me or feel that I am critical of them: everything I say is experienced as not quite right, as badly timed. They may break off the work at a time that seems unexpected to me. I wonder about mistiming between them and the baby.

Of course, in all these cases, pointing out their use of me may help parents think about the dynamic situation with their baby or, indeed, what they expect from other important figures and aspects of their lives. Often parents come describing complex fraught feeding situations and may calm down simply by being listened to and taken seriously. They may tell their confused story as though expecting either an equally confused reaction or the opposite, a very directive organizing reaction. If they get neither, some will be disappointed and quickly go away; others will start to feel held by a steady thoughtfulness and will start to think for themselves.

This style of therapeutic work can also be carried out by health visitors. Helen Stamp, a health visitor who undertook the three-year PG Diploma MA in Infant Mental Health at the Tavistock Clinic, described a case where she helped a mother who had difficulties in getting breastfeeding going, and there appeared not to be enough milk. Helen described the transference relationship between herself and the mother, who "seemed to approach me with intense feelings of need but little hope of them being met". After work in which the mother began to trust Helen, she told her of her traumatic experiences with her own mother. Helen then comments, "I hoped that having opened up a little more to me, having let her story out, she might be more able to let the milk flow too." We see how naturally this body–mind connection is made by Helen. The imagery is compelling. In fact, this work did continue to "flow" and the breastfeeding became much easier.

When babies are being fed constantly, whether by breast or bottle, it does often seem that there is a separation problem (Daws, 1989). Parents and babies are able to be close to each other, but they cannot manage to pull apart. As with some sleep difficulties, it is common to find significant losses in one or other of the parents' lives.

Helping parents to work out the connections between their own experience and their perception of their babies' needs can be useful. Parents' ability to work in partnership is particularly relevant here. Sometimes a mother, enmeshed with her baby, is excluding the father's contribution to the relationship. As well as his direct relationship with the baby, a father can support the mother as she gets to know the baby (Barrows, 2004). He can then help mother and baby become more separate, opening up the value of three-person relationships and the excitement beyond the mother–baby duo. However, when mother and baby are stuck too closely together, this may be dismissed by the mother as "male insensitivity".

As well as thinking about what goes on *between* parents and baby, it is essential to try to understand what goes on *inside* each of them. Early feeding is about the reality of life and death; it is also about *emotions* that have the force of life and death. Mothers have to face the impact of a baby's fears and greed. Infantile emotions of their own will be stirred up by this, and they may feel unable to respond appropriately to the baby's need for feeding. A worker trying to attune to all this will equally be assailed by emotions coming from both baby and mother, ranging from voracious greed to an inability to take in what is offered. Empathy with parents can leave one either drained and exhausted or exhilarated, as though with unlimited resources. Or parents may seem to leave the worry to the professionals, who can feel they are being experienced as critical and persecuting when they express concern about the baby's progress or lack of it. There may be disputes over the actual measurements of the baby's gain or loss of weight, and professionals may argue among themselves about the interpretation of centile growth charts. A vicious circle may develop of the parents feeling empty of any source of good feeding inside themselves and passing on the helplessness to professionals. Any of these feelings need reflecting on, as they may be a key to what either mother or baby feel they have, or what they feel they lack.

This means that the careful listening to and observing of the family must be accompanied by similar listening to one's own countertransference. The information from this may lead to sympathy and getting in tune with a family, and also antipathy to behaviour that is cruel and neglectful. The therapist must be able to stand not being in tune with aspects of behaviour even while understanding how these may have come about. This may help the parents not to split off their own judgement of their behaviour, and not to get professionals to have the only sense of what is a right way to treat a baby.

## Clinical work with sleeping and feeding problems

Six-month old Penny, whom I saw at the baby clinic with her mother, needed feeding on and off throughout the day, and through the night. She could not take solid foods and was solely dependent on the breast. In our first meeting I talked with her mother about how weaning could seem like an unbearable loss: as though comfort—perhaps for both mother and baby—could only come from intimate breastfeeding.

After a week of reflection, mother had said to herself, "Why don't you *let* her go to sleep, rather than *put* her to sleep?" As we talked, Penny woke up. Mother picked her up, and in order to prove to me the progress the week had brought, did not immediately start to feed Penny. I was able to see for myself how painful it was for this mother and baby not to have their instant reunion at the breast. How could they be together and, at the same time, separate? Mother told me that she had begun to wear nightclothes so as not to stimulate Penny with her naked breasts when she picked her up in the night. She felt this was a large factor in helping them both cut down the night feeds. Penny fussed, and mother said: "You're sleepy, go to sleep by yourself." She handed her teething rings, which Penny first pushed away and then took hold of. She cried fussily again. Mother noticed that she had been holding Penny close and in the position for breastfeeding and remarked that this was unfair to her. She put her back in the pram. Penny kept up a low wailing sound, and mother tried to ignore it. I suggested, perhaps fancifully, that the noise was Penny's way of keeping a connection going between herself and mother with her mouth and voice, keeping the link to replace her mouth on mother's nipple. Right or not, my comment helped mother listen to the noise for a while without feeling obliged to feed Penny. As we talked she began to include Penny in the conversation and to think about the meaning of her sounds. She talked to Penny, who stopped wailing and held out the teething ring to her. Mother smiled as she took it and handed it back to Penny, who made little noises as they played the game of to and fro. Babies' speech, or pre-speech, often develops fast after weaning. Their ability to play all sorts of to-and-fro games increases. Their interest in communicating at a bit of a distance is liberated. Perhaps my interest in what was new between Penny and mother helped mother to attune to what her baby was now ready for.

When babies are fed "too little" this is, of course, a much more serious problem. Failure-to-thrive infants are one example where there is a danger that persecuted-feeling parents leave the worry about the infant to professionals, with serious consequences. Here again, transference and countertransference issues are multiple and complex. Often it does seem that there has been a real experience of neglect, deprivation, and hunger in the parents' own lives. Depression in the mother can derive from this and can make her feel she has no resources to give her baby. Therapeutic work has to be able to take account of the seriousness of the negative feelings towards the self, towards the baby, and towards any helping professional (Daws, 1997).

The therapist must judge, consciously or otherwise, to whom to attune at any moment. She may at times feel attuned to both parent and baby. At other times, there is real discordance. I was working with a depressed mother who cried as she talked. Looking at her, with a sympathetic expression, I then found myself looking at her baby who was sitting playing on the floor. He caught my gaze and smiled at me broadly. I smiled in return. He was perhaps grateful for an adult who was not crying; he was probably also showing the means he may often have had to use, a smile to cheer up his depressed mother. In any case, I smiled back at him, then looked up again at his mother and was terribly conscious of my incongruent expression, feeling I had to "wipe the smile off my face". It was a very useful lesson for me of the dilemma for babies of depressed mothers—if their mothers cry, will they make things better or worse by smiling?

Tronick (1989) talks about "the normal, often occurring, miscoordinated interactive state as an interactive error, and the transition from this miscoordinated state to a coordinated state as an interactive repair" (p. 116). He is writing about interactions between parents and infants, but it may equally hold good in thinking about the therapist's attempts to interact with patients. For example, two embattled parents came to me with their sleepless baby. The mother told me that babies need firm boundaries. The father then told me that babies need to be responded to when they cry. A vista of boredom washed over me as I contemplated unpicking each of their assumptions. With spontaneous impatience I said: "I think you're both right." The parents seemed delighted and relieved. It was as though I had managed to contain their hostility and their conflicting opinions. They were then obliged to discourse with each other, not just indirectly through me, and this led to our being able to talk about their own family experiences, where they often felt put in the wrong, and how this had led to their current beliefs about their baby.

Was my quip an enactment, a failure of attunement, or was it perhaps an ability to attune to the complexity of the situation? Both these parents were, as I have suggested, used to being told, "You're wrong," not just by each other in the present but, as I discovered, by their unattuned parents in the past. Also, as we know, parents of crying babies often feel blamed by the baby. So, my charming but rather sarcastic throwaway line may have had its use.

Another family I saw had an English father and a Chinese mother. Their ideas about child-rearing also seemed irreconcilable—until I noticed how comfortably they sat in the room with each other and how, despite their anger, both responded to their children. As the mother poured out her despair about "laid-back English attitudes", I said, "You seem to be a one-woman campaign for Chinese discipline in North London!" Not a very subtle remark, but both parents laughed. When we met again the following week, the mother told me that she had felt listened to properly by father for the first time and that they had been able to talk together. This empathy with both sides of irreconcilable feelings is an art. Sometimes I think, "Why do I have to listen to this?" as hatred spills out around me. At other times, I feel fortunate to be part of a living drama where I have helped emotions to be painfully expressed to some useful end. Whatever you are feeling, you have to not mind and not try too hard to understand or change the situation.

Humour must, of course, not be self-indulgence and must be used as a result of attunement, not as a substitute for it. Baker (1993) quotes Freud (1927d, p. 166) as saying that "Humour is the highest expression of the adaptive mechanisms because it succeeds in restraining the compulsion to make a choice between suffering and denial." Baker regards humour as "an expression of the merging of optimism with pain, seriousness with amusement, uncertainty with the promise of fulfilment". Such qualities, he believes, are not only among those required in a psychoanalyst but, in fact, "suggest a mother–baby relationship of excellent quality" (Baker, 1993, p. 955). Of course, the therapist must attune to the pain before optimism is appropriate (p. 955). Baker also quotes Reik as "the first to draw attention to the psychological significance of surprise in wit" (Baker, 1993, p. 325) and to the importance of surprise as a feature of the most important insights in psychoanalytic treatments.

This takes us back to Stern and his original research on mothers' different ways of making attunements to their babies in order to effect "interpersonal communion" with them (Stern, 1985). He says that as well as "communing attunements" (p. 148) where, in playing, the mother tries to match the baby's internal state—"being with" the baby—there are also misattunements. These include "purposeful misattunements" where the mother, having "slipped inside" of the baby's state, then deliberately misexpresses it, enough to alter the baby's level of activity or affect, but not enough to break the sense of an attunement in process. At best, humorous remarks may have this impact. If mistakenly made, however, they fall into Stern's other category of "true misattunements".

Too much attunement can do families a disservice. Schlesinger (1994) points out that in conversation we often listen "too closely" and lapse into identification with the speaker (quoted in Sternberg, 2005). When listening socially, we assume the speaker means to make sense and we fill in the elisions and ignore pauses. But this, Schlesinger says, is useless in analysis. I similarly find that in observing parent–infant interactions, instead of noticing what is missing, I may fill in the gaps in my own mind and, in a sense, destroy the evidence of what is absent.

## A case example

In one case, sleeping and feeding issues both came up, although they were not the reason for the referral. Separation and individuation became one focus of the work. What also emerged was the need for me as the therapist both to attune to the mother's beliefs about her baby and to have a separate, questioning line of thought.

A mother and her 11-month-old boy, Levi, were referred by their GP after an incident when they were trapped in a lift. No one was hurt, but mother and baby were badly shaken. Levi was sleeping badly; he had screaming fits during the day and screamed out in his sleep.

In our first meeting, mother sat down, took Levi out of the pushchair, and put him on her knee. She started talking to me immediately about her fears that there was something wrong with Levi following the lift incident. Levi was wearing a cotton hat, which shielded his face. I started to try to make contact with him, and he looked warily at a rattle that I shook. His mother relaxed as I listened to her, and, as she began to talk more *with* me than *at* me, Levi took the rattle from me. Mother put him down on the floor, and he stood near her, leaning against the low table, playing with the toy bricks, throwing them on the floor, and then putting one inside the box, and emptying it out repeatedly. He was skilled in doing these movements. At one point I put a brick on top of the others and asked Levi if he could do that. Mother said he couldn't. I agreed (mistakenly!) that he was too young. I commented on how good he was at throwing them, and we laughed.

In this relaxed atmosphere I asked mother to tell me about the lift incident. She told me of the feelings of being trapped, of the sudden jolt when the lift stopped, flinging them to the floor, and the worry of when they would be rescued. Since then she had worried about herself, with shoulder pains and headaches, and about Levi who had been crying a lot. I asked if she had dreamt about it all, and she said not.

As both had been checked out physically, I suggested that the effects of the incident were emotional and psychological but just as real.

I asked her to tell me about the family, and she told me that she was a single parent, as father now worked abroad. Both parents are black, their families originally from African countries. Mother had had a difficult relationship with her own mother—she felt she wasn't there to help her when she needed it. Her father had been violent and left the family. We talked about mother's worry that she couldn't protect Levi from danger—the shock of the incident had led her to feel powerless to comfort him when he showed anxiety in the night. I connected this with her feeling of not being protected by her own parents.

This was very usual "post-traumatic" work. But unexpectedly it led on to thinking about separation issues. I discovered that, since the event, Levi barely ate solid foods. He was still being breastfed, and this was almost his only sustenance. He was also talking less. This was easily explained as regression, but it also fitted in with mother's view that Levi needed her and that any steps towards weaning would be a deprivation for him. Levi was also sleeping in her bed.

I perceived Levi as a sturdy 11-month-old, steady on his feet and exploring my toys. Mother was an intelligent woman with a sense of humour, in spite of her current distress. When I suggested that she was *depriving* Levi of the chance to grow up and be separate from her, that by keeping him tied to her she might be holding him back from many other life experiences, she was startled but amused. However she disagreed with me, saying that she believed the closeness with her would, in fact, give him the security from which to make other relationships.

I asked if Levi fed himself, and she said, "He makes too much mess." I suggested letting him have a spoon to hold while she feeds him from another one, to help his sense of agency. I pointed out that Levi had brought a spoon with him from home (a large one!) and that it must be important to him. Moving on, I asked mother when she thought he should be in his own bed. She said 3 years old, then, perhaps intimidated by me, changed it to 1 year old (I must add that I do not have views about when a baby "should" be in his own bed). She was planning to stop breastfeeding then. Levi's first birthday was in a couple of weeks' time. I said it was difficult to be a single mother—no one to do some "fathering" and help them become more separate.

The next appointment was a few weeks later, a couple of weeks after Levi's first birthday, after the summer holidays. Mother and Levi came in smiling. Mother said Levi had stopped screaming except for one night last week. Levi got into the toys quickly and initiated games with me—handing bricks back and forwards to me—putting toys in and out of the box. I said how well he was standing and developing generally.

We talked about Levi's feeding—he was now eating finger-food. Following one of the themes of the work, I asked if he was now using a spoon, and mother again said he made too much mess. I commented on her not letting him try, and again I suggested they could each have a spoon to hold. She told me how good it had been over the summer—there were no pressures. I suggested that that included not having me nagging her! However, she went on to say that everything had been closed, and it emerged that she and Levi had barely been out. I said it sounded as though she had been depressed and had felt abandoned by me and everyone else.

Mother told me of some voluntary work she had started, where colleagues had not consulted her about an important decision. She had felt angry and had decided to give up the work. She will stay at home with Levi and be a good full-time mother until he is 5 years old. I said she wanted to stay at home with Levi and not go out and see difficult people. She good-humouredly laughed, and we discussed the human need to have contact with other people, including having disagreements. We talked about how dangerous it could be for Levi if they spent all their time together and if he had to be in agreement with her.

These issues of separation continued as the focus of our next meeting—she had made great strides in getting herself back into the outside world and had been accepted onto a part-time training course. She agreed with me about the controlling aspect of not letting Levi hold the spoon himself. She resolved to let him try, and I arranged to phone her the next week to see if she had done it. She told me she had. It seemed that this spoon had real symbolic significance for both mother and Levi (and me) as the key to agency and power!

When mother complained about the "mess" when Levi used a spoon himself, she was confirming Alan Stein's findings (Stein, Woolley, Cooper, & Fairbairn, 1994) that mothers with eating disorders are likely to show conflict with their infants during mealtimes, especially about mess, and about who holds the spoon. Mother herself had been depressed and had stopped eating when as a child she was sent to boarding school. With the emphasis on Levi at that point in the work, it seemed intrusive to discuss with mother whether she had an eating disorder in the present.

The infant's relationship with the spoon is particularly interesting (Daws, 1997). The spoon is the baby's first *tool*, and depriving him of the use of it takes away his sense of agency. The baby using the spoon himself is then a major step towards self-sufficiency. Many mothers who have enjoyed intimate breast- or bottle-feeding of an infant and, following this, have enjoyed getting into the rhythm of turn-taking in spoonfeeding, feel rejected or redundant as their growing baby becomes able to feed himself. Negotiating this new relationship is the first example of many, and it is echoed through childhood and adolescence.

After a troubled start, Levi enjoyed being in a nursery, while mother started her training course. In a way, I fulfilled in our conversations, perhaps even from our first meeting, some of the function of a missing father. As the work progressed, mother allowed her son to become a bit more separate from her, and she began to look for ways to get back into part-time work so that her own intelligence and energy could have a focus outside the mother–child duo.

This was an interesting case, as the referral was to help mother and Levi overcome the stress from the traumatic accident they had experienced. This led on to issues of separation centred primarily on feeding and sleeping that were brought up as problems by me in the first place. Mother had not seen anything untoward in her relationship with Levi but was open to looking at the ideas I introduced to her. In the meetings we had together, I think she was reassured by my interest in her and her son's problems and my genuine confirmation of how well Levi was developing. With the estrangement from her mother she had missed out on a grandmotherly "blessing" on herself as a mother. A therapist may "stand in" at times in the transference for a variety of missing (or present) family members.

She was then able to let me challenge some of her assumptions and I think enjoy the conflict of ideas between us. The separateness of our ideas and her enjoyment of them perhaps enabled her to start noticing the "otherness" of her baby—he changed in her mind from being a passive recipient of her mothering to a separate being whose agency needed to be respected. Babies whose fathers are not present may lack the experience of creative arguments and may feel that disagreement or separate ideas are dangerous. In fact, in work with two parents I often feel that my task is to help them feel that their different views are valuable to the baby and do not need to be explained away. Levi flourished as his mother became more open to his moves to be more independent, and they established a new relationship with a bit more space between them.

## Conclusion

As sleeping and feeding patterns develop, we see how an infant's self-regulation is intimately bound up with his relationship to his parents. The parents' perception of their baby's needs connects with their experiences with their own parents, and beyond.

Much of the pleasure of this brief work lies in helping parent and baby to attain a state of better attunement. Where families cannot spontaneously manage the normal process described by Tronick, where miscoordinated states between parents and babies become coordinated through *"interactive repair"*, the therapist may help to initiate the repair. Other primary-care professionals may also share the satisfaction of developing this approach to the work (Daws, 2005).

Stern's developmental ideas of intersubjectivity and attunement imply that infants get to the stage of seeing that there are "other minds out there". Parents must then reciprocally recognize the infant's separate mind. When parents seem to lag behind in responding to this separateness, the therapist's ability to encompass the idea of minds both at odds and in tune with each other is crucial. The therapist may then give parents and infants the courage to "dare to be different" and to see that individuation need not be the end of intimacy.

### Note

This paper partly has a "classic" function of restating some of my original ideas (Daws, 1989). The later part reflects the title and ventures onto new ground.

CHAPTER 15

# Holding the balance: life and death in the early years

*Elizabeth Bradley*

The death of a child is devastating because it means the loss of so many hopes and dreams for the future. These may even have preceded the pregnancy; during the pregnancy they are elaborated and culminate at the time of the birth. Seeing families soon after the birth of a child, we are familiar with the many hopes for the future the baby can hold at this point. A new baby is experienced as reassurance that life goes on, and when things go wrong the repercussions can be debilitating and long lasting. The loss may continue to affect the family and the lives of future babies in a powerful but not necessarily obvious way (Reid, 1992).

Bourne and Lewis (1984, 1992) wrote about the effects of perinatal loss and the difficulties the next child may have. Women throughout the world continue to suffer from perinatal loss, and however many children parents may have, there is always a place in their memory for the lost babies. Some parents who lose a baby find it difficult to bond successfully with the next child and remain preoccupied with the dead child; this is a theme I shall explore in this chapter.

I shall describe two cases where loss dominated the mother's mental landscape and affected the pregnancies and children that followed.

## The effect of prenatal loss: observation as an intervention

The Thomas family was referred by a clinical psychologist from an Adult Service; Mrs Thomas had been seen for post-natal depression, following the birth of her second child. During an earlier pregnancy, before either of these children was born, she had had a baby diagnosed at 27 weeks with Edwards syndrome (a genetic disorder—Trisomy 18), and the couple had been advised to terminate the pregnancy. It was clear that having to make this decision had been a traumatic experience. The psychologist had offered Mrs Thomas bereavement counselling, as she had felt that the loss of the first baby was contributing to mother's post-natal depression. Mrs Thomas had agreed to this but quickly felt there was no more work to be done on this issue. Rather, she felt she needed help with her children because this was where her anxiety was focused. She was worried by her impulse to place the children in a full-time nursery and work for her husband, where she felt she had a greater sense of control. She knew that in many ways she didn't want this outcome and was keen for help to enable her to feel more confident and able to enjoy her young children.

Mr Thomas was unable to come to the first appointment and told me he was not available for at least two weeks. In order not to delay the first meeting, I decided to offer the family an appointment without him in the first instance.

Mrs Thomas was a 32-year-old Indian woman who appeared pleasant and competent. In the waiting room she cheerfully and efficiently gathered up 3-year-old Ravi and 1-year-old Bella, who was in a pushchair. My first impression of Ravi was of a small boy with intense dark eyes who looked at me sombrely, with curiosity and some hesitation. Bella, who had her hair pulled up in a topknot, was smiling like her mother with no signs of shyness and chose to walk to the room.

I referred to the psychologist's letter and asked Mrs Thomas what it was she hoped to gain from coming to see me. She spoke about her own experience as a child in India, where she had grown up surrounded by siblings and her extended family, and how different she found bringing up children in this country. She described how in India the children had formed a group and spent much of the time outside and away from their parents. She explained that she was a Hindu and that she had had an arranged marriage. I asked her how she had felt about this, and she conveyed that it had worked well for her. She described how, soon after she had met her fiancée, he had gone to England and had then returned five years later to marry her and bring her back to England. She had been pleased to have the opportunity to get away and see the world. This emphasis on getting away contrasted with her earlier description of the warmth and care in the extended family of her childhood; I said it sounded as if she had mixed feelings, both wanting to get away and missing home. Mrs Thomas also told me that she did not live in an Asian community; there was no one to tell her if she was doing things right or wrong. She felt she needed help to find the right way. I said perhaps she was hoping that I would be able to help her find a compromise between the two cultures.

I turned my attention to the children. Ravi was busy playing with the cars and the animals and stopping his sister from having any toys. His mother asked him to share, but that was clearly the last thing he was intending to do. Bella was wanting to play with him; she appeared a robust little girl and was not put off by his definite desire not to play with her. Mrs Thomas explained that they hadn't been together very much. Ravi had been to the nursery from 8.30 am to 5.30 pm during much of the previous year because she could not manage both children, as she had been depressed following the birth of Bella.

She then told me how upset she still was about the first pregnancy. She said that the support group of which she was a member kept inviting her to speak to other Asian women who had lost a pregnancy in similar circumstances. She said she couldn't do this; she became too upset and started crying. Losing her usual articulate manner, she told me she could not speak about it, it hurt her inside. It had taken her three years to get pregnant again, and then after Ravi she hadn't wanted any more children, but her husband did. She had finally agreed when visiting India and watching Ravi playing with his cousins. She could see it would be good for him to have a sibling. I said she still had strong feelings about the first baby and that the tragedy was still alive for her. She spoke at some length about visiting his grave. This melancholy description gave me the impression that she felt stuck and unable to accomplish the normal process of mourning.

Ravi engaged me with the toys, making families with farm animals and saying that the baby animals must have a Mummy and a Daddy. I said perhaps he felt that his Daddy should be here today. He seemed a bright little boy but quite driven in his activity and persistently excluding his little sister, keeping the tub of toys to himself on the couch beside his mother. Mrs Thomas insisted that Ravi give Bella one animal, which she then immediately came and gave to me, following her brother's example.

On reflection after the session, I experienced a feeling of desolation. I was aware how difficult and lonely it must feel for Mrs Thomas to bring up children in a different country, compounded by her anxiety to get it right and with the death of the first baby very much in her mind. I was also aware that the referrer had recognized her need and hoped we were going to provide help. I wondered what effects Mrs Thomas's unresolved feelings about the first pregnancy were having on her parenting of her live children. There was particular difficulty with Ravi, whose birth had followed the termination. My aim in the first meeting had been to hear about her anxieties and conflicts while making a link with the children, who were both keen to make eye contact and engage me with their play. The process of the therapist's attention moving back and forth from the parents to the children slows things down and is helpful in allowing space for the parents to see the children more clearly and make their own observations about them.

Mrs Thomas recognized Ravi's anxiety that Bella was going to take things from him and his general feeling that there were not enough resources to go round. She had linked this to Ravi not having seen much of Bella because he had been at nursery for most of the day. She had now reduced his attendance to five hours a day because she thought it had been too long for him. I was able to talk to Mrs Thomas about how Ravi may feel that Bella had taken his mother over during his long hours in the nursery. This enabled Mrs Thomas to have a different view of Ravi's inability to share, recognizing that he was expressing a feeling that Bella had taken possession of his most prized object—his mother. Therefore, his refusal to allow her anything could be seen as a form of retaliation and a communication of his anxiety that his baby sister would take all the resources for herself.

I was aware that it was necessary for Mrs Thomas to make sense of the overwhelming feelings of grief for which she could not find words. We needed to explore what it was that was unbearable for her so that she could think and speak about it and it could become less toxic and more bearable.

In the second meeting I saw the parents together without the children. Mr and Mrs Thomas sat together on the couch. Mr Thomas seemed quite jovial and comfortable about attending. I asked him if Mrs Thomas had told him about our last meeting. They had both come in holding pieces of paper they had picked up in the waiting room, headed "Sibling Rivalry". Mr Thomas said that he had heard that I thought that Ravi was unable to share things with Bella. Then he read out the list of problems on the sibling-rivalry sheet, saying Ravi had all those difficulties. He asked me why I thought Ravi didn't like to share with Bella. I talked about Ravi possibly feeling left out at the nursery while his Mum had a new baby at home and how he had shown these feelings in his play with the toys. Mr Thomas described how, when he was cuddling Bella, Ravi always noticed and gave him a particular look, seeking comfort from his mother. Mr Thomas said little girls are so cuddly he found it very difficult to resist picking Bella up.

I mentioned how Ravi had told me that the baby animals needed a Mummy and a Daddy and that I thought he had wanted his father there last time. Mrs Thomas agreed that Ravi always sought out his father when he returned from nursery; I said that perhaps it was especially important to have his father's attention now that Bella had arrived. Mr Thomas was interested in this idea.

I referred to what Mrs Thomas had said last time about not wanting any more children and how I understood he had different views. He agreed, saying that he would like many more children, but he had to accept his wife's feelings on the matter. They had thought it was important for Ravi to go to the nursery so that he could have the company that the extended family would have provided in India. Bella had just started spending time at the nursery for the same reason. I said I could see they had positive reasons for Ravi going to the nursery but that perhaps he hadn't quite appreciated this! They said they hadn't noticed how quiet Ravi had been as a baby until they had had Bella; then they realized that he had perhaps been quieter and less confident than he might have been. I commented on how difficult it was to bring up children with two cultures in mind at the same time, and how lonely one can feel without people in the community to offer support and advice. It was clear that this couple desperately wanted to get it right and felt they did not know what to do. The papers on sibling rivalry that they had picked up were something to hold on to, and they took these away with them.

In the third session the whole family attended. Both children went at once to the toy people, Ravi getting out a baby boy and baby girl. He gave his mother the girl and me the boy. His mother asked him who they were. He told us that the girl-baby was Bella but that the boy-baby was *not* him. I asked what he knew about the first boy-baby. His mother said that he often accompanied her to the grave, kissed the stone, and said goodbye, but he didn't understand; I said Ravi seemed concerned about babies and had given me the boy-baby, being quite clear it wasn't him. He must wonder about the baby boy, who has died, when he kisses the stone. Mrs Thomas said she thought he did not understand, and we were able to talk about and clarify his confusion. Ravi remained concerned with babies, and later in the session he got out all the baby pigs and lambs. Following this intervention Ravi appeared much more relaxed and peaceful in this session and managed to play together with Bella, with father's regular participation and attention. I also heard in this session about the pregnancy with Ravi, when they had not wanted any tests. They had been told that there had been a 1:3,000 chance in the first pregnancy of the Edwards syndrome and a 1:100 chance of it happening again. Mr Thomas said they had decided to leave it to God and accept whatever happened. They did have the tests with the third pregnancy and had approached Bella's birth with more confidence. Mrs Thomas's profoundly different experiences of the two pregnancies could account for the differences between the two children. Mrs Thomas spoke more of the shock of the first pregnancy going wrong and not wanting to let anyone know the details. Mr Thomas expressed concern that if his wife didn't manage to get over her upset, she might develop a stress-related illness. Mr Thomas encouraged her to come alone for the next session, and we agreed to meet all together again for the fifth and last session.

## Discussion

The countertransference experience in association with observation has to be used to find a way to form a link with the family. What enables this link to be therapeutic? It must relate to the family feeling heard, understood, and sufficiently supported in their parental role. They can then expand their understanding of the children and see the behaviour that was problematic from a different perspective. They will then be able to contain and manage—in this case, Ravi's feelings of rivalry and Mrs Thomas's feelings of guilt and depression. Mr Thomas was able to give Ravi the attention he wanted in the family session, and he was much calmer. This was observed and commented on and I hoped would be taken into situations outside the session.

A therapeutic alliance is created with the parental couple while recognizing and containing the more infantile aspects of their personalities. Identifying the different feelings in the room—the mother's sadness, loneliness, and guilt, the father's determinedly positive attitude, Ravi's jealousy, and Bella's confident curiosity—is important in helping them to pay attention to each other. It was necessary to find space for feelings of ambivalence and guilt, and this was the area where more work had to be done in the last two sessions.

In these meetings the observations and associated feelings are shared with the family. This can help family members recognize each other's feelings and concerns and shift from a previously stuck view of the problem to a more dynamic view where they appreciate that they have the power to affect the situation by their own behaviour. This can be enough to create sufficient movement for the family to go forward with more confidence to face the next developmental task. This case illustrates some of the therapeutic techniques used in the under-fives work—in particular, how the approach can facilitate the children's communication to their parents, and how the parents can learn from these communications.

The continued presence of the unborn baby, which Mrs Thomas felt she had killed, had important effects, especially on her ability to parent the next child. Ravi was carrying the feelings associated with the dead baby. In working with this problem, it is important to recognize the weight this can be for the living child and to help parents to separate out the feelings that belong to the lost child.

## Holding the balance

The Smith family presented with a very different problem, one that extended my thinking about how to manage issues of loss. Before I saw Ms Smith, I was under the impression that I would be seeing a mother with her dying child. But at our first meeting Ms Smith announced that she was six weeks pregnant with her second child, so I was presented with the prospect of a new baby and a dying child. Emotional life during pregnancy often contains elaborate fantasies about birth and death. In this family there was a possibility of a new life developing alongside another child dying. My role would be to help Ms Smith to think about holding the balance between her hope around the new baby and her despair over her dying child.

Ms Smith was referred by a marital therapist who was working with the couple once a month. They had been seen as a couple for several years, during which time they had been looking after their daughter, Sarah, who had an inherited genetic syndrome that severely affected her development and would lead to her premature death. This was a rare syndrome. When two people who both carry this gene have a child, there is a 1:4 chance of a baby having the syndrome. An affected baby has difficulty in feeding and fails to grow. This is associated with premature ageing of the body. including cataracts and degenerative changes in the brain and other organs. Children with this syndrome are likely to die before they reach the age of 5 years. Sarah was 4½ years old when we first met. Ms Smith had requested time for herself, as the once-a-month marital sessions weren't enough and she wanted to be seen together with Sarah. There was a two-month delay in arranging our first meeting, as Ms Smith was unable to keep the first two appointments offered.

I met Ms Smith and Sarah in the waiting room. Ms Smith was holding Sarah on her lap. Sarah looked like a baby of about a year old until I saw her face, which had a maturity beyond her 4 years. Her pixie-like face and punk blond hair, standing straight up, drew me to her, and I introduced myself; she also extended her arms and I saw her hands, which also had the appearance of someone older. There was something attractive about Sarah that drew people to her and invited their curiosity. Ms Smith later told me there was a constant stream of enquiry and interest as they went about their daily life. Ms Smith appeared pleased to meet me, but initially all our attention went to Sarah.

In the first meeting Sarah was interested in me and looked at me intently, offering me her "Guess how much I love you?" rabbit. We passed the rabbit back and forth, while she looked at me curiously and smiled. Ms Smith said she was always wondering what Sarah was thinking. She felt Sarah enjoyed contact with people; she was unsure how much she could see because of the cataracts. She felt that at any minute Sarah was going to speak, but she never did. I could understand this feeling from my contact with Sarah, in the way she held my attention and made noises, which sounded as if I should be able to understand what they meant. Ms Smith told me Sarah also liked to lie on the floor, which she demonstrated later in the session, keeping an eye on me and occasionally putting her hand out as if wanting to reach out to me.

Ms Smith referred to the long time it had taken us to meet and explained that they had just been on a three-week camping holiday over Easter in France and Spain. It had been important to go and meet again the friends they had met there three years ago. When they had left, three years ago, Ms Smith thought the friends would never see Sarah again, but they had gone back and Sarah was still alive.

I said it seemed she was also conveying a concern about Sarah's survival in relation to our meetings. In this first communication Ms Smith expressed her crucial anxiety: how long would Sarah live?

She also told me early in this first session that she was six weeks pregnant; I noted she had become pregnant in the weeks since the referral was made. I heard that she had had a miscarriage and an ectopic pregnancy during the previous eighteen months. She said she was 42, so she didn't have much time left, but she was worried about whether she could manage to have another unaffected baby when Sarah was not expected to live. Ms Smith told me this was everybody's nightmare situation that she was living through. Despite this she appeared to be a lively woman, wearing all black, polo-neck jersey and jeans, with a slight spikiness to her hair as well.

Ms Smith described how, soon after Sarah's birth when she had been handed the baby, she had had a strong feeling that something was wrong with her. She told me that when Sarah was three months, while she was taking her round to specialists trying to discover the reason for her failure to grow, she read a medical letter that said Sarah might have a rare genetic syndrome. She went straight to read up about the syndrome in a bookshop. This had been a traumatic moment for her. She was unable to tell her husband and was not able to talk about it until later, when she was admitted to a mother and baby psychiatric unit suffering from severe depression.

At the time of discovering the diagnosis, she had rejected Sarah and was unable to care for her. The experience of the mother and baby unit had been positive, and, with the support and help of the staff, she had since then been able to care for and relate to Sarah. I said it was important that the experience of the mother and baby unit had been life-saving for Sarah and had enabled Ms Smith to care for her baby. Perhaps she hoped I would be able to also help her care for the new baby. She was also looking for help with the new situation, which must feel impossibly difficult, to have a new baby, hopefully healthy, and continue to care for Sarah whose condition was deteriorating.

She described how feeding Sarah continues to be her main preoccupation; she has to feed her through a tube going into her stomach, which is linked to a pump. Initially she would have to hold the container of milk up in the air until it gradually, by gravity, went through the tube into Sarah's stomach. It had to go in quite slowly or else Sarah would vomit. She said she needed help with her irritation with other mothers who are so preoccupied by their babies' intake, when she knew that they'd be all right and here she was, four years on, still worrying about Sarah's intake. *She* has the real problem. I said it was difficult to tolerate other people's anxieties when your own seemed to be much bigger. Perhaps she wondered whether I would be able to appreciate how enormous her problem was and be able to give her enough attention when I had so many people's problems to attend to.

She said Sarah went to a children's hospice for thirty days each year to give her parents respite. The staff had previously looked after a child there with this same syndrome. Ms Smith spoke about meeting other parents of children with the syndrome and how important that had been for her. I said she must *feel* alone with Sarah's problem, which was for her so much worse than other people's problems. It must make her feel angry as well. She described how, unlike her, who can feel so angry, her husband had been absolutely constant with Sarah and hadn't had the "blip" that she had at finding out the diagnosis. Together they had shared all the worry, the pain, and the care over the four years.

I heard how Sarah had been attending a special nursery school since she was 2, and this had been successful; she enjoyed going and liked the stimulation of other children. Educational psychologists had told Ms Smith that Sarah was functioning like a 4- to 5-month-old baby in terms of comprehension and communication and like a 13- to 15-month-old in relation to books and reading. Ms Smith found this hard to believe as her experience of Sarah's comprehension was like that of an older child. I agreed with her that Sarah did not relate like a young baby—the feeling was more of a child who was on the verge of speaking.

At first Ms Smith had expected Sarah to die at any moment or at the slightest thing going wrong. She then got used to her continuing to live and thought that the three-monthly check at the hospital worked well. At each visit she thought we will be here again in three months' time. I said we needed a similarly reassuring and regular structure to our meetings, and we agreed on regular fortnightly meetings at a time when Sarah is at school, so that it would be possible for Ms Smith to come without her. The meetings would continue throughout the pregnancy, as five sessions did not feel sufficient.

At the second meeting Ms Smith came alone, eight-and-a-half weeks pregnant, having had a scan, which had been exciting, and she told me how she was now talking about a "baby" and not a "foetus". But there was, ahead, the prospect of the testing to see whether this baby would be normal.

The main anxiety that came over in the second session was when Sarah was going to die and whether Ms Smith would be able to cope with this loss and with a new baby. In her constant wondering about Sarah's survival, she contrasted her feelings with her husband's ability to live for the present and not always be waiting for the end, saying,

"We'll cope with that one when we come to it." He was able to have hope in the present, whereas she was always looking towards death in the future.

The constancy of her anxiety was powerfully transmitted to me, so I would wonder from meeting to meeting about Sarah's survival. At the same time I found myself involved with thoughts of the new baby, hoping it would not be affected and that the hope it represented would be able to be sustained. I commented that my job was to help her to hold the balance between her preoccupation with Sarah dying and holding on to the pregnancy in the belief that she could have a live, healthy baby. Ms Smith wondered whether she wanted a baby mostly for her own selfish reasons. She was worried whether Sarah would die when the baby was tiny and that the baby would have to cope with grieving parents. I said that it seemed to me that she was grieving for Sarah all the time anyway, perhaps in preparation for this. She said she had always been like that; she was always worried about losing what she had. She had been worried about losing her mother all her childhood.

She was pleased that her husband was involved with the new baby, although she felt he had not been as keen as she was about having another child. He thought that something bad in their relationship had produced the damaged child. She thought that maybe they both worried about being able to produce a "good" child.

In the third meeting, when she again brought Sarah, Ms Smith said she had no other space where she could talk about her feelings. She told me she'd had therapy for two years around her thirty-fifth birthday and that this had been helpful; she had immediately become pregnant and attributed this to the therapy. When she found out about Sarah's diagnosis, she felt let down by therapy. She told me she had had a conviction as a small child that she was going to die when she was 35. She had been thinking about having a savings account, and a voice in her head had told her that she wouldn't need savings as she wouldn't live that long. This had been one of the reasons for going to therapy at that time. I said it sounded as if she felt she had had an immunization with the therapy and then bad things still happened to her. I thought she was hoping for a more successful immunization this time from the work here.

She recognized she already had a number of good sources of support, but she felt they weren't enough. She needed the extra time with me to "try to keep her faith" and to counteract what she described as "the deathly streak". My role was to help her with this conflict and to try to support the side of life and hope, which the baby represented, against the deathly streak that said she would lose everything she cared about. Our meetings needed to help her retain the hope in the face of the inevitability of Sarah's death. I said I was aware of a sense that she wasn't entitled to have a healthy baby; she had described this as being selfish, and she felt guilty about getting pregnant. I wondered whether she could turn her attention to a new life when Sarah was going to die or whether this would feel like being disloyal to Sarah.

The tests at 12 weeks showed the baby not to have the syndrome and to be a boy. The fact that the baby was a boy initially caused disappointment; he would not be a replacement for Sarah. Ms Smith told me she was throwing out all the girlie dressing-up clothes as these wouldn't be needed for a boy and that she was sad about the little girl who wasn't going to grow up and get married and have her own babies. As the weeks passed, she recognized how helpful it was that she was going to have a boy.

I continued to have the role of helping her hold the balance in a conflict between life and death. She had many valuable supports: a husband who shared Sarah's care, the nursery where Sarah went daily, friends and family who were interested, the hospice where she had respite care organized, the marital therapist whom the couple saw each month. The list was extensive. I suggested she felt that no one could help sufficiently with the guilt that she was suffering, the guilt of having another baby who could be healthy and strong. I said I knew she felt guilty and selfish about holding on to the hope of a new life, especially because sometimes coping with Sarah was too much and she might wish Sarah would die.

Ms Smith's preoccupation from childhood with the theme of inevitable death predated Sarah's birth. It was not clear from my limited knowledge of her background why the outcome would inevitably be suffering and loss. The risk of dangerous "acting out" was dramatically conveyed when, at 34 weeks, she had a head-on car crash while staying at the hospice. At this time the hoped-for protection given by the therapeutic relationship looked fragile. Ms Smith had to understand and manage her guilt in a different way if the new pregnancy was to survive. The focus of the work was to contain the persecutory guilt so that it became more manageable. This could be described as Old Testament guilt; it was retaliatory, "an eye for an eye, a tooth for a tooth." This is in contrast to the depressive guilt associated with the depressive position, which would give space for her ambivalence—her love and hate in relation to Sarah—and allow reparation to take place. We were able to think about how looking after Sarah enabled her to repair the damage she felt she had done by her anger and rejection when she had first found out about Sarah's diagnosis.

My relationship with Sarah was important to Ms Smith. In one of the early sessions, Sarah walked to me with support and sat on my lap for part of the session. This was a concrete way of holding her, which felt important in the relationship, that I would be willing and able to hold Sarah. On another occasion Sarah vomited and I had to find tissues for mopping up, as Ms Smith did not have sufficient supplies with her. I don't usually literally "hold the baby", but it was important for Ms Smith that I held Sarah and could help mop up as well.

Six months into the pregnancy Ms Smith came one day, saying she was "in a rage with the world". She should not have gone ahead with the pregnancy. Sarah had been vomiting and unwell; she had wanted her friends to ring up and ask how Sarah was. Her sister had phoned to enquire about the baby. Ms Smith had thought she meant Sarah, but she was asking about the new baby. We spoke about how she got them mixed up at times and did not know who was getting the attention and who was being neglected.

She had been speaking to all the doctors about Sarah's prognosis and no one had an answer; she knew there wasn't one. She told her husband she knew she must speak about these things to "Thingy Bradley". She acknowledged my comment that not remembering my name was a way of expressing her irritation with me. She then said she didn't know really where she was going or what her life was about; it all seemed impossible and overwhelming.

The outburst at the beginning of this session was clearly directed at me. I said she was angry with me as much as with the world and felt I had let her down and not made things better. Could she believe that I really understood how she was feeling if I did not provide the answers she felt were missing? Because I had asked permission to write about our work together, I thought she was suspicious about my motives and that the therapy was just for my benefit. She was the one being neglected. My recognition of her anger with me was helpful in this session, where she felt like an angry, complaining child. She linked this part of herself with the person who wanted impossible things from her friends and doctors. I said that part of my job was not to ignore the complaining child while supporting the grown-up parent.

We spoke about this wish for somebody to understand and how important it was to share her present experience with someone while it was taking place. When she couldn't do that, it was unbearable.

She told me how she wouldn't change anything because she had loved being Sarah's mother and Sarah had a powerful influence on others. I said that I was aware of Sarah's capacity to relate and to engage, as she had done with me in the sessions she had attended. I said it was very important to Ms Smith that I recognize that having Sarah was something special and not just an event she would rather not have ever happened. There was something positive in the experience, despite all the difficulties. It is easier to think about Sarah's death when she sees her life as having been worth living. This theme of her ambivalence was always present, as was my need to be able to give recognition and attention to both sides of this ambivalence.

*Discussion*

When unbearable feelings can be spoken about, they lose their toxic power and can be thought about and challenged. In this case it felt urgent, with the pregnancy progressing, to try to find a way of putting Ms Smith's situation into a context where it was possible to bear the sadness of knowing Sarah would not grow up and the hope and excitement of a new and different child. The main task was to hold in mind the very different feelings associated with birth and death at the same time. This was challenging for both patient and therapist.

It was necessary to assist Ms Smith in holding the balance between life and death, to find enough space for both preoccupations, and to recognize that this is a difficult balance to hold. This involved finding sufficient space for negative feelings—her wish to get rid of Sarah, the doctors, the friends, and me—and accepting that these are inevitable feelings that need to be recognized and known about. Then it was possible to engage with and challenge her masochistic guilt and support her entitlement to have another baby.

Melanie Klein (1948) described the paranoid defence against guilt when blame is projected on to another. She regarded it as an important discovery, and it is an easily recognized way of responding to feelings of guilt. It may be that a masochistic response to guilt of a persecutory kind is just as widespread, especially in women. Instead of splitting off and projecting the guilt, the converse happens and it is taken into the self. Understanding and holding these anxieties by giving them consideration allows some space for the hope to grow and develop—in this case, for the new pregnancy to progress. There is then the possibility of challenging the deathly streak—in this case, the self-destructive masochistic forces that are engendered by the guilt.

Bourne and Lewis (1992) thought that it is difficult to engage in a mourning process in pregnancy when the focus is on fostering a new life, but this had to be managed with Ms Smith.

There is a problem for children following the death of a sibling when the mother may continue to be preoccupied with the lost child. The new child may have a sense that he or she can never get it quite right for their mother, as he or she cannot be, or replace, the lost child. The mother may believe that the new baby has to be neglected, because otherwise she is being disloyal or unfaithful to the dead baby.

It is a common misperception that the loss of a child before birth is not as significant as losing a live child. Before birth, the baby will already be carrying many hopes of the parents. The loss of the baby before birth, who is carrying so much for the future, can have a long-lasting effect that continues despite the existence of the children who are alive and flourishing. On many levels, it is often what we have not had that is hardest to lose; it may then be more difficult to recover from this loss, because it represents a loss of many unfulfilled hopes. The child who has lived—even if only briefly and with difficulties—has been known, loved, and cared for.

# *GLOSSARY*

**Autism**  A condition characterized by impairments of emotional and social contact, cognitive capacities, and language development. Children with this condition are distressed by change, and they engage in repetitive ritualistic behaviour as well as idiosyncratic use of their bodies, such as hand-flapping and toe-walking. They typically avoid eye contact and ignore the existence of separate people, who may feel excluded as though by a barrier. Kanner's syndrome children are often mute or echolalic; Asperger's syndrome children have language but tend to use it in unusual ways.

**Container–contained**  An unconscious mental process described by Bion (1962a, 1962b) and performed automatically by most primary care-givers with their infants. Since a baby has limited mental capacities and can become quickly overwhelmed by a flood of often unpleasant (but also intensely stimulating) sensory experiences, the parent needs to be receptive to these states, think about them, and try to make sense of them, returning them to the infant in a more digested, manageable form, by attentiveness to the baby's

---

Compiled from Emanuel (2005) and Rustin, Rhode, Dubinsky, & Dubinsky (1997).

fluctuating emotional states. In this way the care-taker provides some containment to the infant, who internalizes, over time, a capacity to reflect on his own states without being overwhelmed by them.

**Countertransference**   This term has been used in various ways to refer to conscious and unconscious aspects of the therapist's emotional response to the patient.

**Defences against thinking**   Babies and young children who do not have enough experiences of a consistent care-giver who provides attentive containment of their overwhelming states may develop defensive strategies to deal with this "primary disappointment". A baby may resort to challenging, disruptive, or hyperactive behaviour as he attempts to force his feelings into an unreceptive carer, with increasing intensity. He may become withdrawn and cut himself from meaningful contact with others in order to avoid "knowing about" painful feelings of disappointment or loss.

**Defences against thinking and linking**   Bion (1962a, 1962b) describes how one defence against anxiety (linked to painful awareness of feeling helpless, inadequate, and small) may be a process of unconsciously attacking one's own or another's capacity to make meaningful links and connections between ideas and words, or between people in a relationship. This unconscious breaking up of the potential links between people and ideas results in the devaluation of meaningful relationships.

**Depressive position**   A state of mind characterized by the bringing together of splits, so that the baby recognizes that the idealized mother and the hated mother are the same person. Relationships are with whole people for whom love and concern are felt (Klein, 1935). This leads to feelings of guilt for harm done in phantasy, and the wish to make reparation. In the working through of the depressive position, love mitigates hatred, and hope and security increase. If this fails, manic triumph may be resorted to, or paranoid–schizoid trends may be reinforced.

**Infant observation**   A discipline that is part of the preparation for clinical work in many psychotherapy trainings; it may also be pursued for its own sake and as a method of research. An observer visits the family of a new-born baby once a week for two years and makes as full a record as possible of the interaction of family members, while taking care to influence this as little as possible.

The observer pays careful attention to his or her own feelings as well as to the details of the interaction. This is a fruitful way of learning about primitive processes and of understanding how actions express emotion during the preverbal period.

**Internal objects**   Figures to whom the self relates and who have become internalized, so building up the "inner world" of object relationships (Klein, 1940).

**Object**   A technical psychoanalytic term for a person with whom the self (or subject) has an emotional relationship. An *external object* is such a person in external reality, whereas an *internal object* (*q.v.*) has been introjected and thus becomes part of the inner world, coloured now by the subject's perceptions of it.

**Omnipotence**   The belief that one's phantasies are all-powerful and therefore that internal reality is indistinguishable from external reality—for example, *omnipotent destructiveness*, in which destructive phantasies are felt to bring about any damage that takes place in external reality.

**Paranoid–schizoid position**   A term coined by Melanie Klein (1948) to describe a state of mind where "paranoid" anxiety about the survival of the self predominates. The "schizoid" aspect refers to the splitting and projection into others of parts of the self (often hostile feelings), a primitive mechanism of survival. Subsequent fear of the earlier projected hostility returning to harm the self, in the form of a retaliatory attack, may follow. The gradual development of a capacity to integrate loving and hostile feelings leads to a shift towards what Klein terms the "depressive position" (*q.v.*).

**Second-skin defences**   The manner in which, in the absence of a containing, thoughtful adult available to help an infant/child process his difficult emotional states, the child develops alternative ways of coping and holding himself together. He may develop what Bick (1968) calls a "second-skin defence", finding his own ways of preventing himself from a feeling of falling apart, by precocious muscular development, hyperactivity (kinetically holding himself together), or sticking himself in an adhesive way to a person or object so that he feels that the skin-to-skin contact holds him in one piece.

**Splitting and projection**   The unconscious process involving the phantasy of separating off some (usually) undesirable aspects of the self, or painful/unpleasant emotional states, distancing oneself from these traits or feelings by getting rid of them out of the self into another person. (This is, for example, the basis of scapegoating.)

**Symbol formation**   The process by which one thing can be used to stand for another without being confused with it. This underlies all representational activity, linguistic as well as pictorial, and is the basis for creativity in child and adult. In psychotic states, this capacity is interfered with so that a symbol is equated with the thing symbolized, leading to what Segal (1957) has called *symbolic equations*. Thus, a child may feel that a drawing *is* the thing it depicts, rather than a representation of it.

**Transference**   The process first described by Freud (1905e [1901]) by which emotions from the past are re-experienced in the present in relation to the therapist.

# REFERENCES

Ainsworth, M. D. S., Blehar, M. C., Waters, E., & Wall, S. (1978). *Patterns of Attachment: A Psychological Study of the Strange Situation.* Hillsdale, NJ: Lawrence Erlbaum Associates.

Alvarez, A. (1992). *Live Company: Psychoanalytic Psychotherapy with Autistic, Borderline, Deprived and Abused Children.* London: Routledge.

Baker, C. (1993). Some reflections on humour in psychoanalysis. *International Journal of Psychoanalysis*, 74 (5): 951–960.

Balint, E.. (1993). *Before I Was I: Psychoanalysis and the Imagination.* London: Free Association Books.

Balint, E., & Norrell, J. (1973). *Six Minutes for the Patient.* London: Tavistock.

Baradon, T. (2005). *The Practice of Psychoanalytic Parent–Infant Psychotherapy: Claiming the Baby.* New York/London: Routledge.

Barrows, K. (2000). Shadow lives: A discussion of "Reading in the Dark", a novel by Seamus Deane. In: J. Symington (Ed.), *Imprisoned Pain and Its Transformation* (pp. 69–70). London: Karnac, 2000.

Barrows, P. (1996). Soiling children: The Oedipal configuration. *Journal of Child Psychotherapy*, 22 (2): 240–260.

Barrows, P. (1999a). Brief work with under-fives: A psychoanalytic approach. *Clinical Child Psychology and Psychiatry*, 4 (2): 187–199.

Barrows, P. (1999b). Fathers in parent–infant psychotherapy. *Infant Mental Health Journal*, 20 (3): 333–345.

Barrows, P. (2003). Change in parent–infant psychotherapy. *Journal of Child Psychotherapy, 29* (3): 283–301.

Barrows, P. (2004). Fathers and families: Locating the ghost in the nursery. *Infant Mental Health Journal, 25* (5): 408–423.

Benedek, T. (1959). Parenthood as a developmental phase. *Journal of the American Psychoanalytic Association, 7*: 389–417.

Bick, E. (1968). The experience of the skin in early object relations. *International Journal of Psychoanalysis, 45*: 484–486.

Bion, W. R. (1962a). *Learning from Experience*. London: Heinemann. [Reprinted London: Karnac, 1984.]

Bion, W. R. (1962b). A theory of thinking. In: *Second Thoughts* (pp. 110–119). London: Heinemann, 1967.

Bion, W. R. (1970). *Attention and Interpretation*. New York: Jason Aronson. [Reprinted in *Seven Servants*. New York: Jason Aronson, 1977.]

Bourne, S., & Lewis, E. (1984). Pregnancy after stillbirth or neonatal death. *The Lancet, 2* (8393, July 7): 31–33.

Bourne, S., & Lewis, E. (1992). *Psychological Aspects of Stillbirth and Neonatal Death: An Annotated Bibliography*. London: Tavistock.

Bowlby, J. (1979). On knowing what you are not supposed to know and feeling what you are not supposed to feel. In: *A Secure Base: Clinical Applications of Attachment Theory* (pp. 99–118). London: Routledge, 1988.

Brazelton, T. B. (1992). *Touchpoints*. New York: Guilford Press.

Britton, R. (1989). The missing link: Parental sexuality in the Oedipus complex. In: J. Steiner (Ed.), *The Oedipus Complex Today* (pp. 83–101). London: Karnac.

Britton, R. (2002). Forever father's daughter. In: J. Trowell & A. Etchegoyen (Eds.), *The Importance of Fathers*. Hove: Brunner-Routledge.

Chiland, C. (1982). A new look at fathers. *Psychoanalytic Study of the Child, 37*: 367–379.

Corboz-Warnery, A., Fivaz-Depeursinge, E., Bettens, C. G., & Favez, N. (1993). Systemic analysis of father–mother–baby interactions: The Lausanne triadic play. *Infant Mental Health Journal, 14*: 298–316

Cowan, P., & Cowan, C. (2001). A couple perspective on the transmission of attachment patterns. In: C. Clulow (Ed.), *Adult Attachment and Couple Psychotherapy*. London: Brunner-Routledge.

Cowan, P., & Cowan, C. (2002). "Partners, Parents, and Intergenerational Change: What Do We Know and How Can We Help?" Paper given at the Tavistock Marital Studies Institute Summer Conference, London.

Cox, A. D., Puckering, C., Pound, A., & Mills, M. (1987). The impact of maternal depression in young children. *Journal of Child Psychology and Psychiatry, 28*: 917–928.

Cox, A. D., Puckering, C., Pound, A., Mills, M., & Owen, A. L. (1990). *The Evaluation of a Home Visiting and Befriending Scheme*. NEWPIN Final report to the Department of Health.
Cramer, B. (1995). Short term dynamic psychotherapy for infants and their parents. *Child and Adolescent Psychiatric Clinics of North America, 4* (3): 649–660.
Cramer, B., & Palacio-Espasa, F. (1993). *La pratique des psychothérapies mères–bébés*. Paris: Presses Universitaires de France.
Cramer, B., & Stern, D. (1990). Outcome evaluation in brief mother–infant psychotherapy: A preliminary report. *Infant Mental Health Journal, 11*: 278–300.
Damasio, A. (1999). *The Feeling of What Happens*. London: Heinemann.
Daws, D. (1985). Standing next to the weighing scales. *Journal of Child Psychotherapy, 11:* 77–85.
Daws, D. (1989). *Through the Night: Helping Parents and Sleepless Infants*. London: Free Association Books.
Daws, D. (1996). Postnatal depression and the family: Conversations that go awry. In: *Postnatal Depression: Focus on a Neglected Issue—Papers from the Health Visitor/National Childbirth Trust National Conference, London 18 April*. London: HVA.
Daws, D. (1997). The perils of intimacy: Closeness and distance in feeding and weaning. *Journal of Child Psychotherapy, 23* (2): 179–199.
Daws, D. (1999). Parent–infant psychotherapy: Remembering the Oedipus complex. *Psychoanalytic Inquiry, 19* (2): 267–278.
Daws, D. (2005). A child psychotherapist in the baby clinic of a general practice: Standing by the weighing scales thirty years on. In: J. Launer, S. Blake, & D. Daws (Eds.), *Reflecting on Reality: Psychotherapists at Work in Primary Care* (pp. 18–36). Tavistock Clinic Series. London: Karnac.
Elder, A. (1996). Enid Balint's contribution to general practice. *Psychoanalytic Psychotherapy 10:* 101–108.
Emanuel, L. (2002a). Deprivation × 3: The contribution of organizational dynamics to the "triple deprivation" of looked-after children. *Journal of Child Psychotherapy, 28* (2): 163–179.
Emanuel, L. (2002b) Parents united: Addressing parental issues in working with infants and young children. *International Journal of Infant Observation, 5* (2): 103–117.
Emanuel, L. (2005). A psychodynamic approach to consultation within two contrasting school settings. In: A. Southall (Ed.), *Consultation in Child and Adolescent Mental Health Services* (pp. 37–55). Abingdon: Radcliffe Publishing.
Emanuel, R. (1998). The-child-in-the-family-in-the-nursery. In: I. Ward

(Ed.), *The Psychology of Education*. London: Karnac, for The Freud Museum.

Emanuel, R. (2004). Thalamic fear. *Journal of Child Psychotherapy, 30* (1): 71–89.

Fakhry Davids, M. (2002). Fathers in the internal world: From boy to man to father. In: J. Trowell & A. Etchegoyen (Eds.), *The Importance of Fathers*. Hove: Brunner-Routledge.

Field, T. (1992). Interventions in early infancy. *Infant Mental Health Journal, 13* (4): 329–336.

Fivaz-Depeursinge, E., & Corboz-Warnery, A. (1999). *The Primary Triangle*. New York: Basic Books.

Fonagy, P. , Steele, M., Moran, G., Steele, H., & Higgitt, A. (1993). Measuring the ghost in the nursery: An empirical study of the relationship between parents' mental representations of childhood experiences and their infant's security of attachment. *Journal of the American Psychoanalytic Association, 41* (4): 957–989.

Fraiberg, S. (Ed.) (1980). *Clinical Studies in Infant Mental Health*. London: Tavistock. [Reprinted as: *Assessment and Theory of Disturbances in Infancy*. Northvale, NJ: Jason Aronson, 1989.]

Fraiberg, S., Adelson, E., & Shapiro, V. (1975). Ghosts in the nursery: A psychoanalytic approach to the problems of impaired infant–mother relationships. In: S. Fraiberg (Ed.), *Clinical Studies in Infant Mental Health* (pp. 164–196). London: Tavistock, 1980.

Freud, S. (1900a). *The Interpretation of Dreams. Standard Edition*, 4–5.

Freud, S. (1905e [1901]). Fragment of an analysis of a case of hysteria. *Standard Edition, 7*: 7–122.

Freud, S. (1917e [1915]). Mourning and melancholia. *Standard Edition*, 14.

Freud, S. (1927d). Humour. *Standard Edition*, 21.

Freud, S. (1933a). *New Introductory Lectures on Psycho-Analysis. Standard Edition*, 22.

Harris, M. (1966). Therapeutic consultations In: *Collected Papers of Martha Harris and Esther Bick*, ed. M Harris Williams. Strath Tay: Clunie Press, 1987.

Hay, D. F. (1997). Postpartum depression and cognitive development In: L. Murray & P. J. Cooper (Eds.), *Postpartum Depression and Child Development*. New York: Guilford Press.

Heimann, P. (1942). A contribution to the problem of sublimation and its relation to processes of internalization. In: M. Tonnesmann (Ed.), *About Children and Children-no-Longer: Collected Papers 1942–80*. London/New York: Routledge, 1989.

Hopkins, J. (1988). Facilitating the development of intimacy between nurses and infants in day nurseries. *Early Child Development and Care, 33*: 99–111.

Hopkins, J. (1992). Infant–parent psychotherapy. *Journal of Child Psychotherapy, 18* (1): 5–17.

Hopkins, J. (1994). Therapeutic intervention in infancy: Two contrasting cases of persistent crying. *Psychoanalytic Psychotherapy, 8*: 141–152.

Hopkins, J. (1996). The dangers and deprivations of too-good mothering. *Journal of Child Psychotherapy, 22* (3): 407–422.

Johnson, S. (1758). Letter to Bennet Langton. In: *The Letters of Samuel Johnson, Vol. 1: 1731–1772*, ed. B. Redford. Oxford: Oxford University Press, 1992.

Juffer, F., van IJzendoorn, M. H., & Bakermans-Kranenburg, M. J. (1997). Intervention in transmission of insecure attachment: A case study. *Psychological Reports, 80*: 531–543.

Kennell, J. H., Voos, D. K., & Klaus, M. H. (1979). Parent–infant bonding. In: J. Osofsky (Ed.), *Handbook of Infant Development*. New York: Wiley.

Klein, M. (1934). On criminality. *British Journal of Medical Psychology, 14* (1).

Klein, M. (1935). A contribution to the psychogenesis of manic depressive states. *International Journal of Psychoanalysis, 16* (1).

Klein, M. (1940). Mourning and its relation to manic depressive states. In: *The Writings of Melanie Klein, Vol. 1*. London: Hogarth Press, 1975.

Klein, M. (1948). On the theory of anxiety and guilt. In: *The Writings of Melanie Klein, Vol. 3*. London: Hogarth Press, 1975.

Krause, B. (1989). Sinking heart: A Punjabi communication of distress. *Social Science and Medicine, 29* (4): 563–575.

Lieberman, A. F. (2004). Child–parent psychotherapy. In: A. J. Sameroff, S. C. McDonough, & K. L. Rosenblum (Eds.), *Treating Parent–Infant Relationship Problems—Strategies for Intervention*. New York: Guildford Press.

Lieberman, A. F., Padron, E., Van Horn, P., & Harris, W. W. (2005). Angels in the nursery: The intergenerational transmission of benevolent parental influences. *Infant Mental Health Journal, 26* (6): 504–520.

Lieberman, A. F., & Pawl, J. H. (1990). Disorders of attachment and secure base behavior in the second year of life. In: M. T. Greenberg, D. Cicchetti, & E. M. Cummings (Eds.), *Attachment in the Pre-School Years*. Chicago/London: University of Chicago Press.

Lieberman, A. F., & Zeanah, C. H. (1999). Contributions of attachment theory to infant–parent psychotherapy. In: J. Cassidy & P. R. Shaver

(Eds.), *Handbook of Attachment: Theory, Research and Clinical Applications* (pp. 555–574). New York/London: Guildford Press.

Ludlam, M. (2005). The parental couple: Issues for psychotherapeutic practice. *Sexual and Relationship Therapy, 20* (3): 323–331.

Maiello, S. (1997). The sound object: A hypothesis about prenatal auditory experience and memory. In: L. Murray & P. J. Cooper (Eds.), *Postpartum Depression and Child Development*. New York: Guilford Press.

Main, M., & Hesse, E. (1990). Parents' unresolved traumatic experiences are related to infant disorganized attachment status: Is frightened and/or frightening parental behavior the linking mechanism? In: M. T. Greenberg, D. Cicchetti, & E. M. Cummings (Eds.), *Attachment in the Preschool Years*. Chicago/London: University of Chicago Press.

Main, M., Kaplan, N., & Cassidy, J. (1985). Security in infancy, childhood and adulthood: A move to the level of representation. In: I. Bretherton & E. Waters (Eds.), *Growing Points of Attachment Theory and Research* (pp. 66–104). (Monographs of the Society for Research in Child Development, No. 50.) Chicago: University of Chicago Press.

Main, M., & Solomon, J. (1986). Discovery of an insecure–disorganised/disoriented attachment pattern. In: T. B. Brazleton & M. W. Yogman (Eds.), *Affective Development in Infancy*. Norwood, NJ: Ablex.

Main, M., & Solomon, J. (1990). Procedures for identifying infants as disorganized–disorientated during the Strange Situation. In: M. Greenburg et al. (Eds.), *Attachment in the Preschool Years: Theory, Research and Intervention*. Chicago: University of Chicago Press.

McHale, J. P., & Cowan, P. A. (Eds.) (1996). *Understanding How Family-level Dynamics Affect Children's Development: Studies of Two-parent Families*. San Francisco: Jossey-Bass/Pfeiffer.

McHale, J. P., & Fivaz-Depeursinge, E. (1999). Understanding triadic and family group interactions during infancy and toddlerhood. *Clinical Child and Family Psychology Review, 2* (2): 107–127.

Menzies, I. E. P. (1960). The functioning of social systems as a defence against anxiety: A report on a study of the nursing service of a general hospital. *Human Relations, 13*: 95–121. [Reprinted in: *Containing Anxiety in Institutions: Selected Essays, Vol. 1*. London: Free Association Books, 1988; and in abridged form in: E. Trist & H. Murray (Eds.), *The Social Engagement of Social Science, Vol. 1: The Socio-Psychological Perspective*. London: Free Association Books, 1990.]

Miller, L. (1992). The relation of infant observation to clinical practice in an under fives counselling service. *Journal of Child Psychotherapy, 18* (1): 19–32.

Miller, L. (2004). *Understanding Your Two-Year-Old*. London: Jessica Kingsley
Miller, L., Rustin, M., Rustin, M., & Shuttleworth, J. (Eds.) (1989). *Closely Observed Infants*. London: Duckworth.
Morgan, M. (2001). First contacts: The therapist's "couple state of mind" as a factor in the containment of couples seen for consultations. In F. Grier (Ed.), *Brief Encounters with Couples*. London: Karnac.
Murray, D., & Cox, J. L. (1987). Screening for depression during pregnancy with the Edinburgh Postnatal Depression Scale. *British Journal of Psychiatry, 150*: 782–786.
Murray, L. (1988). Effects of post-natal depression on infant development: Direct studies of early mother–infant interaction. In: K. Kumar & I. Brockington (Eds.), *Motherhood and Mental Illness, Vol. 2*. London: Wright.
Murray, L., & Cooper, P. (1997). *Postpartum Depression and Child Development*. New York/London: Guilford Press.
Murray, L., Cooper, P. , & Hipwell, A. (2003). Mental health of parents caring for infants. *Archives of Women's Mental Health, 6* (Suppl. 2): 71–77 [Special issue: Postpartum Depression—Risk Factors and Treatments].
Norman, J. (2001). The psychoanalyst and the baby: A new look at work with infants. *International Journal of Psychoanalysis, 82*: 83–100.
Oakley, A. (1995). *An Evaluation of Newpin: A Report by the Social Sciences, Research Unit, Institute of Education, University of London*. London: KKF.
O'Shaughnessy, E. (1964). The absent object. *Journal of Child Psychotherapy, 1*: 34–43.
Palacio-Espasa, F. (2004). Parent–infant psychotherapy, the transition to parenthood and parental narcissism: Implications for treatment. *Journal of Child Psychotherapy, 30* (2): 155–171.
Palombo, S. (1978). *Dreaming and Memory*. New York: Basic Books.
Parke, R. D. (1990). In search of fathers: A narrative of an empirical journey. In: I. E. Sigel & G. H. Brody (Eds.), *Methods of Family Research. Biographies of Research Projects, Vol. 1: Normal Families* (pp. 154–187). Hillsdale, NJ: Lawrence Erlbaum Associates.
Pozzi, M. (1999). Psychodynamic counselling with under-5s and their families. *Journal of Child Psychotherapy, 25* (1): 51–70.
Puckering, C., Evans, J., Maddox, H., Mills, M., & Cox, A. D. (1996). Taking control: A single case study of mellow parenting. *Clinical Child Psychology and Psychiatry, 1* (4): 539–550.

Quinton, D., Pollock, S., & Golding, J. (2002). *Report to the ESRC: The Transition to Fatherhood in Young Men: Influences on Commitment*. Unpublished manuscript, University of Bristol.

Raphael-Leff, J. (1989). Where the wild things are? *International Journal of Perinatal Studies*, 1: 78–89.

Reid, M. (1992). Joshua—life after death: The replacement child. *Journal of Child Psychotherapy*, 18 (2): 109–138.

Reid, S. (Ed.) (1997). *Developments in Infant Observation: The Tavistock Model*. London: Routledge.

Rustin, M. (1998). Observation, understanding and interpretation: The story of a supervision. *Journal of Child Psychotherapy*, 24 (3): 433–449.

Rustin, M., Rhode, M., Dubinsky, H., & Dubinsky, A. (Eds.) (1997). *Psychotic States in Children*. Tavistock Clinic Series. London: Karnac.

Schlesinger, H. J. (1994). How the analyst listens: The pre-stages of interpretation. *International Journal of Psychoanalysis*, 75: 31–37.

Schore, A. (2001). Effects of a secure attachment relationship on right brain development, affect regulation, and infant mental health. *Infant Mental Health Journal*, 22 (1–2): 7–66.

Schore, A. (2004). *Affect Regulation and the Development of the Self*. Hillsdale, NJ: Lawrence Erlbaum Associates.

Seeley, S., Murray, L., & Cooper, P. J. (1996). The detection and treatment of postnatal depression by health visitors. *Health Visitor*, 64: 135–138.

Segal, H. (1957). Notes on symbol formation. *International Journal of Psychoanalysis*, 37: 391–397. Also in: E. B. Spillius (Ed.), *Melanie Klein Today, Vol. 1: Mainly Theory*. London: Routledge, 1988.

Segal, H. (1973). *Introduction to the Work of Melanie Klein*. London: Hogarth Press.

Segal, H. (1989). Introduction. In: J. Steiner (Ed.), *The Oedipus Complex Today* (pp. 1–10). London: Karnac.

Sendak, M. (1963). *Where the Wild Things Are*. New York: Harper & Row.

Stein, A., Woolley, H., Cooper, S. D., & Fairbairn, C. G. (1994). An observational study of mothers with eating disorders and their infants. *Journal of Child Psychology and Psychiatry*, 35 (3): 733–748.

Stern, D. (1985). *The Interpersonal World of the Infant*. New York: Basic Books.

Stern, D. (1995). *The Motherhood Constellation: A Unified View of Parent–Infant Psychotherapy*. New York: Basic Books

Sternberg, J. (2005). *Infant Observation at the Heart of Training*. London: Karnac.

Sully, J. (1895). *Studies of Childhood*. London: Longmans. [Republished London: Free Association Books, 2000.]

Target, M., & Fonagy, P. (2002). Fathers in modern psychoanalysis and in society. In: J. Trowell & A. Etchegoyen (Eds.), *The Importance of Fathers*. Hove: Brunner-Routledge.

Thomson-Salo, F., Paul, C., Morgan, A., Jones, S., Jordan, B., Meehan, M., Morse, S., & Walker, M. (1999). "Free to be playful": Therapeutic work with infants. *International Journal of Infant Observation*, 3 (1): 47–62.

Tronick, E. (1989). Emotions and emotional communication in infants. *American Psychologist*, 44 (2): 113–119.

Trowell, J., & Etchegoyen, A. (Eds.) (2002). *The Importance of Fathers*. Hove: Brunner-Routledge.

Tydeman, B., & Kiernan, P. (2005). A model for a primary care based child and family mental health service. In: J. Launer, S. Blake, & D. Daws (Eds.), *Reflecting on Reality: Psychotherapists at Work in Primary Care* (pp. 37–55). Tavistock Clinic Series. London: Karnac.

von Klitzing, K., Simoni, H., Amsler, F., & Burgin, D. (1999). The role of the father in early family interactions. *Infant Mental Health Journal*, 20 (3): 222–237

von Klitzing, K., Simoni, H., & Burgin, D. (1999). Child development and early triadic relationships. *International Journal of Psychoanalysis*, 80 (1): 71–89.

Waddell, M. (2006). Infant observation in Britain: The Tavistock approach. *International Journal of Psychoanalysis*, 87 (4): 1103–1120.

Watillon, A. (1993). The dynamics of psychoanalytic therapies of the early parent–child relationship. *International Journal of Psychoanalysis*, 74: 1037–1048.

Williams, G. (1997). Reflections on some dynamics of eating disorders: "No entry" defences and foreign bodies. *International Journal of Psychoanalysis*, 78: 927–941.

Winnicott, D. W. (1941). The observation of infants in a set situation. In: *Through Paediatrics to Psycho-Analysis*. London: Hogarth Press, 1975.

Winnicott, D. W. (1956). The antisocial tendency. In: *Through Paediatrics to Psycho-Analysis*. London: Hogarth Press, 1975.

Winnicott, D. W. (1960). Ego distortion in terms of true and false self. In: *The Maturational Processes and the Facilitating Environment: Studies in the Theory of Emotional Development*. London: Hogarth Press.

Winnicott, D. W. (1963). The development of the capacity for concern. In: *The Maturational Processes and the Facilitating Environment: Studies in the Theory of Emotional Development*. London: Hogarth Press.

Winnicott, D. W. (1971). *Playing and Reality*. London: Routledge.

The Tavistock Clinic *Understanding Your Baby Series* (London: Jessica Kingsley), Series Editor, J. Bradley

*Understanding your Baby* (2004), Sophie Boswell
*Understanding your One Year Old* (2004), Sarah Gustavus Jones
*Understanding your Two Year Old* (2004), Lisa Miller
*Understanding your Three Year Old* (2005), Louise Emanuel
*Understanding your Four Year Old* (2007), Lesley Maroni

# *INDEX*

abandonment:
  fears/terror of, 94, 196, 206
  traumatic feeling of, 230
absent parent, excessive preoccupation with, obstacle to thinking, 188
abuse/trauma:
  cycle of, 2
  history of, 95, 97
  physical, 60–61
  revival of in parents' minds, 154
abusive experiences, re-enacting, 154
Adelson, E., 55, 60, 70, 76, 78, 79, 97, 154, 171, 180
ADHD (Attention Deficit Hyperactivity Disorder), 140, 152
admired figure, "anticipatory identification" with (Alvarez), 149
adult(s):
  infantile anxiety of, 48
  thinking capacity of:
    breakdown in, 132
    about feelings, promoting, 16
"affect attunement" (Stern), 238
aggression/aggressive behaviour, 2, 117, 176
  as defence, 92
  negative effects of on others, 153
  paternal, 179
  unresolved, 224
Ainsworth, M. D. S., 4, 138
Alvarez, A., 149
ambivalence, 128, 132, 183, 243, 259
  over hate and love, 135, 237
  of mother, towards dying child, 266, 267
Amsler, F., 172
anger:
  fear of own, 125
  mother's, towards baby, 126, 266, 267
  and rage, distinction between, 127
"anticipatory identification" with admired figure (Alvarez), 149
anxieties, oedipal, 193
appointment(s):
  cancellation of, by parents, 162, 208, 209
  frequency of, 6, 144, 156
  missed, 162
  speed in arranging, 6, 39, 100
argumentative relationships, transgenerational, 222

Asperger's syndrome, 269
assimilation (Heimann), 181, 183–184
attachment, 2, 3, 4, 55, 62, 67, 75, 168, 237
   disordered patterns of, 154
   disorganized (Main & Hesse), 182
   disturbances of, 76
   figure:
      main, 198
      unresolved loss of (Main & Hesse), 182
   parents' own internal representations of, 71
   and sleeping, 242
   style, and starting in kindergarten, 175
   theory, 72
attention:
   deficit in, 140
   therapist's, moving back and forth between parents and child, 257
Attention Deficit Hyperactivity Disorder (ADHD), 140, 152
attuned responsiveness, 137
attunement:
   and autonomy, 237–238
   excessive, pitfalls of, 248–249
autism, 172, 269
autonomy, and attunement, 237–238

baby(ies):
   actions and vocalizations of, and conversations with parents, connection between, 242
   ambivalent feelings towards, 12
   attunement to, appropriate, 238
   crying of, excessive, and parent's own history, 242
   daily timetable for, asking for details of, 241
   demanding and envious, 206
   hostility towards, by parents, 237, 243
   jealousy of, 19
   mother's identification with, 48
   neglected, out of fear of disloyalty to dead child, 268
   over-identification with, 19
   parents' memories of, from pregnancy to early weeks, 241
   as representation of figures from the past, 55
   transferences onto by parents, 238
Baker, C., 248
Bakermans-Kranenburg, M. J., 72, 75
Balint, E., 100, 112
Baradon, T., 54
Barrows, K., 94–95, 182
Barrows, P., 7, 14, 54, 67, 69–80, 97, 167–169, 171–186, 244
behaviour:
   aggressive and disruptive, 189–194
   child's, over-sexualized, 196
   problems, 151–166
behavioural approaches, 65–66
being hated, need to accept, 93
Benedek, T., 62
benign parental couple, helping parents internalize the functions of, 199
bereavement, 2, 16, 38, 117, 130, 255
   counselling, 255
   failure to come to terms with, 182–183
   projecting anger over into staff, 129–130
Bettens, C. G., 172
Bick, E., 4, 11, 83, 94, 141, 154, 159, 271
Bion, W. R., 3, 6, 11, 13, 14, 53, 66, 77, 78, 139, 154, 160, 166, 187, 189, 269, 270
biting, 4, 143, 144
   severe (case study), 90–95
Blehar, M. C., 4, 138
bonding, 2
boundaries: *see* limit-setting
Bourne, S., 254, 268
Bowlby, J., 63
Bradley, E., 68, 211, 254–268
Brazelton, T. B., 75
brief work (*passim*):
   and attitude towards family, 40
   benefits of, 16–17
   in community setting, 99–115
   early foundations of, 15
   example of, 55–57
   finding the focus in, 111–112
   leading to long-term work, 3
   with parents of infants, 15–37
   psychodynamic approach to, 81–98
   spacing and number of sessions in, 6, 68, 83, 144, 156
   structure and setting, 2, 6
Britton, R., 173, 185, 193, 198–201

Burgin, D., 7, 172

capacity for reflection, enhancing, 74
case studies:
    adult status of parents, loss of, 49–52
    anxiety:
        failure to contain, 160
        and uncertainty over father's
            dependability, 189–194
    baby as representation of negative
        aspects of the parental self,
        58–61
    child-led intervention, 83–88
    excessive biting, 90–95
    extreme splitting between parents,
        96–97
    ghosts in the nursery, 176
    internal parental drama, 90–93
    lack of containment, 41–49
    loss, managing issues of: pregnant
        mother with dying child,
        260–268
    Monster Baby, 20–26
    mother's projection of anger, 127,
        128–133
    oedipal rivalry, 202–210
    omnipotence, collapse of, 156–160
    omnipotent phantasy of splitting
        parental couple, 174
    post-natal depression:
        lack of parental authority, 145–149
        out-of-control child, 142–145
        difficulty looking after baby 30–35
    prenatal loss, effect of, 255–260
    projections of hopelessness into
        therapist, 130–131
    referral by doctor in GP setting,
        102–112
    separation anxiety:
        excessive clinging and fear of
            strangers, 224–230
        panic at being left alone, 217–224
        refusal to be left alone, 231–236
    severe childhood trauma, 63–65
    sleeping and feeding problems:
        difficulties in weaning, 245–246
        mother's over-determined agenda
            relating to father, 194–199
        after trauma, 249–252
    transference cure, 55–58
    unresolved mourning, 26–34

Cassidy, J., 65
change:
    models of, 77–79
    seen as loss, 112
Chiland, C., 172
child:
    development of, 3
    dying/death of:
        effect of on family, 27
        mother's preoccupation with, 268
        and new pregnancy, 260–268
    hostility of towards therapist, 219
    inability of to share, 257
    -led dramatizations, 82–88
    "married to her father", 205
    over-identification with, 201
    and parent:
        anger between, 121–135
        web of mutually constructed
            meanings between, 86
    parental feelings towards, 54
    projection of mother's unrelieved
        anguish into, 129
    as receptacle for parents' anxieties, 85
    severe phobias in, 146
    "symptoms" of:
        as means to separate the parents,
            222
        representative of conflict in
            relationships within family, 110
        as witness to loud parental
            arguments, 217–222
    *see also* baby; infant
childhood experiences, parents', 60, 78,
    207
    making links with, 184
childhood trauma, severe, 63
clinging, 197, 202, 206, 216, 222, 225
cognitive ability, misassessment of, 83
communication(s):
    baby's, rejection of, by mother,
        123–126
    child's, exploration of, 81
    framing for parents, 53
    infant modes of, 40
compliance, compulsive, 61
container and contained, 3, 139, 187, 269
    concept of, 139
        Bion, 187–188
containing function, providing for
    mother, 78

containment, 11–13, 65–66, 83, 88,
        142–148, 184
    of anxiety, 156
    aspects of, 47
    Bion's concept of, 77–78, 139
    and boundaries, 143
    capacity for, 66
    emotional, transgenerational
        transmission of failures in, 5
    failure of, 197
    of infantile emotion, 47
    internal, limited, 36
    by internalized figures, 201
    lack of, 4, 236
        by father, 145–147
        and incontinence, 175
        impact of on learning and
            thinking, 139–141
        and mental pain, 144
        by mother, 194, 197, 270
        and social and cognitive
            development, 6
    by therapist, 148, 209
continuity of work, interrupting, as
        protection from pain, 125
conversations with parents, and babies'
        actions and vocalizations,
        connection between, 242
Cooper, P., 71, 136–139, 251
Cooper, S. D., 251
Corboz-Warnery, A., 172
cot death, 231, 233, 235
counselling:
    chief hazards in, 19
    importance of being emotionally
        available, 49
    and infant observation, 39
countertransference, 3, 37, 40, 55, 169,
        192, 199, 202, 210, 245, 246, 270
    difficulty in bearing in infant–parent
        work, 59
    experience, as means to form link
        with family, 259
    extending concept of, 25
    here-and-now, 216
    and infant observation, 39–40
    as source of insight, 59
    and understanding of "selected fact",
        14
    use of by "therapeutic observer", 82
Cowan, C., 172, 175, 176

Cowan, P., 172, 175, 176
Cox, A. D., 73
Cramer, B., 65, 76, 79, 80, 137, 182
crying, parent's reaction to, 243
cultural issues, relevance of, 103–104

Damasio, A., 5
dark, fear of, 165
daughter, rivalrous, mother's feelings of
        displacement by, 209
Daws, D., 6, 64, 68, 112, 138, 185,
        211–213, 237–253
dead child, preoccupation with, 254
defences:
    manic, 153
    second-skin, 83
defiance, omnipotent, 85
dependency:
    child's anxiety about, 83
    feelings of, resistance to, 141
    of parents, avoiding, 36
    on the therapist, fear of, 209
depression:
    and drinking, 30
    deriving from neglect in mother's
        childhood, 246
    induced in therapist, 48, 77
    paternal, 178
    previous history of, 176
    about separation and loss, 197
    tolerating feelings of, by therapist, 12
    verbalizing, 30
    *see also* maternal depression; post-
        natal depression
depressive position, 152, 266, 270, 271
deprivation and anger,
        transgenerational, 134–135
deskilling, 83
development:
    delay in, 2
    guidance regarding, 55, 64, 66
    psychoanalytic view of, advantages
        offered by, 152
disintegration, fear of, 159
displacement, feelings of, stirred by
        birth of sibling, 201
disruptive and distressed toddlers, 5,
        117, 136–150, 189
distress, evacuation of through rage, 129
disturbance and discomfort, projection
        of into sibling, 204

domestic violence, 176, 178
   parent's failure to respond to
      projection of distress, 132–135
drama, oedipal, 85
dramatizations, child-led, 82–88
dreaming, as means to assimilate
   jumbled thoughts, 242
Dubinsky, A., 269
Dubinsky, H., 269
dying/death of child:
   effect of on family, 27
   mother's preoccupation with, 268
   and new pregnancy, 260–268
"dysregulated attention" (Hay), 138

early intervention, value of, 17–19, 99
early years clinicians, 167
Elder, A., 112
Emanuel, L., 5, 7, 67, 68, 81–98, 118, 119,
   136–150, 153, 168, 173, 187–199,
   269
Emanuel, R., 5, 7, 67, 68, 81, 98, 118, 119,
   136, 141, 150, 153, 168, 173, 187,
   199, 269
emotional communications, child's,
   capacity to be in touch with, 188
emotional containment, importance
   of, 6
emotional development, primacy of
   nature of parental couple, 173
emotional distress, capacity to contain,
   development of, 59
emotional disturbance,
   transgenerational transmission
   of, 94–95
encopresis, 174–175
endings, 112
envy, 152
ESRC (Economic and Social Research
   Council), 175
Etchegoyen, A., 172
Evans, J., 73
exclusion, 198, 200
   feelings of, 204
   and loneliness, feelings of, 204
   mother's childhood feelings of, 207
   oedipal feelings of, 167
experience, dramatization of, 81
extended family, 57, 59, 99, 106, 133, 145,
   215, 255
   lack of, 142, 178

   lack of support from, 156
   nursery as substitute for, 258
quasi-, professional network as,
   108external parental drama, 82
eye contact, avoidance of, 231

failure to thrive, 2, 56, 246
Fakhry Davids, M., 173
false self (Winnicott), 4
family:
   dynamics, facilitating shifts in, 216
   traditions, respecting, 104
   triangle, primary, 199
   *see also* extended family
father:
   absent, 188
      mother's preoccupation with, 197
   childhood anxiety of, 205
   emotionally avoidant, 235
   exclusion, feeling of, 195
      from mother–baby relationship,
         244
   fear of loss of wife, 229
   importance of contribution of, 172
   intimidation of by partner, 177–179
   lack of a positive internal
      representation of, 179
   lack of support from, 145, 147
   as "parentified" child, anger over, 222
   role of, 7, 174
   unreliable, 194–197
   unsupportive or absent, 142
Favez, N., 172
feedback, within community setting,
   100
feeding:
   problems, 237–253
   situation, relinquishing the intimacy
      and exclusiveness of, 201
feelings, terror of being taken over by,
   163
Field, T., 75
firmly set boundaries:
   containment provided by, 143
   *see also* limit-setting
first appointment, 31, 156, 160, 164, 189,
   255
   attendance of by whole family, 156
   contacting client by telephone, 100
   importance of, 49
   rapid response, 100

Fivaz-Depeursinge, E., 172
Fonagy, P., 71, 73, 173, 184
"foreign body", unassimilated, superego as (Freud), 181–185
Fraiberg, S., 12, 13, 54–67, 70, 73, 76, 78, 79, 97, 154, 167, 171, 180, 182, 183, 237
free association, by parents, 241
Freud, S., 3, 40, 165, 168, 180–183, 248, 272

gender-identity issues, 96, 231–236
Gerber baby, 75
"ghosts in the nursery" (Fraiberg), 12, 55, 70, 74, 76, 78, 79, 97, 154, 167, 171–186
Golding, J., 175
good-enough mothering (Winnicott), 125
GP surgery:
  pleasures and problems of working in, 99–101
  under-fives work in, 99–113
grandparents, 96, 103–110, 168, 177, 225, 226
grief, permission to feel, 57
group situations, child's difficulties in, 190–193
guilt, 26, 30, 63, 124, 129, 155, 162, 204, 205, 208, 209, 211, 259, 268, 270
  depressive, 265–266
  immense anxiety stirred up by, 160
  masochistic response to, 267
  paranoid defence against, 267
  persecutory, 265–266
Gurion, M., 168, 169, 200–210

hair pulling, 4
Harris, W. W., 74
hate:
  and love, ambivalence over, 135
  need to accept, 93
Hay, D. F., 138
head-banging, 96–97
Heimann, P., 181, 182
Hesse, E., 168, 182
Higgitt, A., 71
Hipwell, A., 137
"holding" (Winnicott), 11, 13, 65
holding environment, 66

hopelessness, of child, as reaction to stress between parents, 235
Hopkins, J., 11–14, 54–66, 67, 69, 70, 76, 118, 180, 243
hostility, of child towards parents, 152
humour, use of by therapist, 248
hyperactivity, 83, 145

"ideal mother", 123–124
identity, development of, 153
infant:
  direct work with, 74
  effect of improving perceived status of, 75
  mental state of, 74–76
  observation, 12, 18, 36, 39, 40, 45, 46, 48, 49, 53, 122, 138
  –parent psychotherapy, 54–66, 76, 86
  –parent relationship:
    capacity for rapid change in, 65
    parents' own, 62
    treating, 54
  see also baby; child
infantile anxieties/feelings, in adults, 48, 132
infantile aspects, of mother/father, 20
  relation of to clinical practice, 38–53
  as a training tool, 18–20
initial referral, 3
insight, therapist's, importance of, 78–79
"interactive repair" (Tronick), 253
internal object, 17, 76, 181, 271
  dead, 95
  un-mourned, 183
internal parental drama, 82
internal parents, and projective identification, 51
internal representation(s):
  changes to, 73
  damaged, 75
  parents', 72
interpretation(s), 54, 66, 228, 245
intersubjectivity (Stern), 253
intervention process, 6–8
intimacy, avoidance of, by mother and child, 91
introjective identification, 181
irreconcilable feelings, therapist's empathy with both sides of, 247–248

jealousy, 128, 152
  sibling's, 49
"judgements of value",
    transgenerational transmission
    of (Freud), 181
Juffer, F., 72, 75

Kanner's syndrome, 269
Kaplan, N., 65
Kennell, J. H., 137
Kiernan, P., 100
Klaus, M. H., 137
Klein, M., 3, 11, 152, 153, 155, 168, 181, 267, 270, 271
Krause, B., 104

learning:
  limiting factor for, 141
  from others, dependence on, 153
  and primitive unconscious defences, 141
Lewis, E., 254, 268
Lieberman, A. F., 54, 74, 76, 86, 95, 167
Likierman, M., 211, 212, 215–236
limit-setting, 85, 89, 92, 95, 97, 101, 155, 188, 193, 206
  addressing issues of, 83
  challenges to, 166
  failure to, 201
linking, defences against, 270
listening, reflective, 240
longer-term work, 2, 3, 97, 111
loss, 3, 97, 106, 109, 142, 147, 197–201, 236, 245, 270
  addressing feelings of, 107
  of adult status of parents, 49–52
  of attachment figure, unresolved, 182
  avoiding painful feelings associated with, 118, 141
  bereavement in childhood of mother, 142, 147
  change seen as, 112
  of father, 129
  fear of, 91
  immigrants sense of, 13, 57, 58, 68
  and incapacity to mourn, 183
  link to disruptive behaviour, 117
  managing issues of, 260–268
  perinatal, 254
  prenatal, effect of, 255–260
  of self, fears of, 159
  of sense of identity, 166
  and separation, 211–213
  traumatic, 94
  and unmet early needs, 140, 141
  unresolved mourning, 26–30
  untolerated, leading to sense of persecution, 193
  weaning experienced as, 239
  of wife, husband's fear of, 229
love and hate, 237
Ludlam, M., 80

Maddox, H., 73
Maiello, S., 137
Main, M., 65, 71, 154, 168, 182
marital relationship:
  child's feeling of exclusion from, 93
  intimacy of, 97
marriage:
  arranged, 225, 255
  failing, 217
  intercultural, 217–218
maternal care, unmet infantile need for, 64
maternal depression, 136–150, 251
  arising from childhood experiences, 246
  effect of on infant development, 137–138
  infant's contribution to, 138
  infant's defences against, 139–150
  link between mother's speech and infant's cognitive abilities, 138
  see also post-natal depression
maternal function, 188
maternal reverie, 3, 4, 139
  lack of, 77
McHale, J. P., 172
mealtimes, conflicts in, and eating disorders in mother, 251
medication, 7
Mellow Parenting, 73
mental pain, coping with, 117
Menzies, I. E. P., 118
Miller, L., 3, 11–14, 38–53, 67, 69, 77, 78, 117, 121–135, 142, 154
Mills, M., 73
misattunements, by mother, 248

miscarriages, 91, 94, 142, 211
mistiming, 139
   studies, 137
Moran, G., 71
Morgan, M., 74, 186
mother:
   ambivalence of towards baby, 243
   –child relationship:
      early mismatch in, 83
      impact of mother's mental health on, 73
   competitiveness of with baby over partner, 207
   depression of, 73
   effect of mental health of, 73
   effect of observer on, 46
   feeling of abandonment by therapist, 251
   fostered and abused, 234, 235
   gaze of, 46
   hospitalization of, problems arising from, 229–230
   "ideal", 123–124
   infantile emotions of, stirred up by baby, 245
   pregnant, with dying child, 260–268
   overdependency of on child, 138
   therapist's competitiveness with, 19
   unrelieved anguish of, projected into baby, 129
mourning, inadequate, 94
multidisciplinary team, 1
Murray, L., 71, 136–139

need for help, difficulty in acknowledge, 208
negative feelings, 35, 37, 64, 121, 126, 138, 246, 267
negative transference, 12, 52, 55
neglect, cycle of, 2
neuroscience, 3, 5, 152
Newpin, 73
nightmares, 2, 62, 145
"no-entry" defences (Williams), 140
nonverbal communications, 3, 5, 40, 82, 118, 168
Norman, J., 74
Norrell, J., 100

Oakley, A., 73
object(s):
   abandoned, pathological identification with, 183
   past, 79
   relations, 54, 67, 78, 171, 173, 181
      observation of, 199
   theory, 171
   unassimilated, transgenerational transmission of, 181–184
observation, as an intervention, 255–260
observer, effect of on mother, 46
oedipal conflicts, parents', unresolved, 201
oedipal issues, 200–210, 222
oedipal rivalry, 202–203
oedipal situation, 173
   paralysing effect of, potential for, 200
   resolution of, 201
oedipal wishes, 198
oedipal worries, 197–198
Oedipus complex, 165
omnipotence, 119, 153, 166, 196, 206, 271
   collapse of, 156–160
   destructive, testing, 198
omnipotent identification, 157
   failure of, 154
omnipotent phantasies, child's, 198
O'Shaughnessy, E., 215
over-feeding, relationship of, to separation problems, 244
Owen, A. L., 73

Padron, E., 74
Palacio-Espasa, F., 76
Palombo, S., 242
paranoid–schizoid position, 270, 271
parent(s):
   the adult in, 41
   background of, 6, 95
   childhood experiences of, 207
   competition between, 51
   emotionally absent, 188–199
   –infant psychotherapy, 66, 67, 172
      aims of, 71–76
      process of change in, 77
      review of, 70
   interaction between, importance of, 178–180
   investment of infantile selves in child, 52
   lost adult status of, 49–52

mental state of, 71–74
overidentification with child's vulnerable feelings, 206
polarized, dysfunctional, 97
poor communication between, 49
potential for development in, 39
relationship between and with their own family of origin, 241
separated, 188–199
separating from, 152
unconscious expectations of, 112
unhelpful polarization of figures of in child's mind, 193
*see also* single-parent families
parental couple:
attendance of, 94, 96
benign, helping parents internalize the functions of, 199
combined internal, 187–188
containing, 95
effect of role played by, on other parent, 80
functioning of, 167
hidden aggression between, 235
importance of, 171–186
inability of to unite in caring for child, 235
internal, securely based, 201
intolerance of the nature of, 174
polarization of, 95
within the therapy room, 199
unstable, 187–199
well-functioning, cultivating notion of, 187
parental drama:
external, 95–98
internal, 89–95
parental functioning, impact of child on, 81
parental ghosts:
projection of into infant, 180–185
*see also* "ghosts in the nursery"
parental role, child's identification with, 159
parental situation, child's communication of distress over, 224
parenting:
effective, 154
lack of communication between parents over, 223

psychological challenges of, 151
shared, 111
skills, 1
Parke, R. D., 172
past, interpreting the intrusion of, 63
past representations and present realities, effecting a disconnection between, 76
paternal figure, presence in mind of helpful, 111
paternal function, 153, 188
and maternal function, 98
internalizing, importance of for single parent, 189
patterns of relating, transgenerational transmission of, 167
transgenerational transmission of (Freud), 180–181
Pawl, J. H., 76
peacemaker, father as, 179
perinatal project, 1
pets, child's cruelty towards, 146
polarization, 95
polarized parenting, dysfunctional, 97
Pollock, S., 175
port of entry (Stern), 6, 89, 169
possessiveness, 152
child's, 84
post-natal depression, 71, 136, 142, 149, 150, 176, 211, 255
longer-term impact of, 138
*see also* maternal depression
Pound, A., 73
Pozzi, M., 77, 78
pregnancy:
emotional life during, 260
of mother with dying child, 260–268
mourning process in, 268
terminated, unresolved feelings about, 255, 257
premature baby(ies), 123
emotional pressure on staff, 125
prenatal loss, effect of, 255–260
primary maternal preoccupation (Winnicott), 42
primitive anxieties, 13, 19, 37, 121
extreme, capacity to tolerate, 17
prison, separation of mothers from babies in, 2
problems, guarding against premature formulation of, 101

projection(s), 3, 45, 57, 62, 95, 117, 129, 134, 179, 184, 271
    negative, 79
    by the parent of a part of the self into the child, 182
    onto therapist, surviving, 130
projective identification, 3, 5
    with internal parents, 51
psychoanalytic work, 12, 20, 36, 149
    use of observation in, 38
psychodynamic framework, 3, 5
psychological development, successful, 171
Puckering, C., 73

Quinton, D., 175

rage:
    in child, as expression of mother's anger, 192
    communications of, failure to respond to, 143
    as means of eliminating contrary emotions, 129
    as means to evacuate distress, 129
    mother's, over pregnancy and dying child, 266
Raphael-Leff, J., 151
rapid response, as essential part of the Under Fives Service, 100
referrals, 2, 6, 39, 149, 151, 152, 236, 240
    ownership of, 110
reflective self-function (Fonagy), parent's capacity for, 73, 184
Reid, M., 254
Reid, S., 3
representations, sudden emergence of, 64
retaliation, phantasy fear of, 235
reverie, maternal, 3, 4, 77, 139
    lack of, 77
Rhode, M., 269
rivalry, 152
    oedipal, 152, 202–203
    with parent, 201
rules, difficulty in coping with, 161
Rustin, M., 3, 89, 90, 93, 269

Schlesinger, H. J., 248, 249
Schore, A., 72, 152
screaming, 42

second-skin defences, 4, 11, 83, 141, 154, 159, 166, 271
Seeley, S., 137
Segal, H., 153, 201, 272
"selected fact" (Bion), 6, 14
self:
    fear of loss of, 159
    sense of, 153
self-referrals, predominance of, 39
self-sufficiency, 140, 143
    premature, 83, 96
Sendak, M., 151, 154, 164, 166
sense of identity, loss of, 166
separateness, 200
separation, 152–157, 196–201, 207, 212–214, 250–252
    anxiety, 2, 68, 84, 117, 167, 211, 215–236
        transgenerational, 240
    and constant feeding, 244
    developmental milestones, 3
    difficulties with, 158
    early experience of, through breastfeeding, 239
    effect of denying feelings relating to, 118
    and experience of ambivalence, 183
    experienced as cruel or catastrophic loss, 91–94, 97, 117
    managing, 155
    marital, 218
    and mobility, 240
    and night-time/sleeping, 163, 239, 242
    and parent's over-identification with child, 201
    relation of to over-feeding, 244
serial brief treatment, 70
setting:
    atmosphere of, in GP surgery, 101
    containing, 98
setting boundaries, see limit-setting
Shapiro, V., 55, 60, 70, 76, 78, 79, 97, 154, 171, 180
Shuttleworth, J., 3
sibling rivalry, 2, 51, 84, 108, 257–258
Simoni, H., 7, 172
single-parent families, 167, 173, 188, 198
sinking heart (Krause), 104, 110, 113
sleep, "letting go" into, 239

sleeping:
  and attachments, 242
  felt as separation, 158
  problems, 4, 202, 205, 237–253
    and significant losses in parent's life, 244
Solomon, J., 71, 154
splitting, 3, 120, 267, 271
  extreme, 95–97
spoon, use of by child, as sense of agency, 252
Stamp, H., 244
Steele, H., 71
Steele, M., 71
Stern, D., 3, 54, 57, 59, 65, 66, 68, 70–76, 82, 89, 98, 137, 169, 238, 248, 253
Sternberg, J., 3, 67, 68, 99–113, 249
"still-face" studies, 137
Sully, J., 120, 152
superego, 153, 154, 160, 166, 168, 183
  child's, 180–181
symbol formation, 4, 118, 166, 272
symbolic equations, 272
symbolization, 155
symptom, child's, as means to separate parents, 222

tantrums, 4, 38, 84, 89, 96, 117, 119, 120, 123, 130, 145, 151–166, 176
  as defence, 131
  as massive evacuation or rage, 128–129
  as nervous breakdown in miniature, 127, 131
  temper, 2, 143
Target, M., 173
telephone, 2, 6, 39, 42, 193
  initial contact with family by, 100
temper tantrums, 2, 143
therapeutic alliance, 6, 259
therapeutic interventions, 81–98
therapeutic relationship, hoped-for protection given by, 265
therapeutic setting, as "space for thinking", 200
therapeutic task:
  aim of, 74
  "dynamic disconnection between past representations and present realities", 180
therapist:

abandonment by, mother's feelings of, 251
ability of to attune to families, 238
anger toward, mother's, 266
and "couple state of mind", 186
dependence on, fear of, 209
empathy of with both sides of irreconcilable feelings, 247
exclusion of, 208
feelings induced in:
  of desolation, 257
  of helplessness, 219
  of inadequacy, 209
  unacceptable, 123
holding the balance between life and death, 260–268
hostility of child towards, 219
ideal mother figure, 243
judging to whom to attune, 247
listening to own countertransference, 245
as missing (or present) family member, 252
motives, mother's suspicion of, 266
overwhelmed by projections of child, 89
parents' expectations of behaviour of, 243
paternal function, avoiding taking over, 185
sense of intrusion in, 195
as therapeutic consultant/supervisor, 82, 89–95
as therapeutic modulator, 82, 95
as therapeutic observer/director, 82–83
and "third position" (Britton), 185
unacceptable feelings induced in, 123
uncertainty projected into, 203
as unwanted intruder, 205
use of humour by, 248
therapy, mother's suspicion of, 202–203
thinking:
  creating a space for, 200–210
  defences against, 119, 270
  difficulty in, for parental couple, 235
  enabling parents in, 112
  and excessive preoccupation with absent parent, as obstacle to, 188
  framework for, 85
  limiting factor for, 141

thinking (*continued*):
    and managing feelings, 127
    promoting states of mind conducive to, 39
    rigid, 141
thinking object, model of, 77
thinking parent, identification with, 154
third position (Britton), 199
Thomson-Salo, F., 72, 74
transference, 3, 6, 7, 12–13, 37, 40, 41, 59, 202, 272
    communications from parents, 238
    and containment, 77
    cures, 58
    and mind-body connection, 244
    negative, 52, 55
    and neglect, 246
    by parents onto baby, 180, 238
    and parents' expectations of therapist's behaviour, 37, 243
    with single parents, 188
    onto teacher, at nursery, 84
    therapist as missing/present family members, 252
    use of to promote adult capacity in client, 16
transgenerational transmission:
    of failure in emotional containment, 5
    of emotional disturbance, 94
    of monster-baby phantasies, 12
    of patterns of relating, 167, 180–181, 183
"transitional object" (Winnicott), 242
triangular relationship (Britton), 200
"triangular space" (Britton), 198, 201
Tronick, E., 247, 253
Trowell, J., 172
Tydeman, B., 67, 68, 99–113

unacceptable feelings, induced in therapist, 123
unconscious phantasies, 3, 20
unconscious projections, 5, 135
    from clients, effects of, 135
    under-fives, psychodynamic, 152, 155
Under Fives Service (*passim*):
    brevity of work of, 2, 69
    combined paternal/maternal functions, 187
    couple relationships, work on aspects of, 97
    and domestic violence, 168
    dramatic quality of, 81–82
    intervention process, 6–8
    introduction to, 1–3
    model, 99, 100
    and object relations theory, 171
    psychoanalytic approach, 81
    rapid response of, 100
    services offered by, 38–41
    theoretical framework for, 3–6
under-fives work (*passim*):
    process of change in, 69–80
    psychodynamic counselling, 152, 155
    *see also* brief work
understanding, meaningful pattern of, 90
unrelieved anguish, mother's, projected into baby, 129
Urwin, C., 151–166

Van Horn, P., 74
van IJzendoorn, M. H., 72, 75
violent impulses, fear of one's own, 132
voice, tone of, to convey understanding, 106
von Klitzing, K., 172
Voos, D. K., 137

Waddell, M., 3
Wall, S., 4, 138
Waters, E., 4, 138
Watillon, A., 6, 68, 81, 82, 88, 98
weaning, 2, 3, 91, 92, 95, 123, 152, 201, 211, 213, 242–246
    difficulties, 240
        and mother's own childhood, 250
    experienced as loss, 239
    and sleep, 240
wife, husband's fear of loss of, 229
Williams, G., 5, 140
Winnicott, D. W., 4, 11, 13, 42, 66, 74, 125, 153, 155, 242
Wittenberg, I., 11, 15–37

Young People's Counselling Service, 16

Zeanah, C. H., 54